AF531257

Green Hospitality Management

GREEN HOSPITALITY MANAGEMENT

Jayanti Prakash

CENTRUM PRESS
NEW DELHI-110002 (INDIA)

CENTRUM PRESS
H.O.: 4360/4, Ansari Road, Daryaganj,
New Delhi-110002 (India)
Tel: 23278000, 23261597, 23255577, 23286875
B.O.: No. 1015, Ist Main Road, BSK IIIrd Stage,
IIIrd Phase, IIIrd Block, Bengaluru-560085 (INDIA)
Tel: 080-41723429
Email: centrumpress@gmail.com
Visit us at: www.centrumpress.com

Green Hospitality Management

First Edition, 2013

ISBN 978-93-81460-12-2

PRINTED IN INDIA

Printed at Balaji Offset, Delhi.

Contents

Preface

Ecotourism is travel with ethics. It has, in essence, three core tenants- protect and enhance the natural environment, respect local cultures and provide tangible benefits to host communities, and 3 be educational and enjoyable for the traveller. Ecotourism emerged from the environmental movement of the late 1970s. By the early 1990s, it was the fastest growing sector of the tourism industry, expanding globally between 20% and 34% per year. In 2004, ecotourism and nature tourism were growing three times faster than the global tourism industry as a whole. According to Travel Weekly, sustainable tourism could grow to 25% of the world's travel market by 2012, taking the value of the sector to approximately $473 billion a year. The following are current trends in the dynamic field of ecotourism. There is a growing source of international development aid, spearheaded by ecotourism companies, to support community projects in host destinations. Increasingly, conscientious companies and travellers are providing "time, talent, and treasure" to further the well being of host communities. Travelers' Philanthropy projects are helping to empower local.

Closely linked to Travelers Philanthropy is the movement for "Voluntourism," active, hands-on, volunteer vacations that address global issues of environmental degradation and poverty alleviation, while fostering understanding between visitors and host communities. Its origins trace back to the days of healers, explorers, and sailors who travelled while offering services to those in need. With growing awareness of global citizenship and social responsibility, it is no surprise that "voluntourism" is booming. There are increasing concerns about global warming and the effects of carbon dioxide produced from flights, road trips, and other fossil-fuel based recreation. Air transportation alone is believed to produce between 4%-10% of greenhouse gases worldwide. A range of businesses are taking responsibility for reducing their "carbon footprint" by decreasing emissions and donating to tree planting, forest protection, and solar, wind and other renewable energy projects. Organic gardens, native landscaping, solar and wind power, waste water composting, rain water harvesting, gray water irrigation, and recycled building material are a few of the signs of the burgeoning field of 'green' architecture linked to tourism. Small ecolodge owners and luxury chains are beginning to recognize the ecological and often economic benefits of green architecture.

Many family-owned farms are tapping into travelers' interest in rural heritage and lifestyle. Through agroecotourism, farmers generate additional income by hosting visitors, educating the public, and promoting farm products. In Vermont alone, income from farm based tourism activities generated $19.5 million in 2002, representing approximately four percent of the total gross farm income.

The aim of this book is to present a core of this subject knowledge that is desirable for students. Every attempt has been made to keep abreast of the advances in the subject and at the same time to include the fundamentals.

—Author

1

Introduction

Yugoslavia

At the federal level, tourism is under the responsibility of a small department within the Secretariat for Labour, Health and Social Care.

There is no federal policy or legislation on sustainable tourism, since all aspects related to tourism are the responsibility of Serbia and Montenegro. There used to be a small budget allocated by the Federal government to the Tourist Organization of Serbia (TOS) for promotional activities abroad, but such support no longer exists.

Serbia

Present Situation

Tourism in the former Yugoslavia was developed mainly on the Adriatic coast as seaside, summer tourism. Government action to develop the tourist industry did not at that time include the inland parts of the country such as Serbia.

The political events of the past decade have had a marked effect on all sectors of Serbian life and productive activities And, among these, the already limited tourist industry was one of the most affected.

Statistics show that at the end of 1993. when tourism reached an all-time low, domestic tourist traffic was less than half the volume it was at the end of the 1980s, and the number of foreign tourists in Serbia was less than a tenth of what it had been then.

The situation began to improve slowly in 1994, but 2001 data still show only 2,129,128 tourists (of whom 242,525 were foreign), which is 51% of the total number and 26% of the number of foreign tourists in 1989 (4,158,200 and 941,300 respectively).

The Ministry of Trade, Tourism and Services reports that the tourist industry at present accounts for about 2.2% of GDP, a value that is still half of what it was in the prewar period, and the income generated is 10% of 1990 values.

It is estimated that more than 100,00G people (4.5% of the total number employed) work in about 4,000 tourist-related enterprises (about 88% of which arc private).

Data for the year 2001 indicate that Serbia has a total capacity of 92,490 tourist beds, of which only 35,340 (38%) are in hotels.

These figures show a decrease of 23% with respect to 1989.

Table 1: Tourist overnights, 1989-2001

Year	*Tota•*	*Domestic tourists*	*Tourists from Yugoslavia*	*Foreign tourists*
1989	4,158,200	3.216,900	..	941,300
1990	3,949,000	3,067,900		881,100
1991	2.823,779	2.476,512	347,267	
1992	2,669,262	2,522.549		146,713
1993	2,084,536	2,014,393		70,143
1994	2,201.019	1,981,047	137,932	82,040
1995	2,432,107	2,227,956	113,122	91,029
1996	2,197,395	1,950,184	107,817	139,394
1997	2,143,572	1,904.506	99,131	139,935
1998	2,300,840	2,073,385	84,125	143,330
1999	1,443,712	1,319,949	60,234	63,530
2000	2,166,471	2,001,073		165,398
2001	2,129,128	1,886,603		242,525

Source: Ministry of Trade. Tourism and Services. 2002.

Table 2: Accommodation capacity in Serbia, 1989-2001 number of beds

Year	*Total*	*Basic accommodation capacity*			*Complementary accommodation capacity*
		Tota•	*Hote•*	*Other*	
1989	120,540	49,267	37,104	12,163	71,273
1990	116,462	49,214	37,653	11,561	67,248
1991	111,910	48,936	37,716	11.220	62,974
1992	113,262	49.403	38,170	11.233	63.859
1993	109,784	49,558	38.573	10,985	60,226
1994	112,936	49,579	38.609	10,970	63,357
1995	107,684	49,181	38,186	10,995	58,503
1996	105,955	49,125	98,192	10,933	56,830
1997	105,803	49,251	38.437	10,814	56.552
1998	105,438	49,584	38,501	11,083	55.854
1999	104,058	49.751	38,598	11,153	54,307
2000	91,687	46,213	35,016	11,197	45,474
2001	92,490	46,532	35,340	11,192	45,958

Source : M ministry of Trade, Tourism and Services, 2002.

Since 82% of the hotels were built at least 20 years ago, significant renovation is needed. Of these, 69% are classified as B category, while only 16% are classified as A category. Most of them are in the cities of Belgrade, Novi Sad and other major Serbian towns, which indicate that very few high-level hotels are available in rural areas.

Most hotels are owned by public enterprises and may be privatized soon. However, since Serbia is not yet an obvious tourist destination, and since the political situation has been unstable until recently, foreign investors' interest is still not very keen. In addition the road and rail transport network is very limited as far as fast transit is concerned. This is an important obstacle to further development of the tourist industry.

Environmental Problems

Some of the most expensive hotels, with the highest standards, are in the Kopaonic National Park area and are ecological disasters. In most areas with high seasonal tourism, a strong negative impact on natural resources derives from illegal and uncontrolled construction; the pollution of rivers in the vicinity of tourist resorts; high levels of energy consumption; and a lack of facilities for the proper management of both solid and liquid waste.

An environmental impact assessment (EIA) is required by law for the construction of any new tourism facility. However, this is meaningless if regulations are not enforced. Proper and efficient planning for the management of these infrastructure problems is essential for the development of a sustainable tourist industry.

Sustainable tourism includes activities with a low environmental impact such as rural tourism, trekking and cycling. At present, there is insufficient infrastructure in Serbia to support such diversified tourism. Providing good-quality rural hotels or guest houses, hiking trails and cycling circuits would help to support the development of sustainable tourism. In addition, efficient and adequate planning for proper waste management and other support services to guarantee proper protection of the surrounding environment and natural resources is essential.

Prospects for Sustainable Tourism Development

In the past, domestic and foreign tourists were attracted primarily to the mountains, to sports activities and to spas for health-related activities. Although these are the areas with the most obvious development potential, the wide variety of natural and cultural resources in Serbia constitute a valuable base on which to diversify and develop high-level sustainable tourism, including river tourism on the Danube, cultural tourism, transit tourism and ecotourtsm.

This is especially significant in the light of the changing trends of Western tourism, which show a tendency for people to move away from standard mass tourism to more individual, sophisticated and eco-oriented holidays. This requires, as a first step, a sound knowledge of the areas with the best tourism opportunities (e.g. areas of cultural heritage, nature tourism and rural tourism). At the moment, there is no inventory of these areas.

Policy Objectives and Management

The Policy framework

Serbia issued its "Strategy of Tourism Industry Development" in March 1999. It contains the following objectives for the long-term development of the tourist industry:

- The intensification of overall development using existing facilities fully;
- The faster and greater penetration of Serbia in the international market as a tourist destination;
- The creation of conditions for the further development of, a domestic tourist industry;
- The improvement of the overall organization for more efficient management of tourist industry development; and
- The development of economic conditions in tourism.

To achieve these objectives, the Strategy identifies a number of actions to be taken, including support to the tourist industry through fiscal policy, incentives for exports and imports and ad hoc financial credits, the renovation of existing facilities and the construction of new ones up to international standards. It would also improve agency service and booking technologies and train tourist operators. Specific areas targeted for tourist development are big city tourism, mountain tourism, spa tourism, tourism on the Danube and special-interest tourism, such as cultural heritage, rural holidays and ecotourism.

The Strategy addresses the sustainability of the tourist industry in relation to the protection of the environment. It acknowledges that inadequate attention was paid to environmental protection in the past, and it states that the European Charter for Sustainable Tourism in Protected Areas will be taken into account in the development of the Serbian tourist industry. Additional concepts of sustainability are included in the Spatial Plan Law, which contains a framework for the adoption of sustainable tourism strategies through regional and local plans. A master plan for the implementation of the Strategy has not yet been adopted, although the Tourist Organization of Serbia has drafted a proposal for it.

In 1997, the former Directorate for Environmental Protection issued an Action Plan for Sustainable Development in Protected Areas, focusing on pilot projects for sustainable tourism in selected protected areas, education programmes on the protection of natural areas and cultural heritage and the promotion of regional products. However, this document has never been adopted.

The Legislative Framework

A number of laws, draft laws and regulations cover different areas related to the sustainability of the tourist industry, including the following:

- The draft law on the environmental protection system includes articles to protect natural resources and plan for their rational exploitation;
- The Law on Tourism is being upgraded to European standards. The draft should be ready by May 2002 and submirted to the National Assembly in the autumn of 2002. This draft law, however, does not currently contain any reference to eco-standards in the tourist industry;
- A law on ski slopes is being developed under the supervision of a board that includes not only the Ministry of Trade, Tourism and Services and the Ministry of Education and Sport but also the Ministry for Protection of Natural Resources and Environment (as well as the World Ski Association);
- The 1993 Law on Natural Parks sets rules and regulations for the protection of the national parks and limits the activities that are allowed inside them. At present, there is no entrance fee for visiting the national parks, and some of them, for example Konaonic, are suffering significant pressure from the surrounding mountain toutist industry that has developed without adequate infrastructure planning;
- The Regulations on the Categorization of Tourist Places defines criteria for the categorization of areas based on tourist importance, but it does not consider ecotourism; and

- The 1994 Regulations on the Classification, Minimal Conditions and Categorization of Catering Facilities.

There is no strategy or master plan for sustainable tourism that encompasses all of these different regulations. In the absence of a framework, specific sectorial plans, such as those for the sustainable development of tourism in national parks, or tourism along the Danube or in rural areas, have not been drawn up.

Economic Instruments

There is a budget for national parks, and the Law on Natural Parks indicates that a tax is to be paid by the public enterprises using facilities within protected areas, but there are no economic instruments to support the development of sustainable tourism.

The Institutional Framework

The Ministry of Trade, Tourism and Services is directly responsible for Serbia's tourist policies and legislation, but a number of other institutions also have responsibilities for sustainable tourism policy. These include:

- The Ministry of Culture: cultural heritage; and the education and training of operators, the education of schoolchildren, and raising public awareness about the environment and ecotourism.
- The Ministry for Protection of Natural Resources and Environment: national parks and protected areas; environmental impact studies for new tourist structures; the protection and sustainable use of natural resources; the identification of natural regions of significance for Serbia; and the improvement, use and protection of forests and game.
- The Ministry of Construction and Urban Planning: development planning issues.
- The State Enterprise for Forest Management "Srbija sume": hunting tourism and the rearing of pheasants; and congress tourism, schoolchildren and village tourism.

Interviews with representatives of these different institutions made it clear that there is virtually no coordination and no sharing of information or related activities among the ministries on similar issues. There is a similar lack of information exchange between communities and NGOs that are active in tourism. Such a lack of coordination among institutions, organizations and local communities is a significant obstacle to coherent planning and implementation.

Education and Capacity-building

There are institutions for training in the tourism sector. Novi Sad University has a tourism faculty that includes all aspects of sustainable tourism. The Ministry of Education and Sport runs a programme called "Schools in nature" for young children, and, since 1995, it has been obligatory to teach environmental protection issues in primary schools.

There are two higher schools associated with tourism, one for catering and the other for tourism, but neither has a curriculum that addresses sustainable tourism. Seminars for hotel operators, teachers and others are held within the Yugoslav Tourist Agency (YUTA) to raise awareness of sustainable and ecotourism.

Sustainable Tourism Indicators

Statistical data on hotels and tourist numbers are available from the Ministry of Trade, Tourism and Services. These are divided into country of origin and tourist destination. There are no data on national park use.

Data such as the ratio of overnights per tourist arrivals, the ratio of overnights per resident, or the annual value of trade in catering for residents, are not collected at the moment. These are important indicators to develop the monitoring of sustainable tourism.

Montenegro

Present Situation

Although not as developed as on Croatia's Adriatic coast, in the 1980s the tourist industry in Montenegro accounted for a significant part of its GDP with an overall number of overnights close to 11 million.

The political events of the past ten years have seriously damaged the sector and tourism has decreased to 5 million overnights, mostly limited to domestic (Including Serbian) tourists focused on seaside summer tourism. West European tourists has practically disappeared and are only slowly returning.

Due to its natural resources and beautiful coastline, tourism is considered to be one of the main industries to be developed in Montenegro in the next 10 to 20 years, and it is given the highest priority.

Statistics in the Tourist Master Plan for Montenegro, prepared by the German Investment and Development Company (DEG) in March 2001, indicate that of a total number of 95,000 beds available in Montenegro at present, only 26,000 (27.5%) are in hotels, and of these, only about 1% is considered to be of a standard suitable for international markets. Most hotels are owned by public enterprises. In many cases, the land on which they were built was expropriated from private owners, who are now reclaiming their property. This issue, which is being addressed by the preparation of a new law, currently stands in the way of foreign investments.

Another constraint is the transport infrastructure, which is inadequate even for the existing tourism. Interviews with local tourist operators in Budva showed that there was a problem of intense traffic during the peak summer months to such a degree that it becomes difficult to transport tourists from Budva hotels to surrounding destinations such as Kotor and Saint Stefan. Existing roads are slow transit roads, and the standards of the only two airports equipped to receive international flights are very basic.

Environmental Problems

In the main coastal tourist destinations such as Budva, unauthorized building developments have ruined many of the natural characteristics of the sites. Furthermore, such illegal development means both that there has been no environmental planning and that construction has not been accompanied by the essential infrastructure. Basic resources like water and power are short during peak tourist periods.

Sewage is the main problem on the coast. At the moment, this is being partially addressed by the introduction of beach toilets with no outlet to the sea. The Bay of Kotor has no sewerage network; all the houses or groups of houses have their own outlets and discharge directly into the sea. There are no waste-water treatment plants, and the outlets along the coastline are in a bad condition. Budva has four outlets, of which the main one is 2 km out to sea, but the total capacity is still that of 1979. after the earthquake. No upgrading of the drainage systems and outlets has taken place in 23 years. There are other problems with all the aspects of waste management.

If planning regulations are not enforced, Montenegro will lose its potential as a major tourist destination for foreign as well as domestic tourists.

Sustainable Tourism

As in Serbia, Montenegro does not yet have the required infrastructure to support ecotourism activities such as mountaineering, trekking, rural tourism and sailing.

No effort is being made to support local rural activities by including their products in a sustainable tourism development plan for Montenegro.

For example, it was pointed out that the Montenegrin airline is serving Serbian honey on its planes, while local rural communities producing honey do not have the capacity to commercialize it. The same is true for milk; despite the high local production capacity, milk is currently imported. Attention should be paid to local production and efforts made to organize cooperatives to help sustain local rural communities.

Sustainable Tourism Development

Montenegro is a small beautiful republic with a huge variety of natural attractions that have not yet been developed. These include sandy beaches, a rocky coastline and fjords, dramatic mountain scenery enhanced by lakes and river canyons. All of this is enriched by historical sites left by several different cultures that have inhabited the region throughout the centuries.

The Tourism Master Plan for Montenegro (May 2001) has identified the following five main tourist regions:

- The sandy beach of Ulcinj, which, 13 km long, is the only sandy beach on the eastern Adriatic coast;
- The unique Boka Kotorska fjord;

- The rocky coast between Tivat and Ulcinj, which offers many pebble beaches;
- Skadarsko Jezero; and
- The inland mountain region.

Montenegro is endowed with all the basic elements needed for a very high-level, sustainable tourist industry, such as is not found anywhere else in Europe. However, no specific strategy has yet been developed for the immediate future. This is a cause for concern, because there are likely to be intensive efforts to develop the tourist industry without any reference to the environment or sustainability.

Policy Objectives and Management

The Policy framework

The above-mentioned Tourism Master Plan includes all aspects related to the tourist industry such as general infrastructure (transport, waste management, waste-water treatment and water and power supply) and highlights the importance of natural resource conservation. The strategic aim of the Tourism Master Plan is to turn Montenegro into a high-quality summer tourist destination and a provider of specialized, niche tourist products in the winter. It foresees the development of a hotel capacity of 50,000 beds by 2010 and 100,000 beds by 2020, mostly for coastal charter tourism.

A coordination committee for the Master Plan has been appointed and includes all relevant ministries, the municipalities, the main tourist companies, the Public Enterprise for Coastal Management, and the national organization for tourism. The chair of the committee is the deputy president of Montenegro. A smaller committee, composed of only 10 people, meets every 15 days for urgent matters. It includes representatives of the office of the Deputy Prime Minister, the Ministry of Tourism, the Ministry of Environmental Protection and Physical Planning, the Public Enterprise for Coastal Management and private tourist companies.

Development programmes are now being finalized for two of the tourist areas identified by the Master Plan, Kotor Bay and Ulcinj beach. The plans will then be proposed to the local communities for approval and development. The project teams that are responsible for these plans do not include representatives of the Ministry of Environmental Protection and Physical Planning. Montenegro might wish to consider inviting high-level ecotourism experts to design a sustainable development policy to be integrated into the existing Master Plan before implementing specific site plans.

A Plan for the Future of Montenegro's National Parks and Private Enterprise Development was prepared by national park and forest service professionals from the United States (through Flag International) in March 2002. This strategic plan offers a development approach that is complementary to the Tourist Master Plan. At the moment, however, it has no official status.

A strategic spatial plan has been drafted for the whole coast for the next 20 years. This includes guidelines for individual municipal plans and marine transport. It also includes environmental protection concepts for the coast. For example, in the wetland area of Ulcinj, the plan does not allow for any building that might impede bird migration. It also recognizes, for the first time, a sea and underwater area for the protection of marine life and foresees the creation of special underwater parks. Marine areas are not included in the 1978 Law on Nature Protection.

The strategic spatial plan for the coast identifies seven important locations for tourist development, to be studied in greater detail. One of the selected areas, the coastal wetland of Solala near Tivat, is not yet protected, but the plan foresees that the only activity allowed there will be aquaculture.

The planning process was carried out in the traditional way and does not introduce the sustainable development criteria that are included in the recommendations of the European Code of Conduct for Coastal Zones and the UNEP Priority Action Plan (PAP) Regional Activity Centre (RAC) guidelines for integrated coastal zone management. However, it is considered to be more restrictive and protective of the environment than the Tourism Master Plan. At the moment, the strategic spatial plan is just a draft.

International conventions are dealt with by the Federal Government, but given the diverging interests of Montenegro's

Government and the Federal Government, it has been difficult to negotiate conventions specific to the Mediterranean Sea.

Ratification of the Barcelona Convention and membership of the Mediterranean protection and assistance programmes, such as the UNEP Mediterranean Action Plan (MAP) and the World Bank Mediterranean Environmental Technical Assistance Program (METAP) would encourage the Montenegro Government to implement costal protection measures and would make international aid resources available to it.

The Legislative Framework

The Law on Tourism (No. 32/2002) includes new standards for catering, but it does not appear to contain any concepts related to sustainable development. This would have been a good opportunity to introduce eco-standard concepts in the tourist industry.

Economic Instruments

There is a tourist tax on hotel and other tourist accommodation. Of the amount collected, 7% goes to the municipality and 93% to Montenegro's budget, but municipalities use the money for priorities other than tourism and the environment. In addition, there is no reliable mechanism to ensure collection of this tourist tax, and a significant amount of existing accommodation is unregistered. The Ministry of Tourism organizes local inspection bureaux to try to enforce regulations.

No entrance fees are charged for national parks at present.

The Institutional Framework

Montenegro has a Ministry of Tourism directly responsible for tourist policies and legislation but, like Serbia, a number of other institutions are also involved in sustainable tourism policy. These include the following:

- The Ministry of Environmental Protection and Physical Planning: environmental protection issues and aspects related to the management of national parks and protected areas; environmental impact studies for new tourist structures for development planning issues.

- The Ministry of Maritime Trade and Transport: responsible for all matters which concern the sea.
- The Ministry of Culture (Sector of Cultural Heritage): issues related to the development of cultural tourism opportunities.
- The Ministry of Education and Science: the education and training of operators, the education of schoolchildren; and raising public awareness about the environment and ecotourism.

The National Tourism Organization serves as an operative branch of the Ministry of Tourism and is financed by the Government (about E450,000 for 2002). It has a central office in Podgorica and ten local offices, of which seven are on the coast. The Organization is making a huge effort to raise the local population's awareness of the importance both of maintaining the surrounding environment ("Let it be clean" campaign) and of tourism at the community level.

Coastal management is the responsibility of the Public Enterprise for Coastal Management, whose board of directors includes representatives of the Ministry of Maritime Trade and Transport, the Ministry of Environmental Protection and Physical Planning, the Ministry of Tourism, the Ministry of Agriculture. Forestry and Water Management and local municipalities. The Enterprise is responsible for the implementation of the 1992 Law on the Coastal Zene.

Preparation of the beaches and of the coastal zone for the tourist season is also the responsibility of the Public Enterprise for Coastal Management. This is done by leasing parts of land to either public or private companies or individuals for tourist activities through contracts that contain regulations included in the Ministry of Tourism Code for Beaches.

Environmental protection has only recently been introduced as a part of the mandate of the Enterprise. In fact, one of its leasing conditions is monitoring the quality of the sea water through the Institute of Marine Biology in Kotor for biological parameters and through the Centre for Ecotoxicological Research in Podgorica for chemical parameters.

Biological monitoring by the Institute of Marine Biology is active in 55 beach locations while chemical monitoring by the Centre for Ecotoxicological Research is carried out in 8 locations that are mostly urban and port sites. The parameters monitored are those indicated in the monitoring guidelines of the Ministry of Agriculture, Forestry and Water Management. The Enterprise has no direct influence on water management companies.

Education and Capacity-building

There are secondary schools for tourism in Budva, Herzegnovi and Podgorica. A university degree in tourism is offered by the University of Kotor. In addition, a secondary school for spa medicine is available at the health centre of Igalo. Sustainable tourism concepts do not appear to be included in the curricula of any of these schools, all of which are regulated by the Ministry of Education and Science.

No specific training appears to be available for sustainable tourism and no workshops or seminars are available for tourism operators, teachers. students or for general awareness-raising among the population.

Sustainable Tourism Indicators

Statistical data on hotels and tourism are available from the Ministry of Tourism. These are divided into country of origin. There are no data on national park entrances.

Data such as the ratio of overnights per tourist, the ratio of overnights per resident, or the annual value of trade in catering for residents are not collected.

Conclusions and Recommendations

Recommendations to the Federal Government

Ratification of the Barcelona Convention and member-ship in the Mediterranean protection and assistance progra-mmes, such as the UNEP Mediterranean Action Plan (MAP) and the World Bank Mediterranean Environmental Technical Assistance Program (METAP) would help the Montenegrin Government to implement coastal protection measures. It would also make international resources available to it.

Recommendations to Serbia and to Niontenegro

There are many laws and regulations addressing tourism-related issues, from spatial planning, coastal zone management and environmental protection to catering, ski slopes, spas and school programmes. However, there is no overall sustainable tourism policy that could provide a cohesive framework and ensure that sustainability criteria are consistently applied in all relevant laws and regulations affecting tourism development. Once a framework policy has been established, it is important to develop a general master plan for sustainable tourism and a series of individual master plans for specific sites. In order to provide baseline data for the master plan, it is important to make an inventory of all sites of interest (including sites with potential for cultural heritage, rural tourism, river tourism, industrial heritage, nature tourism, and spas). The development plans that are being drafted and will soon be submitted to local communities for approval do not appear to contain sustainable development criteria. Top priority should be given to sustainable development in order to safeguard natural resources and, in particular, Montenegro's unique potential for a "different type" of tourism development.

Recommendation

Serbia's Ministry of Trade, Tourism and Services, in cooperation with its Ministry for Protection of Natural Resources and Environment, and Montenegro's Ministry of Tourism, in cooperation with its Ministry of Environmental Protection and Physical Planning, should:

(a) Each prepare and submit for approval by the Government a policy for sustainable tourism. The policy should serve as a framework for all tourist-related activities. In Montenegro, it should be consis-tent with its declaration as an Ecological State (1991);

(b) Develop a tourism master plan, also based on the overall policy for sustainable tourism, to allow for appropriate economic, spatial and resource planning and the development of the necessary infrastructure in tourist areas. In Serbia, the master plan should be harmonized with the draft action plan for sustainable tourism in protected areas. In Montenegro, where a tourism master plan has already been drafted, the Ministry should ensure that it reflects the (new) sustainable tourism policy;

(c) On the basis of the policy, develop guidelines for tourism development at the local level and introduce eco-standards for tourist premises;

(d) On the basis of the policy, identify the important sustainable tourism indicators and provide the means for monitoring, collecting and evaluating the data accordingly; and

(e) In cooperation with the Ministry of Culture, make an inventory of all sites of tourist interest. As the sites are identified, individual plans for their sustainable development should also be prepared (e.g. for sustainable tourism in national parks).

There are economic instruments for natural resources management in Serbia, including taxes and payments for use of land and forests, and fishing and hunting. There are, however, no economic instruments to support the development of sustainable tourism in Serbia and no charge for entrance into national parks. Serbia could raise revenue through an eco-tax and then spend it on environmental protection projects in protected areas and on improving the infrastructure that is now damaging the environment.

In Montenegro there is currently a tourist tax, although there is no evidence that any of it is applied toward sustainable tourism. At this important moment for shaping the Montenegrin tourist industry and providing for its future development, it is essential that funds should be made available to ensure its sustainability.

Serbia's Ministry for Protection of Natural Resources and Environment and Montenegro's Ministry of Environmental Protection and Physical Planning should establish the following economic instruments to support sustainable tourism:

- Entrance fees at national parks;
- Fiscal incentives for tourist premises that implement eco-standards, such as green hotels that give special attention to the conservation and protection of resou-rces such as water and energy.

Concepts of sustainable tourism are not included in the curricula of either the two Higher Schools for Tourism and Catering in Serbia or the Schools for Tourism in Montenegro. It is important that persons directly involved in tourism are educated in concepts of sustainability and environmental protection, but it is just as significant that municipal authorities and tourists are made aware of such important issues. Therefore, the awareness and education campaign effort should address the public at large. Seminars and workshops should be held for operators of the tourist industry, teachers, students and local authorities to raise general awareness of sustainable tourism and ecotourism. Serbia's Ministry of Trade, Tourism and Services, in cooperation with its Ministry for Protection of Natural Resources and Environment, and Montenegro's Ministry of Tourism, in cooperation with its Ministry of Environmental Protection and Physical Planning, should:

(a) Carry out widespread campaigns to raise awareness of sustainable tourism particularly among hotel managers, tourist agencies, tourists and municipal authorities. The campaign should make use of workshops, community meetings, brochures and posters, among other media; and

(b) In cooperation with Serbia's Ministry of Education and Sport and Montenegro's Ministry of Education and Science, introduce sustainable tourism development into the curricula of the higher schools for tourism and catering.

Recommendations to Serbia

A number of ministries and other organizations are responsible for different areas of importance to tourism. However, there is very little coordination among them, and they rarely share information. At the same time, individual projects are being developed locally by non-governmental organizations. Interaction between the different government bodies and cooperation with the local communities would allow for a more efficient use of human and economic resources and the development of more effective, multidisci-plinary projects.

Recommendation

The Government of Serbia should establish, an inter–ministerial body on sustainable tourism that would also include representatives of local authorities and appropriate non-governmental organizations.

Recommendations to Montenegro

In developing sustainable tourism, it is essential that plans should be formulated within the context of coastal zone management. In addition, more support should be given to the production of local food and other products. Efforts should also be made to organize cooperatives to help sustain local rural communities. A survey of production of rural communities may help in this regard.

> *The Ministry of Tourism, in cooperation with local authorities, should undertake a survey of local products that could be supported and included in a sustainable tourism development plan.*

Monienegro has established a coordination committee to implement its master tourism plan. This is an important step, but it is made up of central government representatives. Interaction between the different government bodies and local communities would allow for a more efficient use of human and economic resources and the development of multidisciplinary projects. There are many very highly motivated and qualified professionals working at the local level. The committee should work with such people to establish strong local ties and develop sensible and sustainable local development strategies.

The coordination committee established for the master tourism plan should establish smaller, more agile thematic working groups, including one dedicated to sustainable tourism and development. The committee should include representations of both local communities and non-governmental organizations.

The situation related to waste management, waste-water treatment, power and water supply and transport in the main tourist areas of Montenegro is critical. Strategic master plans to solve such issues must be given top priority if a tourist industry is to develop at all. Sustainable development criteria should be included in such plans to make the declaration of Montenegro as an ecological State credible.

2

Environmental Consequences of Tourism Development

The relationship between the environment and many forms of tourism is fundamental. From the earliest times, the enjoyment of 'environments'–whether defined in physical or in socio-cultural term – has had a major impact in shaping a succession of tourism geographies. As public tastes for different kinds of leisure environment have developed through time – for example, through the formation of resorts or the changing preferences for scenic landscapes in the nineteenth century; or the quest for amenable climates or the attraction of historic heritage in the twentieth century–so new spatial patterns of interaction between people and environments have been formed.

However, tourism – environment relationships are not just fundamental, but also highly complex. There is a mutual dependence between the two that has often been described as 'symbiotic'. In simple terms this means that since tourism benefits from being located in good-quality environments, those same environments ought to benefit widely from measures of protection aimed at maintaining their value as tourist resources. In England and Wales, for example, the designation of national parks came about partly because these high-quality environments were seen as potentially valuable areas for tourism and the argument for their conservation was strengthened accordingly. Similarly, there is no doubt that the cause of wildlife preservation in East Africa has been assisted by the parallel increase in the appeal of safari holidays to the same region.

As tourism has expanded in the post-1945 period (both in scale and into new destinations) there have, however, emerged very real signs that the nature of that symbiosis has become unbalanced Tourism, far from being a force for enhancement and protection of the environment, actually has shown itself to be a major generator of environmental problems with considerable capacity to destroy the resources upon which it depends. Consequently, more attention is now being focused upon understanding the environmental impacts of tourism and ways of producing more sustainable forms of tourism development that maintain, rather than degrade, key resources.

The complex character of tourism–environment relationships is deepened further by the diverse nature of those impacts and the inconsistencies through time and space in their causes and effects. It is also true that the effects of tourism upon the environment are partial, and one of the practical difficulties in studying those impacts is to disentangle tourist influences from other agencies of change that may be working on the same environment. So, for example, beach and inshore water pollution in the Bay of Naples will be partly attributable to the presence of tourists but will also be a product of the activities of local populations, of farming and of industries that discharge their waste into the Mediterranean.

The diversity of environmental impacts of tourism and the seriousness of the problem vary geographically for a number of reasons. First, we need to take account of the nature of tourism and its associated scales of effect. Impact studies often make the erroneous assumption that tourism is a homogeneous activity exerting consistent effects, there are many different forms of tourism and types of tourist. The mass tourists who flock in their millions to the Spanish Mediterranean create a much broader and potentially more serious range of impacts than will small groups of explorers trekking in Nepal, although paradoxically, where mass forms of tourism are well planned and properly resourced, the environmental consequences may actually be less than those created by small numbers of people visiting locations that are quite unprepared for the tourist. For example, depletion of local supplies of fuel wood and major problems of littering have been widely reported along the main trails through the Himalayan zone in Nepal.

Second, it is important to take account of the temporal dimensions. In many parts of the world, tourism is a seasonal activity that exerts pressures on the environment for part of the year but allows fallow periods in which recovery is possible. So, there may be short-term/temporary impact upon the environment that may be largely coincident with the tourist season (such as air pollution from visitor traffic) or, more seriously, long-term/permanent effects where environmental capacities have been breached and irreversible changes set in motion (for example, reduction in the level of biodiversity through visitor trampling of vegetation).

Third, diversity of impacts stems from the nature of the destination. Some environments (for instance, urban resorts) can sustain very high levels of visiting because their built infrastructure makes them relatively resilient or because they possess organisational structures (such as planning frameworks) that allow for effective provision for visitors. In contrast, other places are much less robust, and it is perhaps unfortunate that a great deal of tourist activity is drawn (by tastes, preferences and habits) to far more fragile places. Coasts and mountain environments are popular tourist destinations that are often ecologically vulnerable, and even non-natural resources can suffer. Historic sites, in particular, may be adversely affected by tourist presence, and in recent years attractions such as Stonehenge, the Parthenon in Athens and the tomb of Tutankhamen in Egypt have all been subjected to partial or total closure to visitors because of negative environmental effects.

In exploring the environmental impacts of tourism, it is helpful to adopt a holistic approach to the subject. Environments, whether defined as physical, economic or social entities, are usually complex systems in which there are inter-relationships that extend the final effects of change well beyond the initial cause. Impact often has a cumulative dimension in which secondary processes reinforce and develop the consequences of change in unpredictable ways, so treating individual problems in isolation ignores the likelihood that there is a composite impact that may be greater than the sum of the individual parts. The effects of trampling of ground by tourists are a good example of this problem.

A second advantage of a holistic approach is that it encourages us to work towards a balanced view of tourism–environment relationships. The temptation is to focus upon the many obvious examples of negative and detrimental impacts that tourism may exert, but, as the concept of a symbiotic relationship makes clear, there are positive effects too. These might be represented in the fostering of positive attitudes towards environmental protection/ enhancement or might be reflected more practically in actual investment in environmental improvement that restores localities for resident populations as well as providing support for tourism.

The third advantage of a holistic approach is that it recognises the breadth (some might say the imprecision) of the term 'environment' and the fact that different types of impact are likely to be present. As is perhaps implicit in the preceding discussion, the term can embrace a diversity of contexts – physical ecosystems; built environments; economic, social, cultural or political environments – and tourism has the potential to influence all of these, in varying degrees. For the purposes of this present discussion, the economic and socio-cultural impacts are discussed in other parts of the book. So for the remainder of this chapter, the focus falls upon the influences that tourism may have upon physical environments, ecosystems and the built environment, together with a consideration of ways in which symbiotic relationships between tourism and the environment may be sustained.

Environmental Impacts of Tourism: A Review

Under first heading, *biodiversity,* are located a number of effects that broadly impact upon the flora and fauna of a host region. The 'balance' of influence here leans strongly towards the group of negative impacts, for whilst tourist demands have occasionally been partly of fully responsible for programmes aimed at establishing zones of conservation in which wildlife and their natural ecosystems are protected (for example, in the national parks in Kenya and Tanzania or on the Great Barrier Reef in Australia), the more commonplace patterns are associated with damage. Such damage may occur in varying forms. Most widely, processes of tourism development (construction of hotels and apartments, new roads, new attractions, etc.) can result in a direct loss of habitats. In the Alps, extensive clearance of forests to develop ski-fields and the loss of Alpine meadows with particularly rich stocks of wild flowers to new hotel and chalet construction has significantly altered ecological balances and, in the case of deforestation, greatly increased risks associated with landslides and snow avalanches.

At a more localised scale, other impacts become apparent. Destruction of vegetation at popular visitor locations through trampling or the passage of wheeled vehicles is a common problem. Typically, trampling causes more fragile species to disappear and to be replaced either by bare ground or where regeneration of vegetation is possible, by more resilient species. The overall effect of such change is normally to reduce species diversity and the incidence of rare plants which, in turn, may impact upon the local composition of insect populations, insectivours birds and possibly small mammals for which plant and insect populations are key elements in a food chain.

Larger animals may be affected in different ways by tourism, even within environments that are protected. The increasing popularity of safari holidays has become a problem in African national parks where the close attention of tourists in vehicles has been held to account for disruption to feeding and breeding patterns of animals and, in some case, their eventual migration to remote areas. (Box 1 provides an example of how quite innocent actions by tourists in one popular location impacts upon a particular species: the Mediterranean loggerhead turtle.) Nor has legal protection necessarily saved some animals and plants from decimation by collectors and tourists. Hunting of animals as a leisure pastime is still widely practised, and poaching to supply a black-market trade in animal souvenirs and trophies is commonplace in Africa, parts of the Mediterranean, the Caribbean and the South Pacific.

The impacts of tourism upon the diversity of flora and fauna link with the second area of concern, *erosion and physical damage,* and this illustrates how environmental problems tend to be interlinked. Erosion is typically the result of trampling by visitors' feet, and, whilst footpaths and natural locations are the most likely places for such problems to occur, extremes weight of numbers can lead to damage to the built environment. The Parthenon in Athens, for example, not only is under attack from airborne pollutants but also is being eroded by the shoes of millions of visitors. However, in such situations, tourism can have positive impacts, for although the activity may be a major cause of problems, revenue generated by visitors may also be a key source of funding for wider programmes of environmental restoration.

Localised examples of such damage can be spectacular. In north Wales, popular tourist trails to the summit of Sundown now commonly reveal eroded ground that may extend to 9 m in width, whilst localised incidence of soil erosion and gullying has lowered path levels by nearly 2 m in a little over twenty years.

The environmental impacts of which the tourist is probably most aware are those associated with *pollution,* particularly the pollution of water. With so much tourism centered in or around water resource, pollution of water is a major concern. Poor-quality water may devalue the aesthetic appeal of a location and be a source of water-borne diseases such as gastro-enteritis, hepatitis, dysentery and typhoid. Visible water pollutants (sewage, organic and inorganic rubbish, fuel oil from boats, etc.) will also be routinely deposited by wave action onto beaches and shorelines, leading to direct contamination, noxious smells and visually unpleasant scenes.

Impact of Tourism on Wildlife: The Example of the Loggerhead Turtle

The Greek island of Zakynthos contains the most important nesting area in the Mediterranean for the loggerhead turtle, a species whose main habitat is the shallow inshore waters that also attract the tourist. Monitoring of turtle populations since 1979 (when the species was formally recognised as 'endangered') has shown a persistent decline in numbers, and whilst the turtles are vulnerable to several natural hazards that include climatic flucturations and a rather wide range of natural predators, the development of tourism on Zakynthos has emerged as one of the greatest risks to the long-term survival of the species. The turtles nest during the height of the summer tourist season, laying eggs in buried chambers in the beach, some 10 to 15 m from the water's edge. This unhappy set of coincidences, although quite inadvertent, directly disrupts breeding in several ways:

* some nesting site have been lost to beach development and improvements (such as tree planting to shade tourists);
* nesting females and young hatchlings (which are positively phototactic – i.e. attracted by light), rather than heading instinctively to the sea, may be disoriented by lights from beach-front bars and cafes, becoming stranded far from the sea;
* noise is also a source of disorientation and confusion;
* vehicular traffic on the beaches compacts the sand, reduces essential oxygen levels within nest chambers and may lead to collapse of nests;
* pollution of the water leads to fatalities as turtles consume plastic bags and food packaging, mistaking these items for natural foods such as jellyfish.

Initiatives by the Greek government to limit the impacts of tourism upon the turtles have so far proven only partially successful. Attempts to limit developments and constrain activities have drawn opposition from local residents who are dependent upon tourism, whilst visitors –although expressing broadly based concerns for the welfare of the animals – also show varying levels of disregard for restrictions aimed at protecting nest sites from intrusion. The authors of the study conclude that a primary goal of policies aimed at protecting the animals must therefore be educative in nature, seeking to alter the attitudes, values and behaviour of both the providers in nature, seeking to alter the attitudes, values and behaviour of both the provides and the consumers of tourism on Zakynthos.

The study shows clearly the incidental manner in which tourism can disrupt wildlife. The animals are neither actively hunted not pursued by tourists with cameras and most of the movement of turtles takes place at night and is largely unseen. Yet routine behaviour by tourists pursued without any disruptive intention whatsoever – is nevertheless having seriously deleterious effects upon the species.

Pollution of water also has a number of direct effects upon plant and animal communities. Reduced levels of dissolved oxygen and increased sedimentation of polluted water diminish species diversity, encouraging rampant growth of some plants (e.g. various forms of seaweed) whilst discouraging less robust species. In some cases, such changes have eventually impacted upon tourists. In parts of the Mediterranean, and particularly the Adriatic Sea, the disposal of poorly treated sewage (supplemented by seepage of agricultural fertilisers into watercourses that feel into the sea) has created localised eutrophication of the water. (Eutrophication is a process of nutrient enrichment.) This has led directly to formation of unsightly and malodorous algal blooms that coat inshore waters during the summer months, reducing the attractiveness of the environment and depressing demand for holidays in the vicinity.

Water pollution is especially commonplace in areas of mass tourism where the industry has developed at a pace that is faster than local infrastructures have been able to match (for example, the Spanish Mediterranean coast), but even in long-established tourism locations, where local water treatment and cleansing services ought to be adjusted to local needs, water pollution is still commonplace In 1996 the UK Environment Agency reported that 11 per cent of beaches in England and Wales failed to comply with EU minimum standards governing faecal contamination of bathing waters. In some regions (such as the North West of England – which covers some of the most popular holiday beaches at resorts such as Blackpool and Southport) as many as 40 per cent of the bathing waters were below EU targets and not a single beach merited the coveted EU 'Blue Flag' for beach cleanliness

Water Quality and Tourism : The Case of Rimini

One of the most recent examples of the mutual dependence between Tourism: Analyzing Impacts on Environmental quality has been the impact of deteriorating water conditions on tourism to the Italian resort of Rimini on the Adriatic. The River Po and its tributaries transport considerable volumes of urban, agricultural and industrial wastes into the Adriatic, to which is added waste from the coastal resorts themselves. The limited tidal range in the Adriatic has meant that pollutants have gradually accumulated, leading to localised eutrophication of the water and the formation, during the summer months, of algal blooms and floating rafts of mucilage. The first manifestation, which was patchy in form, occurred during August 1988, but the algae bloom was far stronger and more extensive in 1989 and attracted widespread media coverage.

The attention of the media and the negative images of polluted, algae-strewn waters had an immediate impact upon tourism, with an estimated reduction by 1990 of between 50 and 60 per cent in organised and intermediate forms of international tourism, although the loss of tourists in traditional, local sectors was much less marked.

Faced with economic catastrophe, the initial responses – from the tourism industry at least – were to treat the symptoms rather than the causes. Some use was made of floating barriers to limit the incursion of the rafts of algae inshore, and mobile bathing pools were erected at more locations. Discounted prices with widely used to try to maintain a market share. However, the long-term viability of resorts with eutrophication problems rests on a more fundamental understanding of water pollution and local environmental systems, and to that end the Emilia-Romagna regional authority has set up programmes aimed at:

* monitoring water conditions;
* undertaking research into coastal currents and sedimentation characteristics in relations to certain pollutants;
* obtaining better understanding of algal development processes.

The European Parliament, noting that eutrophication problems are not confined to the Adriatic but are also manifest in parts of the Baltic and North Seas, has focused attention on the need for more rigorous management and control of agricultural, domestic and industrial pollution as a basic set of causal factors linked to eutrophication.

The recent experience in the resort of Rimini illustrates well the fragile interdependence between tourism and the environment. The resort was already showing signs of deterioration through physical overdevelopment and associated reductions in quality, so the adverse publicity associated with poor water conditions simply acted as a catalyst for extensive relocation of tourists to other areas where environmental problems were not perceived to be present. The extent to which Rimini will be able to recover its position will depend very much upon its ability to resolve the problem of algal blooms and the associated pollution, together with positive marketing to counteract the negative image the resort has how acquired.

Alongside water pollution, tourism is also associated with air pollution and, less obviously, noise pollution. Pollution due to noise is usually highly localised, centering upon entertainment districts in popular resorts, airports and routeways that carry heavy volumes of tourist traffic. However, the dependence of tourism upon travel means that chemical pollution of the atmosphere by vehicle exhaust fumes is more widespread and, given the natural workings on the atmosphere, more likely to travel beyond the region in which the problem is generated. Nitrogen oxides, lead and hydrocarbons in vehicle emissions not only threaten human health but also attack local vegetation and have been held to account for increased incidence of acid rain in popular localities. The St Gotthard Pass, which lies on one of the main routeways between Switzerland and Italy, is one location where atmospheric pollution from tourist traffic has been responsible for extensive damage to vegetation, including are Alpine plants.

A fourth area of concern centres of tourism impacts upon the *resource base.* Whilst tourism may be an agency for the promotion of resource conservation measures, it will exert negative effects associated with depletion or diversion of key resources. The attraction of hot, dry climates for many forms of tourism creates particular demands for local water supplies, which may become depleted through excessive tourist consumption or be diverted to meet tourist need for swimming pools or well-watered golf courses.

In parts of the Mediterranean, tourist consumption of water is as much as six times the levels demanded by local people. Tourism may also be responsible for depletion of local supplied of fuel or perhaps building materials. Paradoxically, the removal of sand (for concrete) from beaches is not uncommon.

The final area of environmental impact concerns *visual and structural changes,* and its is here that there is perhaps the clearest balance between negative and positive impacts of tourism. The physical development of tourism will inevitably produce a series of environmental impacts. The natural and non-natural environmental impacts. The natural and non-natural environment may be exposed to forms of 'visual' pollution prompted by new forms of architecture or styles of development. Land may be transferred from one sector (for example farming) to meet demands for hotel construction, new transport facilities, car parks or other elements of infrastructure. The built environment of tourism will also expand physically, whether in the form of accretions on growth on existing urban resorts, new centres of attraction of second homes in the countryside.

However, set against such potentially adverse changes there are significant areas of benefit. First, tourist-sponsored improvements to infrastructure, whether in the form of enhanced communications, public utilities or private services, will have some beneficial effects for local residents too. Second, tourism may provide a new use for formerly unproductive and marginal land. The rural environments in central Wales, north-west Scotland and the west of Ireland, for example, have all been partly sustained by the development of rural tourism. Third, tourism to cities has helped to promote urban improvement strategies aimed at clearing dereliction. Examples include the programme of national and international garden festivals held in several British cities during the 1980s which took derelict industrial sites and created new tourist attractions out of the wasteland. In Britain, continental Europe, the USA and Canada, the regeneration through reuse of redundant areas – dockland and water frontages being favoured targets – has been as recurring theme in contemporary urban development.

Towards a Sustainable Relationships Between Tourism: Analyzing Impacts on Environment

The evident problems that surround tourism and the

environment have led to the formulation of a range of management responses to the perceived difficulties. This has been mirrored both in the development of site-specific management techniques and also, more fundamentally, in strategies and approaches aimed at developing sustainable forms of tourism.

There are number of tourism management techniques that have been widely applied in areas where protection of environments is a key consideration – for example, within designated national parks. These techniques normally focus upon:

* spatial zoning;
* spatial concentration of dispersal of tourists;
* restrictive entry of pricing.

Spatial zoning is an established land management strategy that aims to integrate tourism into environments areas of land that have differing suitabilities or capacities for tourism. Hence zoning of land may be used to exclude tourists from primary conservation areas; to focus environmentally abrasive activities into locations that have been specially prepared for such events; or to focus general visitors into a limited number of locations where their needs may be met and their impacts contained and managed.

Zoning policies are often complemented by strategies for concentrating tourists into preferred sites (sometimes referred to by recreational planners as 'honeypots') or, where sites are under pressure, deflecting visitors to alternative destinations. Honeypots are commonly provided as inter-ceptors – planned locations that attract the tourist by virtue of their promotion and on-site provision (e.g. information, refreshment, car parking, etc.) and which then effectively prevent the further penetration of tourists into more fragile environments that may lie beyond. (Commercial tourist attractions, tourist information and visitor centres, country parks and heritage sites are all examples of locations that can act as honeypots and assist in the wide environmental management of tourism.)

In contrast, where conditions requires a redistribution of tourist activity, devices such as planned scenic drives or tourist routes may have the desired effect of taking people ways from environmental pressure points.

In some locations, regulation of environmental impacts of tourism is now begin achieved via pricing policies and/or exclusions and controls. The nature and scope of such practice varies considerably from place to place. In the USA, for example, entry to many of the national parks is subject to payment of an entry toll. whereas in England and Wales, entry if free. However, policies of exclusion and control are commonplace and becoming more so through time as the pressures of tourism grow. The stated policy of the Dartmoor National Park authority, for example, is to deffect as much tourism development as is possible to the periphery of the park, in order to protect the open moorland environment that lies at its core. Within the park, visitors are encouraged (through patterns of access and planned provision) towards a relatively small number of higher-capacity sites, whist movement of vehicles is subject to a park-wide traffic policy which both restricts and segregates vehicles to prescribed routes according to size and weight.

In some senses, however, these practical techniques for harmonising tourism and the environment are simply building-blocks that lead towards the much broader goal of securing sustainable forms of tourism development. Sustainable development is a concept that has entered the language in a diversity of contexts — population growth, natural resource development, energy consumption and, not least, tourism – and advocates of sustainability argue its merits as the most effective, long-term resolution of a range of environmental and resource-related problems. But what does the term 'sustainable development' actually mean, both as a general principle and in the context of tourism?

Sustainable Tourism

The concept of sustainability has been defined by the World Commission of Environment and Development as 'development that meets the needs of the present with compromising the ability of future generations to meet their own needs'. When viewed in these terms, the relevance of sustainable forms of development to tourism is obvious, given that it is an industry with a high level of dependence upon 'environments' as a basic source of attraction but also one, as we have seen, with a considerable capacity to erode the long-term viability of those self-same environments. Tourism therefore needs to be involved in sustainable development.

However, the outwardly simple definition of sustaina-bility cited above conceals much controversy and debate over who defines what is, or is not, sustainable and what sustainable development might therefore mean in practice.

The concept implicity recognises that there are basic human needs (e.g. food, clothing, shelter) that processes of development must match and that these needs are to be set alongside aspirations (e.g. to higher living standards, security and access to discretionary elements such as tourism) that it would be desirable to match. At the same time, however, there are environmental limitations that will ultimately regulate the levels to which development can actually proceed, and if principles of sustainability are also to embrace implicit notions of equity in access to resources, and the benefits that they bring, then sustainability is likely to prove an elusive target in the absence of some radical shifts in attitudes and beliefs. For this reason, the concept of sustainability has acquired a diversity of interpretations ranging from, at one extreme, a 'zero-growth' view that argues that all forms of development are inherently unsustainable and should therefore be resisted, to very different perspectives that argue for growth-oriented resource management based around the presumed capacities of technology to solve environmental problems and secure a sustainable future.

For the further development of tourism (as for most areas where sustainability is an issue), a middle path between these extremes – one which manages growth within acknowledged resource conservation limits – is generally held to offer the best prospects. Sustainable tourism needs therefore to :

* ensure the renewable resources are not consumed at a rate that is faster than rates of natural replacement;
* maintain biological diversity;
* recognise and value the aesthetic appeal of environ-ments;
* follow ethical principles that respect, livelihoods and customs;
* involve and consult local people in development processes;

* promote equity in the distribution of both the economic costs and the benefits of the activity amongst tourism developers and hosts.

Approaches to the Evaluation of Environmental Impacts and Sustainable Tourism

The central attributes of sustainable tourism may be mapped relatively easily, but the more practical difficulties of how to measure sustainable forms of development are less easily resolved. This particular challenge has focused attention onto alternative approaches to evaluation the environmental impacts of tourism; in particular, the concept of carrying capacity; the limits of acceptable change; and the use of environmental impact assessments.

The concepts of carrying capacity is a well-established approach to attempting to understand the ability of tourist places to withstand use and is inherent in the notion of sustainability. It recognises that for any environment, whether natural or non-natural, there is capacity (or level of use) which when exceeded is likely to promote varying levels of damage and/or be associated with reduced levels of visitor satisfaction. Carrying capacity has been visualised in several distinct ways; for example:

* as *physical* carrying capacity – which is normally viewed as a measure of absolute space, such as the number of spaces within a car part;
* as *ecological* capacity – which is the level of use that an environment can sustain before damage to the environment is experienced;
* as *perceptual* capacity – which is the level of crowding that a tourist will tolerate before he or she decides a location is too full and relocates elsewhere.

Although carrying capacity is easy to conceptualise, the value of the idea as a tool for measurement of impact is more limited. Ecological capacities are difficult to anticipate while perceptual carrying capacities, as personalised responses, are prone to variation both between and within individuals and tourist groups, depending very largely upon circumstance and motives. Capacity will also vary according to prevailing management practices whereby a site that is actively planned for tourism is likely to have a higher set of capacities than one that is not.

As a result of these limitations, alternative approaches to impact assessment have become more popular. The limits of acceptable change (LAC) technique was developed in the USA as a means of resolving development-related conflicts in conservation areas. The central features of the method are:

* the establishment of an agreed set of criteria surrounding a proposed development;
* the representation of all interested parties within decision-making;
* the prescription of desired conditions and levels of change after development;
* the establishment of ongoing monitoring of change and implementation of agreed strategies to keep impacts of change within the established limits.

The LAC approach therefore embodies several key aspects of sustainable form of tourism development. It recognises that change is an inevitable consequence of development but asserts that by the application of rational planning, overt recognition of environmental quality considerations and broad public consultation, sustainable forms of development may be realised. However, the approach does suffer practical weaknesses too. There are technical difficulties in agreeing and assessing qualitative aspects of tourism development and the process is dependent upon the existence of a structured planning system and sufficient resources in expertise and capital to operationalise the monitoring and review stages. Hence the contexts in which LAC would be most beneficial – for example, in shaping tourism development in Third World nations – often prove the least suited to the technique in practical terms.

The same constraint is also true of the third possible approach to realising sustainable development, the use of environmental impact assessment (EIA). EIA is becoming a widely used methods for evaluating possible environmental consequences of all form of development and is potentially a valuable tool for translating sustainable principles into working practice. In particular, EIA provides a framework for informing decision-making processes that surround development, and a widening number of industries are routi-nely required (or advised) to undertake EIAs and produce written environmental impact statements (EISs).

The methodologies of EIA are diverse and may embrace the use of key impact checklists, cartographic analysis of spatial impacts, simulation models or predictive techniques. Their strength are that when properly integrated into the planning phases of a project, they should help developers anticipate environmental effects, enable more effective compliance with environmental standards and reduce need for subsequent (and expensive) revision to projects. The overall goal of a sustainable form of development is also a more achievable object when environmental impacts have been evaluated in advance. However, EIA has also attracted criticisms, which have included tendencies:

* to focus on physical and biological impacts rather than the wider range of environmental changes;
* to application on a project-specific basis and/or at the local geographic level, thereby overlooking wider linkages and effects;
* to require a range of scientific and other data as a means of assessing likely impacts;
* to advocate technocratic solutions to environmental problems, which some advocates of sustainable development view as inappropriate.

Thus, as with LAC, EIA has practical limitations that will inhibit its application in many tourism development contexts, especially those that might benefit most from the technique.

The relative recency with which sustainable tourism has become an active issue means that practical cases that exemplify the application of sustainable principles and the methodologies outlined above are still not widespread, Box 3 presents an outline summary of two contrasting cases that do show how sustainable forms of environmental management are being applied in tourism areas. In the first example, attempts to protect a rare ecosystem on the Great Barrier Reef in Australia are outlined, whilst in the second case, a successful programme of sustainable water management at the desert resort of Palm Springs, California, is described.

Sustainable Tourism in Practice: Australia's Great Barrier Reef and Palm Springs, California

The Great Barrier Reef, Australia

The Great Barrier Reef off the northern coast of Queensland, Australia, provides one of the largest systems of coral reefs in the world. A maze of some 600 islands, 300 cay (reef islands) and nearly 3,000 sumerged reefs, the Great Barrier Reef region is home to 1,500 species of fish, about 350 types of coral, over 400 sponges and more than 4,000 molluscs. Apart from some small areas of development the reef has been largely unaffected by human activity and remains in excellent condition.

However, in recent years there have been significant increases in the presence of tourists. Over a fifteen-year period up to around 1990, tourist bed spaces increased from 785 to over 2,000; the charter vessel fleet grew from 135 to 300 boats and numbers of registered speedboats from 15,000 to 24,000.

In 1988, over 900,000 tourists visited the reef and the growing popularity of tourism to the area has begun to exert a range of environmental impacts. These have included physical destruction of reefs by trampling effects of divers standing on the coral and damage by boat anchors; localised water pollution from sewage and boat fuel; and removal of corals and specimen fish as souvenirs.

As a direct response to these problems, the Great Barrier Reef Marine Park (which at 350,000 km^2 is the largest protected marine area in the world) was set up by the Queensland Federal Government in 1975 to manage the conservation and use of the Reef. The Marine Park Authority has a broad remit that includes research, preparation and implementation of management plans, educational programmes and the regulation of commercial fishing.

The main strategy within the park management is zoning system based around three primary categories:

* 'General use' zones (which cover about 80 per cent of the park) permit most activities, provided they are ecologically sustainable.
* 'National park' zones allow only activities that do not remove living resources.
* 'Preservation' zones permit only scientific research.

Within zones, specific local variations may also be enforced, particularly limitations on building.

Tourism (and its associated development) may occur in all zones except the preservation zones, subject to the issue of permits. The factors considered in issuing permits will include the objectives of management within the zones in question; the size, extent and location of the use; access conditions; likely effects upon the environment in general and the ecosystem in particular; and likely effects upon resources and their conservation. Proponents of large-scale developments are also encouraged to conduct an EIA and to produce an EIS as a routine part of development applications. The tourists themselves are targeted via educational strategies, reinforced by local controls and prohibitions, aimed at encouraging responsible behaviours that help to conserve the marine environment.

Palm Springs, California

The development of the desert resort of palm Springs is a remarkable example of sustainable tourism in a difficult environment. Located in the Coachella Valley some 160 km south-east of Los Angeles, Palm Springs in a true desert region with mean July temperatures of 42ºC and less than 75 mm of rain per years.

However, the presence of springs fed from a substantial aquifer initially allowed the development of irrigated farming and, more recently, the growth of a fashionable tourist resort. More than 2 million visitors annually visit Palm Springs and, with over 200 hotels, 7,500 swimming pools and more than 80 golf courses, the Coachella Valley has become a major recreational environment within southern California.

The success of the resort has, however, depended entirely

upon the sustainable management of its water supplies. They key to the development was the construction in 1948 of the Coachella branch of the All-American Canal, which transfers water from the Colorado River near Yuma to the valley. This new supply not only helped to recharge the main groundwater sources, which farming had already begun to diminish, but also created a surplus of water that permitted the expansion of the resort. Diverted water is trapped in intake basins from where it percolates into underground storage, and despite the increasing demand for water in Palm Springs, groundwater reserves have actually increased in recent years, rather than diminished.

To reinforce the effectiveness of the scheme for recharging groundwater, a wide-ranging programme for managing water supply and demand has been implemented. This has included :

* improved extraction techniques to maximise the potential of groundwater sources;
* improved application systems, including computer-controlled drip irrigation systems and metered supplies;
* increased charges to moderate demand;
* increased reuse of waste water.

The latter policy, in particular, has benefited the tourism industry as some 3 million gallons a day of cheap reclaimed water is distributed to parks, urban amenity spaces and particularly, the resort's golf courses.

Sustainability has also been increased by complementary moves towards more water-efficient urban design and landscaping in Palm Springs. New golf courses are now encouraged to limit watered turf to only the essential parts of the course mainly the greens, tees and key sections of fairway – whilst urban parks, hotels, civic buildings and even private residences have been persuaded to adopt the practice of low-water-use landscaping using desert plants and natural surfacing.

Although extensive areas of lush, green ornamental space still adorn the resort, the wider use of desert-style landscaping has permitted a 10 per cent reduction in outdoor use of water in five years, even though parkland and amenity acreages have actually risen.

Sustainability and Alternative Forms of Tourism

The examples of the Great Barrier Reef and the desert resort of Palm Springs demonstrate sustainability in the context of conventional forms of tourism, but, in concluding this chapter, one further question merits brief attention. How far do the so-called 'alternative' forms of tourism provide templates for sustainable tourism in general?

There is perhaps a natural temptation to view the mass forms of packaged tourism as the least sustainable and the style of tourism that is most likely to bring widespread environmental change. In contrast, alternative forms of tourism (which are often characterised by their smaller scale, the involvement of local people, a preference for remoter areas and a predilection to place enjoyment of nature, landscape and cultures at the centre of the tourism experience) outwardly appear more in tune with principles of sustainability.

Further, the alluring names that are commonly given to alternative form of tourism – 'green tourism', 'eco-tourism', 'soft tourism', 'responsible tourism', even 'sustainable tourism' – tend to reinforce a popular belief the sustainability can only be equated with alternative tourism.

Such views do, however, need to be accorded considerable caution, for although the underlying philosophies of alternative tourism may strongly reflect the concept of sustainability, the experience of alternative tourism in a growing number of places suggests that such forms may be highly potent as agents of change and generators of impact. In fact, alternative tourism can be just as problematic, in development terms, as mass forms of tourism.

Several potential problems have been noted. First, alternative tourism usually penetrates far deeper into the personal lives of residents than the more aloof forms of mass tourism, with similarly enhanced capacities to generate a range of environmental, economic, social and cultural impacts. Second, lack of local expertise in catering for alternative tourists can mean that inappropriate practices are implemented and local resources over-exploited for short-term gain. Third, there is an evident risk that the alternative from of tourism simply represent the pioneering stages in new practices of mass recreation. In this way, alternative tourism simply becomes a mechanism for constructing new geographies of travel and its associated impacts, centered on the exotic and the distant.

There is ample evidence in high-street travel agencies that destinations that until quite recently were the domain of the alternative tourist – for example, the Himalayas, China, such-Saharan Africa-are now being opened up to the package tourist, albeit at the luxury end of the market for the present.

Perhaps most fundamentally, alternative tourism – whilst perhaps embracing many principles of sustainability – does not in itself provide a model for sustainable forms of mass tourism. As several writers have noted, alternative tourism is not a replacement for mass tourism.

It lacks the physical capacity, logistics and organisation to meet the growing levels of demand, it lacks the economic scale that has become so important to many national, regional and local economies, and the style of alternative tourism fails to match the tastes and preferences of many millions of holidaymakers and travellers word-wide.

So, whilst there are aspects of alternative tourism that certainly provide lessons in how to forge sustainable relationships between tourism and the environment, alternative tourism is not a natural (sustainable) replacement for the supposedly problematic mass forms of travel. Solutions to the problem of sustainability therefore need to be forged within the context of mass tourism, and that suggests that if the symbiotic relationship between tourism and the environment is to be maintained, careful management and planning of tourism development – whether guided by sustainable principles or not – must be a central component the future growth of tourism. The role of planning in tourism form the in focus for the next chapter.

Summary

Many forms of tourism are dependent upon the environment to provide both a context and a focus for tourist activity, yet those same activities have a marked capacity to devalue and, occasionally, destroy the environmental resources upon which tourism is based. Environmental effects of tourism are broadly experienced in impacts upon ecosystems, landscapes and the built environment, although specific impacts very spatially – reflecting differences in the nature of the places that tourists visit, the levels and intensity of development, and the skills and expertise of resource managers. As the environmental problems associated with tourism have become more apparent, greater attention has been focused upon ways of producing sustainable patterns of development and alternative forms of tourism that produce fewer detrimental effects upon the tourist environment. However, truly sustainable tourism has often proven to be elusive, whilst there are evident risks that alternative tourism, in time, develops into mass forms of travel, with all the attendant problems that such practices tend to produce.

3

Hospitality and Environmental Protection

Tourisni's Relationship with the Environment

Tourism relationship with the environment is complex. Given its scale and global extent, it is inevitable that tourism has important environmental impacts. *These impacts are related to resource consumption,* as well as *to pollution* and *waste generated by tourism activities, including impacts from transport.* At the same time, *beaches* and *mountains, rivers, forests and biodiversity make the environment a basic resource upon which the tourism industry depends to thrive and grow* and *grow* and *threats to the environment threaten the viability of the tourism industry.* Lastly, tourism can contribute to environmental protection.

Tourism continues to grow rapidly and is expected to increases by 4 per cent each year over the next five years. It is expanding in all regions, including in remote and sensitive areas.

Environmental Impacts of Tourism

The main potential adverse impacts of tourism on the environment include

Pressure on Natural Resources

The main resources at threat are:

Land and landscape: sand mining/beach and sand dune erosion, soil erosion, urbanisation, toad and airport building leading to land degradation, loss of wildlife habitats, deterioration of scenery

Marine resources: recreational impacts. (scuba diving, snorkeling, sport fishing), damage to coral reefs and subsequent impacts on coastal protection and fisheries.

Atmosphere : high levels of energy use in tourism facilities and in transportation

Freshwater overuse of critical water resources for hotels, swimming pools and golf courses. This is of particular concern in recions such as the Mediterranean where water resources are scarce and each tourist consumes more than 200 liters a day.

Pressure on other local resources: for example energy, food, and other raw materials which may be in short supply locally.

Harm to Wildlife and Habitats, with Associated Loss of Biodiversity

The main harm to wildlife and habitats is:

Biological resources: disruption of wildlife habitats, clearance of vegetation for tourism developments, increased pressure on endangered species due to trade and hunting; extra demand for fuelwood, forest fires

Ecologically fragile areas: such as rain forests, wetlands, mangroves, coral reefs, sea grass beds. If not properly planned and managed nature tourism threatens the world's most ecologically fragile areas including parks and natural world heritage sites

Pollution and Wastes

Pollution and wastes contaminate:

Land: solid wastes and litter (a tourist produces an average of about 1 kg of waste a day)

Freshwater: pollution by sewage

Marine waters and coastal areas: sediment run off, pollution from land-based hotels and marinas; waste and litter linked with marine sports and cruises : for example in 1995, it was estimated that cruise ships in the Caribbean alone produced more than 70,000 tonnes of waste each year.

Air: at local level, air pollution from tourist transportation, global impacts, especially from, CO_2 emissions, related to energy use in transportation, air-conditioning and heating of tourist facilities, etc.

Noise: Related to ground as well as air transportation.

Social and Cultural Pressures Related to Conservation and Sustainable use of Biodiversity

Social and cultural impacts: tourism means disturbance to the local way of life and disturbance of social structures, and can adversely affect traditional practices that contribute to the conservation and sustainable use of biodiversity

Adverse impacts on livelihoods and lack of benefit sharing with those who bear tourism related costs to both the human and natural environment.

Resource use conflicts: competition between tourism and local populations for limited resources of water, sanitation and energy, competition with traditional land uses, especially in heavily used areas such as coastal zones.

Contribution of Tourism to Environmental Conservation

Tourism can contribute to environmental protection, the conservation of biodiversity, the sustainable use of natural resources and provide much needed resources.

The tourism industry can contribute to the conservation of areas that are assets for their development: parks, protected areas, cultural and natural sites, through financial contributions, provision of environmental infrastructure and improved management. Financial contributions are being made for a limited number of initiatives by the tourism industry and this trend should be further developed.

Tourism also helps raise awareness of the local population with regards to the financial value of natural and cultural sites, makes them proud of this heritage and allies for its conservation. More widely, the involvement of local communities in tourism development and operation appears to be one important condition for the conservation and sustainable use of biodiversity.

This possible contribution of tourism to conservation is one of the reasons explaining the current interest given to the development of nature tourism. However, for sustainable tourism, there is a need to better understand not only the benefits but also the costs of tourism. There is also a need to develop both a more systematic analysis of direct and indirect costs and benefits from tourism as well as green accounting approaches.

However, all types of tourism should fully integrate environmental and social considerations. The current focus on nature tourism should not obscure the major challenge to also make mass tourism sustainable.

Environmental Challenges for the Private Sector

Progress Achieved

The tourism industry has developed a number of voluntary initiatives for addressing environmental issues:

environmental management of tourism facilities *and especially hotels is being widely promoted, and progress is being made, particularly for larger hotels, in waste reduction handling, management and disposal, energy and water consumption. This has been promoted by main international industry associations. Numerous industry associations at the regional and national levels have also promoted it. UNEP has taken part in these efforts. A few tour operators also have implemented environmental programmes and raised environmental awareness of their clients.*

a number of environmental codes of conduct have also been developed *by the tourism sector (cf UNEP publication in references) as well as Action Plans (example of the Caribbean Action for Sustainable Tourism)*

the tourism industry is also increasing/v interested in ecolabels *as a means of promoting their facilities and destinations (ef. UNEP publication in references)*

However., efforts up to now have been concentrated on measures which result in short term economic benefits and there are still many major problems to be solved to put the tourism industry on the path towards sustainability.

Key Remaining Environmental Challenges

The key remaining challenges are to:

Promote wider implementation of environmental management,

particularly in the many small and medium enterprises that form the backbone of the tourism industry, and spread initiatives to all sectors of the tourism industry

Use more widely environmentally-sound technologies, in particular to reduce emissions of CO_2 and other greenhouse gases and ozone depleting substances as set out in international agreements

Raise the awareness of tourism clients of the environment and social implications of their holidays, and of opportunities for their responsible behaviour

Develop a better dialogue with the local communities in travel destinations and promote the involvement of local stakeholders in tourism ventures

Work with governments and other stakeholders to improve the overall environmental quality of destinations

Report publicv on environmental performances and address the key issues of siting and more ecoefficient design of lourism facilities.

For the tourism industry to remain credible in their commitment to sustainable development, it needs to address the above issues.

Environmental Challenges for Governments

Progress Achieved

A number of initiatives have been taken by governments, in all parts of the world to :

Develop national strategies or master plans for sustainable development of tourism

Develop appropriate regulatory mechanism and tools such as, environmental assessment, development of building regulations and of environmental standards for tourism

Create terrestrial and marine protected areas

Support voluntary initiatives by the tourism industry

However, in many counties the coastline is being overbuilt due to tourism development. Unfortunately, the same are being repeated.

Too often, action is delayed until loss of revenue and cultural and environmental degradation has occurred. The damage can be irreversible. To achieve sustainable tourism preventative approaches must be adopted.

Key Remaininge Environmental Challenges

Facts and figures demonstrate the need for urgent actions to avoid irrecersible damage from tourism, particularly in coastal and mountain areas.

Further Develop and Implement the Legislative and Policy Framework

Ratify, if not already done and work toward continued implementation of international and regional environmental conventions

Integrate more fully tourism development into the overall plans for sustainable development and develop participatory approaches

Develop more widely land use planning and protect the coastline through building restrictions (for example legislation in France, Spain, Denmark and Egypt where it is forbidden to build with in defined distance from the coast)

Identify and adopt the most appropriate mix of regulation and economic instruments and, in many cases, develop economic instruments to address environmental issues

Work towards the real enforcement of regulations and standards.

2. Raise Awareness, Build Capacity and Promote Effective Action for Sustainable Tourism

Improve the understanding of the benefits and burdens of tourism in environmental, social and economic terms, for the areas under their jurisdiction

Strengthen capacity for the management and control of tourism in their sphere of responsibility and establish and maintain procedures for coodination with neighbouring authorities and with relevant state authorities

Provide support through pilot projects and capacity development, including capacity development at local government level

Ensure the participation of all stakeholders affected by or involved in tourism and its development, especially indigenous and local communities

Ensure that tourism makes a positive contribution to economic development and that the economic benefits of tourism are equitably shared

Encourage and catalase industry initiatives for sustainable tourism across all sectors of the tourism, including accommodation, land, air and sea transportation, tour operations, travel agents, attractions sectors, etc.

Promote changes in consumer behaviour in both tourist originating countries and destinations towards more sustainable forms of tourism

Develop Monitoring of Progress Towards Sustainable Tourism

Develop activities to monitor, control and mitigate adverse effects that may arise from tourism activities and development.

Example: Sustainable Tourism in The Mediterranean

A group of experts on sustainable tourism meeting at Antalya, Turkey, 17-19 September 1998, under the framework of the Mediterranean Commission on Sustainable Development, highlighted the means to make sustainable tourism a reality for the region. The meeting looked at conventions, framework agreements, procedures and protocols; financial mechanisms, such as taxes on the environment, tourism taxes, requirements to reinvest profits in regions with tourism installations, fines for non-compliance, subsidies for the environmental upgrading of facilities, development of agro-tourism, and tourism development in difficult areas; technical Assistance and advice; and land use planning and protective laws.

The meeting noted that efforts currently being put into these mechanisms throughout the region do not yet match the needs for widespread effective action, and that better integration of Mediterranean tourism with sustainable development demands major efforts on training, awareness raising, and exchange of experience and best practice information, as well as organisation of the strong participation of the local population. Action is also needed on:

(a) financial mechanisms to enable the tourism sector to contribute to the quality of destinations

(b) network of pilot projects and establishment of a "Mediterranean electable" for environmental quality of destinations and installations

(c) capacity building for states, regions and tourist destinations to bring about successful integration of tourism with sustainable development

(d) measures to support tourism in the Mediterranean island regions

Challenges for Non-governmental Organ Isations

Progress Achieved

Many NGOs have already made significant steps in modifying consumers preferences and behaviour, making sensitive issues public and highlighting problematic areas and thus influencing decisions. They have also increased the environmental awareness and educational level with great positive results. An example among others is the "Blue Flag" campaign, conducted by the Foundation for Environmental Education in Europe, which contributed to the improvement in the quality of European beaches and marinas.

Key Remaining Environmental Challenges

More specifically voice their views in tourism policies and strategies

Con tribute to development, and implementation, of' environmental standards for tourism

Develop or participate in raising awareness and education activities for sensitising tourists towards improving guest consumption patterns

Assist with monitoring tourism activities and development and progress towards more sustainable tourism.

Environmental Policy Challenges for the International Community

Progress Achieved

Many international organisations have, in line with their mission and held of expertise, developed programmes and activities to help put tourism on the path towards sustainability.

Unep's Contribution to Sustainable Tourism

- *Global efforts by the Industry and Environment Centre (IE),*

  IE, in co-operation with partners, such as the World Tourism Organization, and UNESCO and industry associations, published technical reports on best practices in the tourism industry (and organised conferences and workshops to share experiences.

- *Regional Efforts through the Regional Seas Programme:*

  The Caribbean Environmental Programme (CEP) developed with USAID the Caribbean Environmental Network to improve environmental practices in the tourism industry in the region (training, pilot studies)

  The Mediterranean Action Plan provided information on sustainable tourism and has set up an expert group on this topic within the framework of the Mediter-ranean Commission on Sustainable Development.

- *Thematic efforts.* The secretariats of the international conventions and, in particular, the convention on biological diversity, have provided information and catalysed action for sustainable tourism in their areas.

The World Tourism Organisation has also been active focusing in particular on planning at the national and local levels and on indicators for sustainable tourism and in addressing sustainable tourism in a number of regional events.

A number of other international organizations have developed activities for sustainable tourism and, in particular, UNESCO: tourism in World Heritage Sites, cultural tourism etc.

Many regional organisations and in particular the various UN Economic and Social Commissions have also developed activities to support sustainable tourism in their region

To help catalyse appropriate action UNEP has recent/v proposed · Principles for Implementation of Sustainable Tourism". The Principles are being designed to provide a coherent framework for more specific guidelines to be prepared by the various Conventions: Biological Diversity, Climate Change, Regional Seas Action Plans, and other international agreements, that have already or will address tourism issues; and to help Governments, intergovernmental, private-sector and other organisations in applying the general concept of sustainable tourism in practice.

Key Remaining Environmental Challenges

The key remaining challenges are to:

- Assist and support governments in development of national strategies or master plans for sustainable development of tourism and of environmental land use and building regulations and standards for tourism
- Raise awareness and build capacity of all stakeholders by providing information on best practices for sustainable tourism
- Encourage the private sector to develop and apply codes and guidelines, environmental management systems, and promote the development of the use of environmental reporting by companies in the various branches of the tourism sector
- Assist in assessing the environmental effectiveness of existing voluntary initiatives in the various branches of the tourism sector and present corresponding recommendations
- Promote the transfer of Environmentally Sound Technologies (ESTs), practices, and management tools adapted for the tourism sector, and disseminate information on ESTs to governments and the tourism industry
- Work with other stakeholders to establish, and disseminate lessons from, Best Practices projects on sustainable tourism
- Provide support through pro vision of information and capacity development programmes particularly on the costs and benefits of tourism development, the use of

economic incentives to promote sustainable tourism, and on destination management

- Assist in establishment of monitoring of progress towards sustainable tourism.

Emerging Issues

Developing partnership: For sustainable tourism the involvement and commitment of all stakeholders are essential. However, public, private and academic sector partnerships are still underdeveloped and therefore need to be encouraged.

Involvement of the banking and insurance sectors: banks and insurance companies could greatly expedite progress of sustainable tourism by incorporating environmental and social criteria into assessment procedures for loans, investments, and insurance. Ney could neap finance environmentally-sound technologies and provide incentives for sustainable tourism. This approach has worked well in other contexts. Widespread involvement of the banking and insurance sectors should be sought.

Use of economic' instruments: the tourism industry consumes increasingly scarce natural resources. The costing of energy and water in particular could expedite greatly ecoefficiency in the tourism industry and raise revenue for the improved management of these resources. Governments should consider the development and widespread use of economic instruments for sustainable tourism.

Involvement of tourism boards: Often, marketing strategies and messages are not in line with the principles of sustainable tourism. There is the need to better and involve tourism boards in sustainable tourism efforts.

Capacity building of local government: In many countries, local governments have important responsibilities regarding tourism development. Capacity building programmes should be implemented to help them understand these responsibilities, develop integrated and participatory approaches and define and implement policies for sustainable tourism.

Greater focus on transport: There is a continued development of long-haul travel. Economic, technological and management approaches should be developed to reduce emissions. Waste and pollution resulting from tourism transportation. Changing consumption patterns should also be considered. Emerging types of tourism: Tourism is rapidly diversifying. Emerging forms of tourism should also develop according to sustainability criteria. Currently, the increase of cruises and the current trend towards megaships, necessitate that the cruise ship industry develops a socially and environmentally responsible approach.

Improve monitoring: Careful monitoring of impacts and results as well as the adoption of corrective measures are conditions for sustainable tourism. All stakeholders at all levels should thus develop monitoring. As previously stated, the private sector should develop monitoring and public reporting of their activities. Local and central governments should develop, more widely, monitoring tools such as indicators, and incorporate the results into their decision making process. Where appropriate, participatory approaches should be used. Monitoring is currently uncommon and this should be a priority.

4

Environmental Implications of the Hospitality Business

Environmental management in the United States over the past several decades has focused on regulating production industries, such as manufacturing and mining. However, there has been increasing interest in the environmental effects of the service industry.

Generally speaking, a service is as an activity done for others. A perhaps even broader definition of a service is "anything sold in trade that cannot be dropped on your foot". The service industry therefore comprises a variety of activities, from restaurants to hospitals to financial institutions. It accounts for 75% of the U.S. gross domestic product ($3.8 trillion in 1997) (U.S. Census Bureau, 1998) and 80% of U.S. employment.

The service industry merits attention because of its large size and consequently its potential for environmental impacts (both negative and positive). There is a small but growing body of literature discussing the influence of the service sector on environmental quality. Three categories of influence have evolved from these discussions:

1. direct impacts of the service itself,
2. upstream impacts, arising from the service provider's ability to influence its suppliers, and
3. downstream impacts, where the service provider can influence its customers' behavioural or consumption patterns.

It is necessary to look at all three categories to develop a complete picture of the influence of the service sector on environmental quality.

The tourism industry is one of the largest components of the service sector, and has considerable ability to influence environmental quality. Travel and tourism contributed $91 billion in revenue into the U.S. economy in 1998 (World Airline News, 1999), supporting 16.2 million jobs directly and indirectly. Over forty-three million tourists visited the United States in 1998 (U.S. Department of Commerce, International Trade Administration, 1999). Furthermore, the tourism industry is projected to be the largest U.S. private employer by 2000, and now represents 10% of the national private gross domestic product.

Tourist destinations tend to be places of the highest amenities, whether the amenities are social, cultural, or natural. These destinations, due in part to their high quality, are often in short supply relative to demand (Robert Healy, Nicholas School of the Environment, Duke University, personal communication via email, November 28, 1999). This scarcity leads to the potential for degradation of tourist areas, as they reach and in some cases exceed their carrying capacity.

The tourism industry is complex; being fragmented into several industries that, taken together, constitute what is commonly referred to as the travel and tourism industry. It comprises components of other industries that do not cater exclusively to tourists; therefore a discussion of the environmental impacts of tourism needs to consider what percentage of use is related to tourism in each industry. Sectors of the tourism industry include transportation (e.g., airlines, buses, automobiles), lodging, restaurants, the cruise industry, amusement parks and resorts, and general retail and merchandise stores. Included in the definition of the tourism industry is the associated development (e.g., tourist infrastructure) of tourist destinations, and tourist activities.

We have identified impacts from tourist-related transportation, tourist-related development, tourist activities including some recreational activities such as boating, and direct impacts of the lodging and cruise industries. Quantitative data help to illustrate impacts where available; otherwise qualitative data supported by relevant examples are used. Although this discussion focuses on environmental impacts in the United States, some international examples are drawn upon when applicable. After presenting these impacts, we analyze the influence that providers of tourism services can have on their suppliers as well as the tourist. While there are many more industries that provide services to tourists, this discussion focuses on the upstream and downstream leveraging potential of four service providers: the lodging industry, the cruise industry, travel agents, and tour operators.

Section 1 presents both beneficial and adverse environmental impacts of tourism, including tourist activities, development, transportation, and direct impacts of the lodging and cruise industries.

Section 2 explores the relationships among travel agents, tour operators, and service providers, and tourists. The structure of selected components of the tourism industry is presented, and opportunities for upstream leverage on suppliers and downstream leverage on tourists are discussed. Finally, this section briefly analyzes the impact of technology on travel services.

Section 3 discusses steps within the tourism industry as well as government to lessen the adverse environmental impacts of tourism. This section concludes with a brief presentation of the benefits of educational efforts to minimize impacts.

Environmental Impacts of Tourism

Definition of Tourism

Tourism is "the temporary movement of people to destinations outside their normal places of work and residence, the activities undertaken during their stay in those destinations, and the facilities created to cater to their needs". It is often difficult to distinguish between tourism and recreation, as they are interrelated. Tourism involves traveling a distance from home, while recreation is defined as the activities undertaken during leisure time (McIntosh & Goeldner, 1990). Outdoor recreation is even more closely related to tourism. The extent of the overlap depends in part on the length of time of the activity and its location. For example, a boater who uses his or her boat for one day and who stays near his or her home may be considered a recreational boater; while a boater who travels on his or her boat overnight to a destination may be considered a tourist. Therefore while this discussion paper focuses primarily on tourism, selected recreational activities and their impacts are considered as well.

The degree of environmental impact varies, depending on the type of tourist and the intensity of site use (Gartner, 1996). There are day tourists, who visit a destination for a day and then leave; summer residents who are in effect tourists for a season; and tourists on bus tours and other trips that may visit a location for a few minutes or a number of days. Day tourists have an impact on the environment through their transportation to their destination as well as their activities once there. This is true for summer residents, but these tourists also have a cumulative impact, as they are in one place for a longer period of time. For example, nutrients leaching from the septic systems of tourists' waterfront homes can accelerate eutrophication and contribute to depletion of dissolved oxygen supply of the adjacent water body. On the other hand, summer residents often are an important force in preserving the natural beauty of an area (e.g., the Adirondacks). Tourists who visit an area for longer than a day and choose to stay in hotels contribute to the impacts that the lodging industry has on the environment. In addition to the length of stay, tourist impacts depend on the type of activity undertaken. Passive activities such as birdwatching have different impacts than more active pursuits, such as snowmobiling or boating.

There are environmental impacts from the travel to a destination, the tourist activities in and of themselves at that destination, such as hiking or boating, and from the creation, operation., and maintenance of facilities that cater to the tourist, such as hotels. This discussion addresses impacts from tourism-related transportation, development, the lodging and cruise industries, and tourist activities including selected forms of recreation.

Transportation

Airlines

In 1995, twenty percent of U.S. commercial air travel was attributed to leisure, including rest and relaxation, sightseeing, and outdoor recreation (U.S. Department of Transportation, 1997). Aircraft emit the most carbon monoxide of any of the five listed air pollutants, but it is a small amount relative to other modes of transportation. In total, aircraft are responsible for approximately one percent of the total ground-level emissions from mobile sources; therefore tourism-related air travel is responsible for only.2% of total ground-level emissions. Furthermore, tourism-related air travel contributes less than 1% of total U.S. emissions of each of the listed criteria pollutants.

Although aircraft contribute only a small amount to total air pollution, emissions from this source is increasing. Between 1970 and 1995, hydrocarbon and NOx emissions from aircraft sources have grown 53%. Projections to 2010 indicate that aircraft emissions will continue to increase. Aircraft emissions in nonattainment areas with large airport facilities in particular are projected to represent a growing percentage of regional sources of air pollutants (EPA, The projections indicate an increase in the aircraft component of total regional emissions between 1990 and 2010 in ten metropolitan regions (nine of which are currently not in attainment of the National Ambient Air Quality Standards (NAAQS) for ozone; the tenth city has attained the ozone standard, but is considered an ozone "maintenance" area). The 2010 percentages are still relatively low, ranging from 0.2% volatile organic compounds (VOC) in Philadelphia to 5.1% VOC in Charlotte; and 1.8% NOx in Philadelphia to 7.6% in Charlotte (EPA, 1999). The percentages are higher in Charlotte in part because other sources contribute less.

The EPA has had regulations for smoke and hydro-carbon emissions from aircraft engines in place since 1984. In 1997, the agency promulgated new emission standards for nitrogen oxide, and carbon monoxide. This rule was adopted to codify the existing voluntary emission standards of the United Nations International Civil Aviation Organization (ICAO) The DOT's Federal Aviation Administration (FAA) is responsible for enforcing these aircraft emissions standards.

Noise Pollution

In addition to air pollution, aircraft contribute to noise pollution. The FAA is responsible for addressing the noise abatement issue. The 1990 Airport Noise and Capacity Act authorized the FAA to reduce aircraft noise by requiring replacement of louder planes with quieter aircraft. In fact, airlines have spent billions of dollars to address this problem. Stage 2 aircraft are now being replaced by Stage 3 aircraft, which are 50% quieter; and the goal was to have only Stage 3 planes flying by 2000. There are also noise impacts from air tour operators, such as those that take 800,000 passengers a year on scenic overflights of the Grand Canyon. In an effort to reduce unnatural noise, the FAA proposed new rules in August 1999 that would cap the number of overflights in the Grand Canyon ("A Cramped Grand Canyon," 1993). However, again, as tourism-related travel represents only 20% of commercial air travel, and airplanes are only one source of noise pollution, tourism's contribution to total noise pollution is minor.

Ground Transportation

Much of the tourism-related air pollution comes from automobiles. Thirty-five percent of people traveling for leisure in 1995 used personal automobiles as their means of travel. Four-hundred million leisure trips are taken in automobiles per year in the United States; 80% of those trips are 250 miles or les. In 1997, light duty vehicles (passenger cars up to 6,000 lbs. G.V.W.) emitted an average of 1.53 grams of exhaust hydrocarbons per mile, 19.86 grams of carbon monoxide per mile, and 1.51 grams of nitrogen oxide per mile (DOT, 1998). Automobiles emit by far the most carbon monoxide, nitrogen oxide, and volatile organic compounds in comparison to other transportation. Personal automobiles emit 32% percent of the total national carbon monoxide emissions, and 12% of total national nitrogen oxide emissions (in 1996). However, it is difficult to separate the amount of tourism-related automobile travel from all automobile travel.

One area where it is possible to distinguish between tourism-related automobile travel and other travel is within national parks. Exhaust from tourists' cars affects air quality and vegetation in some national parks. Adverse impacts on vegetation have been attributed to automobile exhausts in Yosemite. Almost three-quarters of in national park superintendents surveyed cited exhaust from tourists' cars as a significant factor affecting air quality within the parks. Indeed, one national park report noted that "the impact of automobiles (air and noise pollution, acreage for roads, gasoline stations) may be more significant than the impact of the visitors themselves."

Tour buses have an impact on air quality as well. Often referred to as the motorcoach industry, the tour bus industry includes 3,000 companies and 25,000 vehicles. Companies are classified as intercity or charter-tour. The latter constitutes more than 50% of the market. Charter-tour bus trips have increased, while intercity trips have declined. Specific emissions data on tour buses are not available, but most tour buses belong in the category of heavy-duty diesel vehicles. In 1997, these vehicles emitted 1.468 million short tons (mst) of carbon monoxide, and 1.886 mst of nitrogen oxide.

Another form of ground transportation that has grown in the past twenty years is the recreational vehicle (RV) and off-road recreational vehicle (ORV) sector. These non-road recreational vehicles do not include sport utility vehicles, or SUVs. These data suggest that this segment of tourism-related transportation does not contribute

Ground transportation can also have an impact on natural habitat. This impact occurs primarily through road construction. However. Some vehicles such as ORVs can have a direct impact. As noted earlier, the distinction between tourism and recreation is a difficult one to make. While ORVs can be considered to be primarily recreational, some ORV users travel significant distances (e.g., from New Jersey to Cape Cod, Massachusetts) to participate in a recreational activity. When ORV use occurs during a trip away from home (as part of a larger tourist trip), it can be considered a tourist activity as well as a recreational one.

Off-road vehicles have damaged dune systems and salt marshes in Barustable, and Provincetown, Massachusetts. A study done by the National Park Service Cooperative Research Unit at the University of Massachusetts found that even low-level use can cause severe environmental degradation. Only 50 passes of an ORV at the foot of dunes halted growth of beach grass that stabilizes the dune. This causes erosion of the dunes, which in turn increases the risk of damage from flooding, as dunes provide natural flood protection. In addition, the use of ORVs by tourists has proven destructive to wildlife in some areas. Cape Cod National Seashore has had to initiate seasonal and spatial permits for ORV users to protect Piping Plovers during their nesting period. An ORV race across the deserts of California and Nevada has been permanently cancelled as a result of the damage the vehicles were doing to the desert tortoise populations.

Recreational Marine Vehicles

Recreational marine vehicles are included in this discussion because their use can be considered tourism when part of a longer trip. For example, recreational boaters who take their boats to Block Island from the coast of Connecticut can be considered tourists (because they are visiting a destination away from home). The impact of this activity occurs in transit to a tourist destination.

Recreational marine vehicles, can, therefore, affect air quality during transit to a destination and while their owners boat in and around that destination. Recreational marine vehicles do not emit as much carbon monoxide as automobiles, but they do emit significantly more of it than recreational land vehicles (such as off-road vehicles) and aircraft. The EPA found that nonroad hydrocarbon emissions represent 10% of urban summertime HC emissions. Recreational marine engines were responsible for 30% of the nonroad engine emissions. In addition, two-stroke engines, such as those found on personal watercraft, are rather inefficient and typically release 25-30% of oil and gas into the surrounding water (Robert Healy, Nicholas School of the Environment, Duke University, personal communication via email, November 28, 1999). However, emissions from marine recreational vehicles represent only a small percentage of total national emissions; therefore their effects are less pronounced than with automobiles.

The Clean Air Act Amendments of 1990 gave the EPA authority for the first time to regulate emissions from nonroad engines and vehicles (EPA, 1996, August). The EPA set emissions standards for new spark-ignition gasoline marine engines in 1996, including outboard engines, personal watereraft engines, and jet boat engines. These are designed to reduce hydrocarbon emissions from these types of engines 75% by 2025. These emissions standards do not apply to inboard motors, as they emit fewer pollutants, but they do apply to outboard engines sold starting in 1998, and to personal watercraft (such as jetskis) engines sold starting in 1999 (64 Federal Register 62293, 1999).

Development and Land Use

The environmental impacts of the construction and development of facilities needed to support the industry are both immediate and gradual. Development associated with tourism includes accommodations, roads, retail stores and restaurants, tourist attractions, tourists' seasonal waterfront homes, water supplies, and waste disposal facilities. Cumulative effects over time are particularly problematic because the developer in question is often out of the picture before impacts become obvious. An example of a gradual impact is the leaching of nutrients from septic systems of tourists' waterfront homes into the waterbody, accelerating eutrophication and depleting dissolved oxygen supplies.

Tourist infrastructure can also adversely impact water quality because more wastewater is created in one place and reduced someplace else, putting more pressure on sewage treatment plants or septic systems in the tourist destination. When a sewage treatment plant receives more effluent than it can treat, the excess can flow directly into water bodies untreated, creating a potential health hazard. The sewage problem with tourist facilities is further exacerbated by the seasonal nature of many tourist areas. An area which off-season may have the capacity (either through septic systems or treatment plants) to properly treat sewage may be overburdened during the tourist season.

Sewage effluent can damage coral reefs because it stimulates the growth of algae, which cover the filter-feeding corals, hampering their ability to get food. Furthermore, the algae impede the transmission of sunlight to the plant cells (zooxanthellae) living within the corals' tissue, hindering their ability to grow and provide the coral with needed nutrition. This damage has occurred on the Hawaiian island of Oahu, where the discharge of partially treated sewage effluent stimulated the growth of a particular algae, destroying parts of the reef. However, it is difficult to separate the effects of rapid urbanization of Oahu on the sewage treatment plants with the effects of an increase in tourists to the area. An area where the degradation of coral reefs due to sewage discharge can be attributed to tourism is in Jamaica. Damage to the corals there resulting from sewage discharge from tourist resorts along a 160-kilometer stretch of coastline was observed as early as 1973.

Tourist facilities increase the amount of impervious surfaces, causing more runoff to reach water bodies. This runoff contains nutrients, suspended particles, and oil and gas. Excess nutrients added to a water body can accelerate the process of eutrophication, causing an overgrowth of algae, which in turn uses up excess dissolved oxygen as the algae decays, causing fish kills. The overgrowth of algae is also a nuisance to swimmers. Furthermore, if masses of algae wash up on shore, they can create a foul-smelling area and a breeding ground for biting flies. A relevant example is the accelerated eutrophication of Lake Tahoe since the 1950s. Increased development to accommodate tourism and recreation contributed to the degradation of water quality for two primary reasons: (1) the increase of impervious surface, which in turn led to increased runoff of nutrients into the lake, and (2) the destruction of wetlands needed to filter those pollutants.

Construction of facilities supporting the tourism industry can damage wetlands, mangroves, coral reefs, and estuaries. Wetlands have been destroyed to make way for roads, airports, marinas, sewage treatment plants, and recreational facilities. This destruction is problematic because wetlands provide many crucial functions, including acting as a nursery ground for a diverse aquatic community, and helping to buffer the impacts of pollutants to the water body. In Cancun, Mexico, the natural environment of mangrove wetlands was almost completely destroyed by the development of tourist hotels and their associated infrastructure. Similarly, in Jamaica over 700 acres of wetlands have been destroyed since the 1960s for tourism development. In the Rocky Mountain National Park, the construction of a high level road increasing human accessibility led to the destruction of 95% of the vegetation cover in some areas close to the road.

Although tourism has been the impetus for much destructive development, it has also been the motivation for preserving sensitive ecosystems. Some of this motivation stems from economic benefits, as natural parks serve as attractions for tourists. An example on an international level is the Parc des Volcans in Rwanda, which provides ecological benefits through protection of the local watershed, and economic benefits, as it is the country's third largest source of foreign exchange. Everglades National Park in Florida is a domestic example of a sensitive wetland and estuarine environment where tourism has spurred preservation efforts.

Tourism with an emphasis on cultural and historic sites has been called "heritage" or "cultural" tourism, and is one of the fastest growing trends in the industry. Heritage tourism focuses on sharing the historical and cultural resources of an area with travelers, while still maintaining the integrity of each site. This type of tourism has been the impetus for the rehabilitation of existing historic sites, buildings, and monuments, such as the facelift that historic houses, lighthouses, and piers received on Cape Codth in the name of tourism. Similarly, the 18 century capital of the former British colony of Virginia, Williamsburg, has been transformed from ruins to a thriving historic site and tourist destination. Renovations to the Custer House at Fort Abraham Lincoln State Park in North Dakota were completed in part to attract additional tourists. A final example where heritage tourism has been the catalyst for improvement is the rural, somewhat neglected farm town of Fort Benton, Montana. It was transformed into an international tourist attraction because of several historic sites that were restored, including a Lewis and Clark memorial, the Museum of the Northern Great Plains, and the Museum of the Upper Missouri.

A related benefit of tourism can be the revitalization of derelict urban areas. Two examples are the Gas Lamp District of San Diego and the South of Market Area (SOMA) in San Francisco. The Gas Lamp District was transformed from an area resembling skid row to a thriving tourist area, thanks in part to municipal funding. City officials took advantage of the area's prime location between downtown and the city's convention center by building restaurants, clubs, and other tourist attractions that were subsequently also used by local residents. Similarly, in San Francisco's South of Market Area, an area dominated by abandoned warehouses grew into a thriving tourist destination due in part to the construction of a convention center there in 1983. The tourist development led to residential development, and now SOMA is considered a good place to live. Other urban centers such as Washington, D.C. and New York City have also benefited from an expansion of tourism. The revenue generated from tourists and their activities allows these areas to maintain sites and buildings that would not otherwise be as well kept.

Another benefit of tourism development is its role in fostering an appreciation and understanding of nature. Tourism development can facilitate an increasing awareness and appreciation of the natural world. For example, the development of mountain railroads and athletic resorts in Switzerland made it possible for people to visit and appreciate the previously unknown area. Similarly, tours into the Canadian tundra have increased their visibility to people other than hunters and scientists.

Development undertaken to cater to tourists in coastal areas can have adverse impacts. Jetties and breakwaters built to create artificial harbors can increase erosion of those areas on the downstream side of the littoral drift (i.e., the movement of sand along the nearshore underwater propelled by the prevailing current). In addition to their physical impacts, these structures can detract from the aesthetics of an area. The construction of marinas can alter water levels and nutrient concentrations, as well as destroy habitat.

However, tourism-related development can benefit a coastal zone as well as harm it. Public access, for example, often increases with tourism development, as some states have legislation requiring developers to maintain some public access with development. Furthermore, tourism injects the resources along a coast and adjacent waters with political and economic value, helping to ensure their protection.

The political value stems from the significant constituency of summer residents and day tourists who want to maintain their recreation area. Slightly more obvious are the economic benefits from fostering tourism along the coast, as revenue is generated from entrance, parking, and other fees, as well as from sales and employment.

Tourism-related development has an impact on wildlife, also. Development in the lower elevations of mountain resorts (where it usually is located) restricts the migratory winter range of certain wildlife. Impacts on wildlife associated with tourist development can be indirect as well as direct. For example, automobile headlights, streetlights, and resort illumination on beachside roads can disorient marine turtles. This disorientation causes them to head inland instead of towards the sea. The growth of tourist communities can affect wildlife habitat. For example, residential subdivisions in Jackson Hole, Wyoming, adjacent to National Elk Refuge, have decreased the amount of habitat available for grazing by the elk.

Impacts on National Park Gateway Communities and Other Host Communities

Communities adjacent to national parks that cater to tourists are called "gateway communities." Development of these areas is often undertaken without consideration of the natural landscape. Indiscriminate and scattered development tends to detract from the local character of such areas and homogenizes the experience for the visitor. For example, Tusayan, the gateway town to the south rim of the Grand Canyon, is "dominated by a gaggle of fast-food restaurants, motels, and trinket shops along the highway, [and] has been likened to a strip mall on the entry way to the Vatican". An example of new development that is not integrated into the natural landscape is a resort community currently being built around an IMAX theater in West Yellowstone (Culbertson, 1997). It is important to note that development adjacent to national parks is a trade-off for less development within the parks. If it is a question of one or the other, then it is preferable to develop outside of the parks. However, there is no reason why areas adjacent to the parks cannot be developed in accordance with the natural environment and local character.

Many resorts have ribbon or sprawl developments that are unattractive and are not well assimilated into the surrounding area. High-rise hotels along the coastal zones of Atlantic City and Miami are examples of visual pollution. Hawaii was one of the first tourist destinations in the United States to experience this problem, prompting articles about it as early as 1969. Becker

(1969) noted that "statehood and the jet airliner have transformed the Hawaiian capital from a picturesque crossroads to something approaching an outpost of Southern California." The character and architectural beauty of Jerusalem was similarly marred by the construction of several high-rise hotels in an attempt to stimulate tourism.

A more subtle impact of tourist facility development is the gradual yet persistent transformation from a natural to a built environment. As the number of tourists in an area increases, the demand for facilities increases, and thus their supply. Eventually, the built environment almost wholly subsumes the natural environment, with contrived, artificial attractions becoming the focus of tourists. Relph (1976) described this process as "the destruction of the local and regional landscape that very often initiated the tourism, and its replacement by conventional tourist architecture and synthetic landscapes and pseudo-places." For example, visitors to the Dells, Wisconsin initially went there to see the natural sandstone cliff formations. However, the increasing number of tourists every year led to an expansion of the built environment, and the attractions now receiving the most attention from tourists have names such as "Western World" and "Robot World," along with water parks and a greyhound racing track. The natural sandstone cliffs are a peripheral attraction, if they are seen at all.

There are positive economic impacts associated with tourism in gateway communities and host communities. More visitors can mean increased employment opportunities and an improved standard of living. Other economic benefits of tourism reported in the literature include improvement of public utilities and transport infrastructure, and an increase in tax revenues (Ap & Crompton, 1998).

Direct Impacts of the Lodging Industry

Energy Use

The lodging industry consumed slightly below 0.5 quadrillion British thermal units (Btu) of energy in 1995 (DOE/EIA, 1998). This amount was approximately 9.4 % of the total energy consumption of all commercial buildings. In that same year, the lodging industry consumed 125 thousand Btu per square foot, which was more than the average of 90.5 thousand Btu per square foot for all commercial buildings (DOE/EIA, 1998). The lodging industry has the fifth highest rate of energy consumption according to principal building activity (out of 13 categories) (DOE/EIA, 1998). The lodging industry consumes less energy than both the health care and food service industries. While some hotels have been successful in reducing energy usage since the early 1970s, it remains a concern of the lodging industry. There is increasing pressure to reduce energy use further because of the greenhouse gas emissions associated with energy use (Stipanuk & Roffmann, 1996).

Water Use

Water is used at lodging facilities for drinking, cleaning, recreation (if there are pools), fire safety systems, and bathing and sanitary purposes. Water usage depends on the size and type of the hotel. Larger hotels often offer amenities that use large quantities of water, such as swimming pools and extensive landscaping. Furthermore, large hotels are more likely to have a central chilled water plant, which consumes a large quantity of water (Redlin & deRoos 1990). Stipanuk and Roffman (1996) estimated that hotel water usage ranges from 101 gallons per available room per day in a hotel with less than 75 rooms, to 208 gallons per room per day in a hotel with 500 or more rooms. This amount averages out to 1.54 gallons per available room per day, or 56,210 gallons of water per room per year. Since tourists constitute about 30% of the total number of guests in U.S hotels (Gee, et al., 1989), tourism is responsible for about 16,863 gallons of water per room per year. The entire lodging industry has been estimated to use 154 billion gallons per year (Stipanuk & Roffman, 1996), with tourism therefore accounting for about 46.2 billion gallons per year. Total freshwater withdrawal for offstream uses (e.g., withdrawal of surface and groundwater for public supply, commercial, irrigation, livestock, industrial, mining and thermoelectric power uses) in the United States in 1995 was 340 billion gallons per day, of which tourism-related hotel water use was less than.04% of the total (Solley, 1997).

Solid Waste Generation

The amount of solid waste generated is dependent upon the

size and type of the hotel, as well as the existence of waste management facilities. A pilot study by the Florida Department of Environmental Regulations, the Central Florida Hotel and Motel Association, and the University of Florida found that the average rate of solid waste generation at hotels ranged from 132.7 pounds per room per month for a Comfort Inn to 220.3 pounds per room per month at an upscale Hilton in the Walt Disney World Village (Shanklin, 1993). Therefore, waste generated from tourism would range from 40 pounds per room per month to 66 pounds per room per month (at 30% of total). Another study reported similar numbers, with the addition that the numbers doubled on checkout days (Shanklin, et al., 1991).

Direct Impacts of the Cruise Industry

The cruise industry is the fastest growing segment of the tourism industry, moving from 500,000 passengers a year in 1970 to over five million in 1995 (Dickinson & Vladimir, 1997). Industry statistics suggest an increase in those numbers to seven million passengers in 2000. The United States has an interest in the potential environmental impacts of the cruise industry in part because six of the world's eight leading cruise markets are in or adjacent to U.S. waters (National Research Council [NRC], 1995). Direct impacts of the industry are presented below, as well as a discussion of the regulatory framework surrounding the impacts.

Solid Waste

As with recreational boats, the amount of solid waste (excluding sewage) generated by the cruise industry is difficult to document. A cruise ship carrying 2,700 passengers can generate at least a ton of garbage per day. An average passenger generates 2 pounds of dry garbage. I and a half pounds of food waste, and disposes of two bottles and two cans (U.S. House of Representatives, Coast Guard and Maritime Transportation Subcommittee 1998). One estimate had the industry generating only 1.1% of the total annual garbage generation by U.S. maritime sectors (NRC, 1995), with recreational boaters generating the most. However, the National Research Council developed its own estimates and found that cruise ships produce the second most garbage by weight (24% of the total), followed by recreational boaters (NRC, 1995). The NRC believed that Canton, et al. (1990) underestimated the amount of garbage produced by the cruise industry because they underestimated the number of passengers and because the fleet has increased substantially since 1990 (NRC, 1995).

These discrepancies reveal the importance of assumptions in using data, and how different assumptions can lead to very different results. In addition, as with recreational boating, these figures represent the amount of garbage generated; it is even more difficult with cruise vessels to determine how much gets tossed overboard. It is nearly impossible to monitor the vessels, and (as with recreational vessels) it is difficult to distinguish shipboard waste from land-generated waste once onshore. Evidence of illegal dumping of solid waste must therefore come from passengers on board or other vessels. For example, passengers on board a Princess Cruise Lines vessel, the Regal Princess, witnessed the illegal dumping of 20 trash-filled bags overboard during the late evening in October 1991 5 miles off of the Florida Keys ("Expensive Rubbish Disposal," 1993). Under the Marine Plastic Pollution Research and Control Act of 1987, any willful discharges of plastic within 200 miles of the United States shoreline are punishable by up to $500,000 in fines for the company involved. Princess Cruise Lines received the maximum fine.

Cruise vessels have addressed the waste issue through the use of onboard waste incinerators that meet the requirements of the International Maritime Organization (IMO). The cruise industry is attempting to move towards zero discharge of these materials. Total waste on cruise vessels has been reduced by almost 50% over the past 10 years (U.S. House of Representatives, Coast Guard and Maritime Transportation Subcommittee, 1998).

Air Pollution

The cruise industry has the potential to affect air quality through engine emissions. Most marine fuels are residual fuels with higher concentrations of contaminants such as sulfur. Recent studies have suggested that ocean-going vessels have the potential to affect air quality in coastal regions, port areas, and heavily traveled trade routes where annual sulfur emissions from ships equal or exceed land-based emissions. However, passenger vessels (cruise ships) contribute only 5% of nitrogen emissions from ships and 6% of sulfur emissions from ships. The cruise industry contributes the least of all categories of ocean-going vessels to total nitrogen and sulfur emissions. The IMO approved global emission limits in September 1997, with NOx regulations applying to new ships or major ship conversions after January 1, 2000. Sulfur fuel levels are currently limited to 4.5% of the total fuel mixture.

Oil and Chemical Effluent

Cruise ships also produce toxic chemicals and hazardous waste from dry-cleaning procedures, used batteries, and paint waste from brush cleaning (Malbin, 1999). Waste oil is produced from normal leakage from the main engines and generators, the cleaning of fuel filters, losses during maintenance, and leaks from hydraulic systems (U.S. House of Representatives, Coast Guard and Maritime Transportation Subcommittee, 1998).

In 1997 passenger vessels (cruise ships) had 136 oil spills in U.S. waters, totaling 1,778 gallons. This amount represents only 1.6% of the total oil spills in the United States that year (U.S. House of Representatives Coast Guard and Maritime Transportation Committee, 1998). While this is a small percentage, it is important to note that these figures represent only incidents reported to the U.S. Coast Guard. It is more difficult to discern how many illegal discharges occur.

There has been a recent example of illegal discharges. The world's second largest cruise line, Royal Caribbean, recently plead guilty to 21 felony counts for dumping oil and hazardous chemicals from its cruise ships and then lying about it to the Coast Guard ("Cruise Line Paying $1 8M," 1999). The cruise ships used bypass pipes to illegally discharge these materials, usually in the middle of the night, and crewmembers constantly falsified logbooks. One of the chemicals the company admitted to illegally dumping was perc, a toxic dry-cleaning fluid ("Royal Caribbean Takes Steps," 1999). While this may not be the norm in the cruise industry, it is important to consider the unreported incidents that have an impact on the environment. Based on the available data for reported incidents, however, it does not appear that the cruise industry's impact on the environment through oil spills is as significant as other sources.

Introduced Species

The introduction of non-native species through discharge of ballast water is another potential environmental impact of the cruise industry. The Council on Environmental Quality found that over 130 non-native species have been introduced to the Great Lakes since 1800, with almost a third thought to have been carried by ships (EPA, 1996, October). It is impossible, however, to distinguish how many of those ships were cruise ships. Introduced species cause problems because they can disrupt the food web of the ecosystem and clog the intake pipes of power plants and water treatment facilities (EPA, 1996, October). The International Maritime Organization has recognized these problems, and promulgated guidelines to minimize transfer of organisms.

Regulatory Framework of the Cruise Industry

The cruise industry is highly regulated. The inter-national Convention for the Prevention of Pollution from Ships, or MARPOL 73/78 as it is called, is the primary regulatory framework for the industry (as well as other maritime transportation). MARPOL comprises five annexes that describe the discharge regime of certain substances. The three annexes most relevant to the cruise industry are Annex one (I), Annex four (IV), and Annex five (V). Annex one prohibits the discharge at sea of oil in designated "special areas," and limits other discharges to a specified percentage of the cargo. Bilge water can only be discharged outside 12 miles from the U.S. coastline, established in the Law of the Sea Treaty. In addition, oil discharged from cruise ships must be no more than 15 parts of oil per million parts of oily water mixture (U.S. House of Representatives, Coast' Guard and Maritime Transportation Subcommittee, 1998). Oily waste that does not meet this standard must be kept on board and/or taken to a reception facility.

Annex IV prohibits the discharge of untreated sewage within 3 miles of the nearest land, and allows only treated and disinfected sewage to be released between 3 and 12 miles from land (EPA, 1997, September). Annex V prohibits disposal or dumping of any garbage (solid wastes, excluding sewage) within 3 miles of the United States. From 3 to 12 miles it is illegal to dump plastic, dunnage, paper, rags, glass, crockery, metal, or food not ground to 1 inch in diameter. From 12 to 25 miles it is illegal to dump plastic and dunnage, and it is illegal to dump plastic anywhere. The United States ratified Annex V in 1987, and passed implementing legislation called the Marine Plastic Pollution Research and Control Act (NRC, 1995). The Coast Guard is responsible for enforcing these standards, and has promulgated regulations to that effect (33 CFR Part 151). They inspect vessels four times a year to check for properly operating marine sanitation devices and oily water separators (Anthony Furst, lieutenant commander, U.S. Coast Guard Vessel Compliance Division, personal communication, August 13, 1999).

Positive Impacts of the Cruise Industry

It is important to comment on some of the positive impacts of the cruise industry. The industry contributes to the economy of destination areas. For example, Holland America line, which carried 178,822 passengers in 1995, estimated that their passengers spent $90 million in Alaska (primarily Anchorage, Juneau, and Fairbanks), their crew spent around $1.4 million on shore, and the combined in-state payroll of the Holland America partners was about $18 million ("Holland America: State Benefits," 1996).

In addition, the exposure of tourists to beautiful, pristine areas such as those in Alaska can improve understanding of the need for conservation. To that end, both Holland America and Norwegian Cruise Lines (NCL) have programs to foster environmental awareness. Holland America has shore excursions that focus on ecology, nature, indigenous culture, and environmental responsibility, and NCL offers the same through their "Dive Into Adventure" programs. Holland America donates time, money, medical materials, and other resources to the Alaska Raptor Rehabili-tation Center; in addition they also donated 17 acres of recently purchased land to the center.

The cruise industry can aid in raising awareness of threatened or endangered species. For example, Discovery Cruise Line has adopted the "Manny T" as its mascot to increase recognition of the plight of the manatee. The line also donates money raised through shipboard sales of selected items and other shipboard events to the Save the Manatee Foundation, and is participating in a television public service campaign concerning the manatee.

Tourist Activities

Hiking, Snorkeling and Diving

Many tourist activities occur in fragile ecosystems, such as coral reefs. While snorkeling and diving in and of themselves do not cause much damage, inadvertent related activities, such as stepping on coral do cause damage. With such activities, it is the cumulative nature of the damage that is most problematic. One or two tourists may not cause much harm, but hundreds of them over time can do considerable damage to an ecosystem. Coral reefs are also affected by tourism as a result of the market for souvenirs. Tourists break off pieces of coral themselves, or the reef is dynamited by locals to sell the pieces. The cumulative effect is relevant here as well, as one tourist may not understand her impact when aggregated with other tourists. Damage to coral reefs from tourists in the above-mentioned manners has occurred in Tanzania, Kenya, and Madagascar, among other places (Salm, 1986).

Tourists hiking along mountain ranges can harm the ecosystem by littering and by trampling vegetation. The greatest impact of tourists on vegetation usually occurs during initial contact with an area, with the most sensitive species affected first. The cumulative impact of tourists on vegetation gradually shifts species composition, because only the most resilient plants can survive in an area under constant pressure from tourist activities. Excessive hiking on trails has caused damage to the sequoia redwoods in California. Increased visitation at Arches National Park has contributed to the deterioration of the soil there, which can take up to 250 years to recover after being trampled (U.S. General Accounting Office [GAO], 1996). Alpine tundra in the Rocky Mountain National Park also has been damaged by human trampling (Willard & Marr, 1970). Hiking on the soil can also damage wildlife habitat. Constant pressure can damage or destroy the burrows of reptiles, mammals, and underground-nesting birds. Tourists' use of trees for firewood and tent poles has diminished tree populations, altering the age structure of the plant community. In addition, fires started by tourists for camping have caused major damage in the forests of California.

Littering not only contributes to visual pollution, but can also change the nutrient composition of soils and prevent light from reaching plants. Furthermore, tourists have unwittingly carried exotic species to ecosystems, thereby upsetting their balance. Littering by tourists has caused wildlife, such as bears, to frequent the garbage area of campsites to scrounge for food. As animals become accustomed to human food, their behaviour becomes more aggressive and can be potentially dangerous to humans. When Glacier National Park implemented management plans to restore normal feeding patterns for bears, there was a decrease in injuries to tourists.

Recreational Boating

The most significant problem associated with recreational boating and water quality is the discharge of sewage into waterbodies with limited flushing or nearby shellfish beds. Sewage contains pathogens (fecal coliform is used as an indicator of the amount of pathogens contained in the sewage) which can adversely affect human health and contaminate shellfish. Diseases that can be potentially transmitted through human contact with fecal discharge and/or ingestion of contaminated shellfish include typhoid fever, dysentery, infectious hepatitis, and nonspecific gastroenteritis.

Significantly higher fecal coliform counts have been found in waters with a high recreational boating population during peak usage (summer). One study reported that at three different sites on Puget Sound 70%, 91%, and 62% of shellfish sampled had levels of contamination higher than that allowed at the commercial wholesale level. Two of the three sites failed to meet the Washington State Department of Ecology Class AA Extraordinary Water Quality Standard. The lack of other sources of contamination at these sites (all sites were used by recreational boaters) suggested to the authors that the contamination resulted from boat sewage discharge.

Under Section 312 of the Clean Water Act, the EPA requires vessels to have Marine Sanitation Devices (MSDs), that physically and chemically treat boat sewage before it is released into the water. The three types of MSDs each provide a different level of treatment, depending on the vessel's length. A vessel must be equipped with one of the three types of MSDs, if it has an installed toilet as of January 30, 1980. In addition to sewage discharges, recreational boats can impact the environment through oil spills. In 1997, recreational vessels were responsible for 535 oil spills in U.S. waters with a total volume of 4,217 gallons, and an average spill of 8 gallons. This represents 6.2% of total spill incidents in U.S. waters (U.S. House of Representatives, Coast Guard and Maritime Transportation Subcommittee, 1998). While this is a small percentage, it is important to note that the data represent spills reported to the U.S. Coast Guard. It is likely that some spills are not reported. However, given the available information, oil spills from recreational boats do not seem to be a significant threat to the environment.

Another way that recreational boating can adversely affect water quality is through the discharge of solid waste (garbage). The National Research Council has listed some of the adverse impacts of marine debris in the environment: (I) aesthetic degradation of surface waters and coastal areas; (2) physical injuries to humans; (3) ecological damage resulting from the interference of plastics with gas exchange between surface waters and deeper waters; (4) alterations in the composition of ecosystems because opportunistic organisms use debris as their environment; (5) entanglements of birds, fish, turtles, and cetaceans; and 6) ingestion of plastic by marine mammals (NRC, 1995).

It is difficult to determine the amount of solid waste generated by recreational vessels. One study estimated that recreational boats generated 51.4% of the total annual garbage generated by U.S. maritime sectors (NRC, 1995). However, the National Research Council estimated that recreational boats contributed only 19% of the total (NRC, 1995). Furthermore, those figures represent the amount of waste generated; not how much of that waste is dumped overboard.

Although the amount of waste generated on a daily basis is minimal due to the relatively short duration of trips, the cumulative effect has the potential to be significant. There are approximately 7.3 million recreational boats in the United States, more than in any other maritime sector (NRC, 1995). Recreational boaters operating within 3 miles of shore (that is, most of them) are required to store their garbage on board and dispose of it onshore.

Recreational boating can cause damage to marine habitat and animals such as coral by running aground or dragging anchor over the habitat. This damage has happened within some national parks with marine or freshwater components. For example, in 1997, 161 vessels ran aground in Biscayne National Park in Florida. These events damaged 8,000 square meters of submerged seagrass beds, which are important because they serve as a nursery for many commercial and sport marine species. In addition, seagrass beds help stabilize sediments, reduce wave energy, and filter pollutants. The manatee in Florida has been threatened by the propellers of powerboats. The wash generated by motor boats can induce erosion of plant roots, and propellers can cut macrophyte growth. Although there are no data currently available on the effects of wakes from boats, these impacts are confined to localized and sensitive areas.

The movement of tourists' vehicles can also adversely affect wildlife by separating the young from their parents. It is possible that whale-watching boats have this impact because studies have shown that, if young whale calves lose contact with their mothers, they sometimes attach themselves to the side of a ship. The noise made by these boat engines and propellers are also thought to interfere with the whales' communications systems.

Recreational boating can have positive impacts on the environment as well. Recreational boaters provide funding indirectly for conservation and recreation efforts through a tax on motorboat and small-engine fuel. This tax is mandated in the Internodal Surface Transportation Efficiency Act, which earmarks the funds for the Federal Aid in Sport Fish Restoration Program of the U.S. Fish and Wildlife Service. Revenue from this fund is used by states to stock fish, acquire and improve sport fish habitat, fund fisheries research and education, and to provide recreational access to water through boat ramps and piers.

Tourist Activities Within National Parks

Visitor and Traffic Congestion

Visitor and traffic congestion exists in many tourist destinations, and national parks have been greatly impacted by this problem. Over 2.5 million people visit Zion Canyon each year, with half of those driving in the park. A summer day can see 2,000 vehicles in the canyon corridor, creating congestion, air pollution from vehicle exhaust, and vegetation damage along overflow parking areas. To help alleviate this problem, the park plans to launch a shuttle system in 2000. Although this system is expected to reduce some of the traffic-related impacts and provide a higher quality experience, it could also have the effect of increasing the number of visitors to the park. The next management question will then be how best to manage the volume of people.

Similarly, the entrance to Yosemite National Park in California has had to be closed several times due to gridlock during the summer months when visitation is at its peak. With over 5 million visitors a year, Grand Canyon National Park suffers from congestion as well. The huge volume of traffic is more than just an inconvenience. There are physical impacts, such as air pollution from exhaust, and there are social impacts that also degrade the overall experience, such as honking horns and blaring radios. The superintendent of Grand Canyon National Park has commented that "we've taken this special place that is different from everything in your life and we've homogenized it so it's just like your life. It's full of cars, you re constantly looking for parking spaces, you're standing around in lines." ("A Cramped Grand Canyon," 1999).

An increasing number of tourists have been using snowmobiles as a form of recreation while visiting some national parks. Snowmobiles have the potential to adversely affect air quality over time because they use two-stroke engines that produce relatively high emissions of carbon monoxide and unburned hydrocarbons, and they are not equipped with pollution control equipment. Recent studies by state and federal agencies and the University of Denver found that snowmobiles account for 94% of the annual hydrocarbon emissions at Yellowstone National Park, 78% of carbon monoxide emissions, 37% of particulate matter, and 3% of nitrogen oxide emissions at Yellowstone (Llanos, 1999). Currently, no federal law regulates these emissions.

Tourist activities can alter the integrity of cultural resources. This damage includes vandalism and looting of sites of cultural significance. Historic structures and archeological sites were harmed by tourist activities at Gettysburg National Military Park (GAO, 1996). Damages to cultural resources can be more serious than those to natural resources, as the natural resources can recuperate over time.

While the environmental impacts on the parks from tourists and their activities are important and significant in some areas, it is important to note that many parks do not experience these problems. As always, there is scientific uncertainty about the effects of visitors on park ecosystems. Furthermore, some parks are underused, with low densities of visitors.

Upstream and Downstream Influence

The previous section discussed the direct and indirect impacts of selected aspects of the tourism industry. This section first presents the structure of selected components of the industry, and then discusses how each sector can influence other parts of the industry as well as tourists. It is possible for tourism service providers such as hotels and travel agents to leverage their influence on other parts of the supply chain to encourage more environmentally responsible tourism. The "supply chain" in the tourism industry consists of those industries that supply accommodations, transportation, and make arrangements for travelers. "Upstream" influence refers to a sector's ability to influence an actor "above" them in the tourism services supply chain. A hotel's influence over a supplier's products is an example of upstream influence. "Downstream" influence refers to the influence an industry has over other sectors (including tourists) or industries "below" them in the tourism services supply chain. An example of this type of influence is a travel agent's influence over a tourist's choice of vacation type and destination.

Structure of Selected Components of the Industry

As mentioned previously, the tourism industry is not one industry, but rather a conglomeration of many industries and sectors. A full characterization of this complex and fragmented industry is beyond the scope of this paper. However, the structure of selected components of the industry is presented to demonstrate the potential for upstream and downstream influence. This discussion focuses on the lodging and cruise industries, travel agents, tour operators, and some nonprofit groups that offer trips. The tourism industry has changed substantially in the past ten to fifteen years, with more change likely. The airline industry is expected to consolidate further, along with continued decreases in fares. Development of new technology such as the Internet has already had some effect on the distribution of travel, and it is very likely that more change will occur. This change is discussed later in this section.

The Lodging Industry

The lodging industry is in and of itself large, with over 51,000 establishments and over 3.1 million rooms in the United States (Patricia Griffin, president of Green Hotels Association, personal communication, October 21, 1999).

The industry employs over 1.6 million workers, and accounts for 1.3% of the gross national product. It comprises hotels, motor hotels, motels, bed and breakfasts, and condos. There has been a trend in the lodging industry over the past thirty years of consolidation, as the number of chain and franchise affiliations has increased and the number of independently owned and operated properties has decreased. However, industry predictions suggest a decrease in the franchising trend, with a subsequent increase in control over properties by the chains. The fastest-growing segment of the industry is the bed and breakfast sector. This segment has the ability of generating tourism revenue in smaller communities where larger chains do not have a presence.

The Cruise Industry

As mentioned previously, the cruise industry is the fastest growing segment of the tourism industry, moving from 500,000 passengers a year in 1970 to over 5 million in 1995 (Dickinson & Vladimir, 1997). This growth is also reflec-ted in the increase of the number of berths, with 5,000 new berths added during the first half of 1996 (Godsman, 1997). The industry is planning on adding 41 new vessels by 2002, increasing passenger capacity by 57% (International Council of Cruise Lines [ICCL], 1999). An average of 113 cruise ships visited or operated from U.S. ports between 1990-1995 (USCG, 1995 of Executive Summary). The industry has a significant economic impact, creating $11.6 billion in expenditures in goods and services in 1997, including passengers and suppliers (ICCL, 1999). The most visited U.S. ports of call for cruise ships are all in Florida: Miami, Everglades, Canaveral, and Tampa. Other U.S. ports of significance are located in Alaska, California, Louisiana, New York, Texas, and Massachusetts (ICCL, 1999).

Travel Agents

There are currently around 39,000 travel agencies in the United States (Whitley, 1998, on-line). Traditionally, the industry has comprised many smaller agencies, with an average agency employing seven people. There is an increasing trend, however, of consolidation and concentration within the industry, as an increasing number of large networks of agencies act under a common brand name. Two-thirds of travel agencies belong to co-ops or consortiums. While there are more small agencies (with sales less than $2 million), two-thirds of the sales are done by agencies with $2 million or more in bookings. The development of technologies such as the Internet has spurred this consolidation, as small agencies need to combine with others to make a profit.

Large travel agencies get the majority of their revenue from commissions paid by airlines, with airlines spending $6.4 billion each year on travel agent commissions. Slightly less than 66% of the total dollar volume of travel agents comes from the sale of air travel (Mill & Morrison, 1985). However, this allocation is changing as airlines move to cap commissions to travel agents. For example, instead of the previous flat rate of 10% for domestic trips, Delta airlines has limited commissions for these tickets to $50 regardless of the ticket price. Airlines are doing this for economic reasons, as commissions are now the fourth largest operating expense for U.S. carriers after labor, fuel, and maintenance.

Travel agents book 95% of cruises, 90% of airline tickets, and only 25% of hotel rooms. There is an emerging trend in the travel agent industry where the larger agencies focus on corporate clients, and the smaller agencies focus primarily on tourists and small businesses. These smaller agencies are inclined to concentrate on revenues from tours arid cruises, rather than airline revenues.

Tour Operators

Tour operators have an interesting niche in the tourism industry because they act as an intermediary between travel agents and suppliers of travel services. Tour operators plan and organize all aspects of a vacation by putting down large deposits for block reservations (e.g., at hotels and other lodgings), and then usually sells them to the public through travel agencies or airlines. This industry has grown from around 300 operators in 1975 to over 1,500 in 1990, with the 50 largest having 50% of the business. It comprises three segments: the independent tour operator, the airline working with a tour operator business, and the travel agent that packages tours for clients. Operators generate more than $10.5 billion annually in North America.

Other Organizations Functioning as Travel Agents/Tour Operators

Organizations such as the American Automobile Association (AAA) and nongovernmental organizations (NGOs) perform many of the same functions as traditional travel agents and tour operators. Although AAA is primarily known for its automobile services, it generated travel sales of $2.15 billion in 1995, with leisure travel accounting for 81% of that. It has significant potential for downstream influence on its customers, as it can reach a large audience. AAA has 960 agency locations and around 35 million members in the United States. Industry representatives believe AAA has not yet realized its full potential as a travel agency. AAA executives hope to increase their hotel, airline, and cruise line sales through a Windows-based booking system that will allow easy access to its members travel data. They currently have 23 preferred cruise and tour suppliers, and three airline preferred suppliers. In fact, AAA signed a 5-year preferred supplier deal with Carnival Cruise Lines in 1996. The organization could use its growing influence in the travel industry to work with and promote environmentally friendly suppliers.

NGOs that have ecotourism links and/or conduct nature, adventure, and eco-tours include the World Wildlife Fund, the Nature Conservancy, the Audubon Society, Conservation International, Africa Wildlife Foundation, and the Sierra Club. These organizations use the trips as a way to raise money, and to increase awareness and understanding of natural systems. The Audubon Society offers trips to places such as the Galapagos

Islands, Greenland and Hudson Bay, and the Pacific Northwest. World Wildlife Fund (WWF) takes travelers to Alaska, Antarctica, and Africa, among other destinations.

Upstream and Downstream Influence

Each of the above sectors of the tourism industry has potential for upstream and downstream influence on the environmental impacts of tourism. The three primary types of influence are supplier relations, channeling of activity, and education. Each is presented below, with a concluding discussion of the impacts of technology on the tourism industry.

Supplier Relations

The lodging industry can leverage its influence "upstream" on suppliers by demanding products that have less of an environmental impact. For example, a hotel chain can wield its influence on a supplier by requiring paper towels made out of recycled materials for their bathrooms. The extent to which a hotel can leverage its suppliers depends upon several factors, including type of hotel (e.g., large chain or small independent) and type of supplies. Some larger hotel chains have national corporate purchasing agreements with different vendors. Often these chains will purchase supplies based only on these corporate purchasing agreements for the sake of convenience or because it is less expensive to do so (Mark Petruzzi, program director, Green Seal, personal communication, October 5, 1999). It might be most effective, then, to exert upstream leverage at this national level because franchises follow whatever contract is negotiated by their larger chains.

An example of an organization exerting upstream leverage is the Green Seal program; an independent, nonprofit organization dedicated to protecting the environment by promoting the manufacture and sale of environmentally responsible products. The organization has a pilot project underway to negotiate contracts where suppliers provide environmentally friendly cleaning products to large hotel chains and their franchises (Mark Petruzzi, program director, Green Seal, personal communication, October 5, 1999). The Green Seal program has also published an environmental purchasing guide for hotels, providing specific product and brand recommendations. Another program underway to encourage environmental responsibility through supplier relations (among other things) in the lodging industry is the International Hotels Environment Initiative (IHEI).

Created in 1992, this is a nonprofit organization developed by the international hotel industry that serves over 8,000 hotels. It is governed by an International Council of 12 multinational hotel company executives, whose goal is to promote the benefits of environmental management as an integral component of hotel business. The group influences supplier relations with hotels through its supplier program, created in 1998. This program facilitates hotels' leverage on suppliers in three ways:

1. by creating a "Registry of Industry Suppliers" who have an environmental policy and can also demonstrate that their products meet the best environmental standards (accessible to hotels through a CD-Rom, the Green Hotelier magazine (quarterly publication focusing on hotel environmental issues), and directly through IHEI to the corporate Vice Presidents responsible for purchasing in each member hotel group);
2. by establishing and publishing environmental specifications for products or product groups; and
3. through the creation and disbursement of a comprehensive buyers guide with a list of all registered suppliers, guidelines for purchasing of products that minimize their.

IHEI suggests several ways hotels can influence their suppliers. These include insisting on buying products made from recycled material or that are recyclable, writing to competing suppliers to explain why the hotel chose to do business with a more environmentally aware supplier, and demanding that suppliers minimize their packaging. In order to determine how environmentally friendly a supplier is, a survey can be distributed to them.

A third organization dedicated to fostering environmental stewardship within the lodging industry is the Green Hotels Association (GHA). This mail order business and trade association was founded in 1993 to help hotels develop and maintain environmentally friendly practices (Patricia Griffin, president of Green Hotels Association, personal communication, October 21, 1999). Like the IHEI, the GHA facilitates hotels' leverage on suppliers through publication of a catalogue of environmental products for the lodging industry, with items such as a toilet-tank fill diverter, which saves around three-quarters of a gallon of water per flush. The GHA currently reaches less than 1% of all U.S. hotels (it has about 170 member hotels; there are over 51,000 in the U.S.) (Patricia Griffin, personal communication, October 21, 1999).

The cruise industry has a similar ability to influence upstream suppliers. There are several large firms that supply products to cruise lines. A large cruise line such as Carnival Cruise Lines generally has a good deal of influence on its suppliers because competition for business is strong (Deborah Lauder, Carnival Cruise Lines, personal communication, October 7, 1999). Upstream leveraging efforts are focused primarily on the environmental quality of the shipboard products they purchase. They can encourage suppliers to use more environmentally friendly packaging. Recently, cruise lines belonging to the International Council of Cruise Lines have begun replacing plastic products such as cups, shampoo, and straws with biodegradable, reusable, or recyclable material (U.S. House of Representatives, Coast Guard and Maritime Transportation Subcommittee, 1998). Carnival Cruise Lines has reduced the amount of plastic brought on board their ships through working with their suppliers. To further reduce the amount of plastic on board, Carnival has eliminated plastic from the shotgun shells used for skeet shooting and has completely eliminated driving golf balls off the ships (Lincoln, 1994).

Royal Caribbean Cruises is another example of a cruise line using leverage with suppliers to encourage use of products that minimize environmental impact. Through a Quality Supplier Development Program (QSDP), the cruise line has convinced suppliers to reduce packaging and substitute more environmentally benign materials. In the last five years they have reduced packaging by 35% through several different routes including ordering ketchup and chili sauce in 5-gallon pouches instead of tin cans, ordering some beer in kegs rather than cans, putting fountain syrup in 5-

gallon boxed bags, which saves 250,000 syrup cans annually, and purchasing soda in cans without plastic rings.

Travel agents are intermediaries between providers of the tourist product (including airlines, cruise lines, and hotels) and the tourist, and, as such, are able to influence the decisions of suppliers. Their influence is currently stronger with cruise lines and airlines, as they book the majority of those trips. However, the relationship between travel agents and hotels has strengthened, with travel agents' bookings constituting a growing segment of the hotel industry (Bush, 1989). This growth has occurred for several reasons. The hotel business has become more competitive, therefore hotels need to explore more marketing avenues. Secondly, once. The association estimates that this practice alone can save 5% on the cost of hotel utilities (GHA, 1999).

It has been suggested that an effective way to implement changes favorable to the environment is by starting with hotel employees in areas such as laundry, housekeeping, and engineering. These employees have first direct contact with some aspects of the hotel business that have an impact on the environment (such as washing linen and sheets). The Saunders' Hotel Group solicits employee input and recognizes their input through its SHINE program, or Saunders Hotels Initiative to Nurture the Environment. This program began in 1989 as a recycling program and has since grown into a much more comprehensive environmental program, with investments in energy-efficient lighting and windows as well as an improved recycling program.

The cruise industry has a significant opportunity for downstream influence on the environmental behaviour of its passengers, as the industry's vessels carried over 5.5 million North American passengers in 1997 (ICCL, 1999). Cruise vessels determine where their passengers travel, and they can exert downstream influence to minimize environmental impact by limiting the number of tourists that go ashore at sensitive destinations, and by avoiding environmentally sensitive areas. Orient Cruise Line limits the number of tourists for certain shore excursions, such as visiting an albatross colony.

Cruise lines also influence personnel and passenger environmental behaviour by: (1) making announcements over the public address system and putting daily notices in ship newsletters that caution against throwing trash overboard; (2) placing signs in crew and passenger areas encouraging environmental protection; (3) offering training programs in pollution prevention; (4) placing environmental information booklets in crew cabins and lounges; and (5) meeting with officers and crew of all departments to discuss more effective environmental protection (U.S. House of Representatives, Coast Guard and Maritime Transportation Subcommittee, 1998).

Travel agents have the opportunity to have "down-stream" impacts because they can influence where and how a tourist travels. Over 40% of tourists have only a general idea of their destination and mode of travel when they first visit a travel agent (Mill & Morrison, 1985).

The highest percentage of tourists seek advice from travel agents about hotels. This number suggests that travel agents have the most opportunity to steer their clients towards hotels that have established good environmental practices and policies. A U. S. Travel Data Center study found that 85% of travelers indicated they would be "very likely" or somewhat likely" to support or patronize travel companies perceived to be environmentally friendly.

Given this receptivity, it is clear that travel agents have the opportunity to influence the type of travel and the company a customer chooses. The concept of "responsible tourism" was the focus of a 1997 New Travel Expo, where over 125 travel agents discussed how they might influence tourists. The segment of tourists who actually do choose travel suppliers based on environmental principles (as opposed to stating that they would be likely to) is small now, but will most likely increase as children who have received more environmental education come of age.

Because tour operators interact with all travel suppliers, such as lodging and transportation services, they, too, have an opportunity to exert influence on suppliers. Tour operators can leverage suppliers to provide a more environmentally friendly product by fostering demand for it among their clients. An international example of a tour operator exerting leverage is the boycott of Pattaya, Thailand as a destination by German tour operators because they objected to the environmental degradation in the area.

As more tourists become aware of potential environmental degradation caused by tourism, the demand for more environmentally oriented trips (sometimes referred to as "ecotours") increases. This increase in turn leads to more visibility for groups offering environmentally oriented trips. A group called International Expeditions has reaped this reward, as travel agents increasingly seek information from them to meet tourists' increasing demand for such trips; in 1990 International Expeditions arranged trips for 300 groups a year (about 3,500 clients), compared with two tour groups in 1980.

Education

The environmental impacts of the tourism industry can be partially mitigated through education of tourists and service providers. For example, efforts to educate about marine debris have targeted cruise line operators and owners. The Shipping Industry Marine Debris Education Plan, launched by the Marine Entanglement Research Program (MERP) of the National Marine Fisheries Service, educates cruise line operators and owners by writing articles for cruise trade journals, presenting MARPOL information at cruise trade meetings, producing and distributing brochures about the problem, and presenting workshops about MARPOL compliance for members of the cruise industry.

Many educational efforts to minimize the environmental impacts of tourism are incorporated into ecotourism trips. Ecotourism attempts to minimize impact on the social, cultural, and physical environment. It can mean the development of tourism facilities in an environmentally responsible manner, recreational programs that promote a greater awareness and appreciation of nature, and a mode of travel that is sensitive to the host community. The Ecotourism Society calls ecotourism a nature-based form of specialty travel that is responsible, conserves the environment, and sustains the well being of local people (Ecotourism Society, 1998). Eight million U.S. travelers had taken at least one ecotourism trip, and 30% (35 million) said they were planning on doing so in the next three years (Ecotourism Society, 1998). Samples of ecotourism have been used internationally to guide discussions of tourism's impact on the environment. For example, the 1992 United Nations Conference on Environment and Development produced Agenda 21, a document concerning sustainable development. In 1996 the World Travel and Tourism Council, the World Tourism Organization, and the Earth Council developed an Agenda 21 for tourism, called "Agenda 21 for the Travel and Tourism Industry: Towards Environmentally Sustainable Development." This document advises travel and tourism companies to incorporate the sustainable development concept into tourism. Priority areas include waste minimization, energy efficiency, fresh and wastewater management, hazardous substances, transportation, land-use planning and management, and involvement of staff, customers, and communities in environmental issues.

A potential benefit of ecotourism is the ability to raise revenues for protected areas (Robert Healy, Nicholas School of the Environment, Duke University, personal communication via email, November 28, 1999). For example, park entrance fees can be used to support management plans and ecological studies. However, currently this idea is for the most part unrealized, as most protected areas are unable to generate enough revenues to be self-sustaining. One successful example is Ecuador's Galapagos Islands National Park, where international visitors are charged higher fees than Ecuadorian citizens.

The American Society of Travel Agents (ASTA) proposed recommending environmentally sensitive tours to their clients at a 1990 conference. They have developed guidelines for travelers to minimize their impact on the environment. These are called the "ten commandments" on ecotourism, and encourage tourists to "respect the frailty of the earth," "leave only footprints, take only photographs," and educate themselves on the local customs. The guidelines are no more than general advice, and it is hard to determine how much they influence travelers. A perhaps more useful and pragmatic commandment" is to ask the travel agent to identify those travel suppliers that subscribe to ASTA's Environmental Guidelines.

Tour operators also have an opportunity to influence customers through education. However, when discussing educational efforts of tour operators, it is useful to distinguish between those operators that cater to "mass tourists" and those that focus on a specific market, such as "ecotour" operators. Ecotour operators and tour operators that cater to mass tourists are both primarily economically motivated. The critical difference is in their clientele; people who seek out ecotours are more likely to care about their impacts on the environment, so it is in the best interests of the ecotour operators to take steps to minimize a trip's impact. Tour operators catering to mass tourists are less concerned with the needs of a particular destination because environmental protection is generally not a primary concern for the mass tourist. Therefore, these operators are less likely to be concerned with the environmental impacts of tourism.

One of the ways ecotour operators attempt to minimize impacts on the environment is by using guidelines to educate tourists. These guidelines range from specific methods to preserve and minimize impact to general platitudes that may have little effect on the tourist. Other methods used by self-identified ecotour operators include pre-trip orientations, printed information packs, videos or slide shows, lectures, discussions, and talks during the trip.

Problems with Ecotourism

The numerous names and definitions make it difficult to ascertain how environmentally responsible ecotourism is. There are important distinctions among nature tourism, adventure travel, and ecotourism. Nature tourism implies enjoyment and appreciation of nature, yet it often does not include protection of the environment. Adventure travel utilizes local resources often without consideration of impacts. Ecotourism, as the above definition suggests, is concerned with the concurrent enjoyment and preservation of the natural environment.

Aside from the uncertainty and discrepancies surrounding the labels, there are also problems with the term ecotourism itself. It is possible that some travel suppliers that call themselves "eco" are only paying lip service to a marketable concept that is gaining popularity. Some travel outfitters use the label "eco" for short-term economic gain without truly abiding by environmental principles. One tour operator suggested in a survey that the label eco-tour' should be given only to those tour operators that directly benefit the culture or environment; otherwise they should be known as adventure travel" operators.

The development of industry standards or regulations about the definition of ecotourism would be a productive first step in differentiating these groups. The Ecotourism Society (TES) established guidelines in 1993, which are fairly comprehensive and can be used as a starting point for developing an industry standard. These guidelines include educating travelers to minimize impact, ensuring that the tour company minimizes impact by example (by offering environmentally friendly accommodations), and contributing to the economy of the region visited. The guidelines are voluntary and are therefore not moni-tored or enforced. One study suggested that tour operator compliance with the TES guidelines is strongly influenced by whether or not they can gain economically from them. Therefore, emphasizing the potential for economic gain from abiding by these ecotourism guidelines would increase compliance with them. An accepted industry standard such as the TES guidelines can help identify the tour operators that conduct truly environmentally friendly tours. This identification would in turn aid travel agents in recommending qualified groups to interested tourists.

The Green Travel Network (GTN), a Washington, D.C.-based company that is partnered with Conservation International (a nongovernmental organization promoting international sustainable development), has on-line resources for tourists interested in environmentally friendly trips. GTN attempts to ensure that ecotour operators are truly taking steps to minimize their impact on the environment by requiring that any that wish to advertise on its Web page complete a responsibility form. This form asks these operators several questions to ascertain their level of environmental responsibility, such as whether or not they have a waste management policy, and if visitation to fragile areas is monitored. GTN interviews clients of these ecotour operators to ensure that they are actually doing what they had indicated on the responsibility forms (Amaro, 1999).

Ecotourism can adversely impact the environment in the same way as traditional, mass tourism. Two examples are the destruction of coral reefs in the Caribbean and the disturbance of breeding habits of birds in Antarctica. In January of 1988 an Argentine naval vessel carrying paying tourists ran aground off the coast of Antaractic, spilling 250,000 gallons of fuel, damaging rookeries of 24,000 perguins. A less dramatic type of damage is the disruption of wildlife when ecotour operators get too close to their habitat. The Virginia Eco Tourism Association suggests that educating tour operators is the first step in preventing this type of damage. To that end, they are in the process Coastal Services Centre, 1999).

Another problem with ecotourism is that it is often exclusive because eco-trips are usually more expensive. Therefore the "mas" tourist is less likely to participate. Wheeler argued that "the 'green' concept allows the tourist industry to improve its own image while in reality continuing its familiar short-term commercial profits strategy." An example of an attempt to promote ecotourism to the mass tourist is the "green travel" campaign of an environmental nonprofit organization in Europe called Ark. Ark partnered with Manchester Airport, the European Commission and Thomson Holidays to show in-flight videos and provide magazines that encouraged tourists to care for the culture and environment of their destination. The campaign reached three million tourists in 1992.

Impact of Technology on Travel Services

As yet, the Internet has had little impact on travel distribution methods, in part because there is not yet an easy way for customers or agents to access all the necessary information through one avenue. Therefore, the telephone still remains the preferred channel. However, the newly created Open Travel Alliance, an industry group comprising air, car, hotel and travelagent industry representatives, is trying to change this by creating an industry-wide information standard, called the Open Travel Initiative (1998). The goal is to create and promote electronic commerce standards that improve information exchange among travel suppliers, distributors, and consumers ("Consortium of Travel Suppliers," 1999). The group's proposal to create a multi-channel distributions system would allow customers and travel agents to differentiate among alternatives. Such a system could make it easier for travel suppliers that are more environmentally aware to promote their policies, for travel agents to sell products and for consumers to access those suppliers directly.

Initiatives such as these signify that although the growth of the Internet has not had a significant impact on the tourism industry thus far, it has begun to change the relationships among travel agents, suppliers and consumers and has the potential to have an even larger effect. In fact, the president of the U.S. tour Operators Association noted that almost all relationships among suppliers, tour operators, travel agents and tourists in the future will be electronic (Whitely, 1998). Some industry analysts feel that the emergence of the Internet will lead to a shrinking role for intermediaries.

For example, the sophistication of information technology has already begun to allow tourists to bypass the travel agent. In 1976, 40% of airline tickets issued in the United States were written by travel agents; by 1985 this amount had increased to 80%, due in part to the increased competition and more complex fare structure created by the Airline Deregulation Act of 1978. However, the rapid growth of the Internet has allowed and encouraged more prospective travelers to interact with airlines directly. An example of this is the ability of travelers to purchase tickets online ("ticketless travel"). Southwest Airlines now sells most of their tickets without the use of travel agents. Another example is the Air Travelers Homepage, which provides links to airlines, online reservation systems, and other tourist information. The increased use of the Internet may decrease travel agents' ability to leverage upstream and downstream impacts because the consumer is interacting directly with the supplier.

On the other hand, the.growing ease with which travelers can use the Internet for travel purposes can also strengthen the relationship between travel agents and tourists. For example, the Internet Travel Network allows travelers to book their trips through a travel agent. The amount of upstream and downstream leverage that travel agents will be able to maintain, therefore, depends in large part upon their Internet presence and accessibility.

Similarly, the Internet's effect on the ability of tour operators to leverage upstream and downstream influence will depend in part on the extent of their presence on the Internet. As an increasing number of travelers shop for their vacations on the Internet, tour operators are attempting to capitalize on that market. This trend has the potential to make it easier for tourists to interact directly with tour operators (e.g., via Web sites), thereby potentially increasing the downstream influence of operators and the upstream influence of tourists. Overall, the interactive nature of the Internet allows for the values of tourists to register directly with providers of tourist services. If there is strong demand for environmentally sensitive services, it is quite likely that the demand will be met.

Steps to Lessen Adverse Impacts

As the environmental impacts of tourism have become more obvious, efforts to minimize or avoid further impacts have developed. There are existing initiatives within the tourism industry to minimize impacts. Potential improvements include voluntary efforts by industry sectors and government initiatives, developers' initiatives to design and build tourist infrastructure with minimal impact on the environment, and nonprofit tours that espouse environmentally friendly travel ethics.

Voluntary Efforts by Industry Sectors and Government Initiatives

There has been growing recognition within the tourism industry as well as without of the need for tourism that is environmentally responsible. This recognition has been exemplified by industry and government initiatives aimed at fostering more sustainable tourism. The World Travel and Tourism Council (WTTC) developed a "Green Globe" program through which travel and tourism companies can commit to improvements in their environmental practice ("World Travel and Tourism," 1994). The WTTC membership consists of 70 corporate executive officers from all sectors of the tourism industry, including accommodation and transportation. Members commit to mitigating their environmental impacts using the WTTC "Environment Guidelines" published in 1991 or industry guidelines accepted by the Green Globe board. They participate in annual surveys, and pay a fee in exchange for access to publications and guidelines, an advisory network, a members directory, and promotional support (e.g., a logo and annual achievement awards) ("World Travel and

Tourism," 1994). The recreational boating sector has made some attempts to mitigate its environmental impacts. Regulation of this sector is not always effective because enforcement is difficult. More often than not, it is up to the goodwill of the individual boater to minimize potential impacts. A potentially effective strategy to encourage this goodwill is through boater education. Such a program is run by the National Safe Boating Council, a group of private citizens and boating organization representatives who advise the U.S. Coast Guard on several matters. During their National Safe Boating Week Campaign, the group teaches recreational boaters about safety and environmental issues.

The National Park Service has several initiatives planned or underway to help reduce visitor congeston and its associated impacts. Thirty-nine parks offer some form of alternative transportation, such as buses and vans. The National Park Service is planning to build a 3,500-car parking lot six miles south of the Grand Canyon in Tusayan and by 2002 use a light-rail transit system to ferry people back and forth. In addition, two unappealing hotels will be replaced by a "heritage education campus," which will blend better with the surrounding environment. Once at the canyon's edge, visitors will have the option to walk, bike, or take alternative-fuel shuttle buses along the edge.

The Park Service is also trying to reconcile economic needs with aesthetics. Environmental groups have supported a proposed development in Tusayan, a gateway community to the Grand Canyon National Park, that would include 1,220 hotel rooms and 250,000 square feet of commercial and retail space. However, the space would also include a large interpretive and education centre, incorporate "green building" practices, and use river water from 100 miles away to preserve groundwater. This type of development attempts to minimize the physical and aesthetic disruption that can occur from tourist development. It allows for retention of the community character of the landscape while still providing a healthy economy.

Some hotels recognize the need to reduce environmental impact and have developed various programs to that end. Efforts to minimize solid waste generation at hotels involve source reduction, waster transformation, recycling, and refuse. A Dallas hotel donates

250 sheets and 100 tablecloths three times a year to a local shelter, and Days Inns of America initiated a similar program called "Hotel-to-Shelter Recycling". All new U.S. Hyatt Hotels and Resorts constructed after 1992 have on-site recycling centers. Hotels will most likely be willing to minimize waste if it can be demonstrated that such efforts will be economically beneficial. A study of 13 corporate executives of hotel chains found that the two most important factors that contributed to their decision to implement a should waste management program were waste disposal fees and the betterment of public image. There are also efforts in place to minimiz water sue. 77% of U.S. hotels use low flow showerheads, and 33% use low consumption toilets. However only 4% of hotels reclaim their laundry wastewater, and 2% use their gray water for irrigation.

Examples of Development that Minimizes Environmental Impact

Three example of tourist infrastructure that minimize environmental impact and incorporated local people's needs are two eco-resorts in the U.S. Virgin Islands, and a reverberant park in Detoit, Michigan. Maho Bay Camps and Harmony Resort were built in the 1970s, and are two of the best known and successful eco-resorts. Wooden walkways minimizesoil erosion and vegetation damage from trampling. Communical toilets and captured rainwater reduce water usage, and reliance on solar and wind power along with computer monitoring of electricity and water use help reduce energy use. The "Detroit Linked Riverfront Parks Plan" is a good example of effective tourism planning. In lieu of indiscriminate development based solely on economics, planners first determined the needs of the local people, and then designed the area accordingly.

Nonprofit Groups

The Audubon Society has recognized the potential for adverse effects of tourism, and has developed a "Travel Ethic" for tour operators that provide wilderness trips. The Travel Ethic encourages tour operators and cruises to stay on trails to protect vegetation, keep a minimum distance from wildlife, refrain from destruction of coral reefs, maintain and enforce an antidumping policy, and educate tourists about the types of souvenirs not to buy (such as sea turtle products and ivory). The Sierra Club also educates its members on methods to minimize their impact on the environment. The club's concern about the potential impact of member travelers on the environment started as early as 1970, when its leaders commissioned a report from three professors about any adverse impacts Sierra outings had, and how they could be mitigated. These "Wilderness Manners" include traveling on durable surfaces, camping away from water bodies and trails, reducing litter by repackaging used food and carrying out all trash and garbage, minimizing use and impact of fires, and respecting wildlife and other travelers. The World Wildlife Fund uses the trips it sponsors as a way of fulfilling one of the tenets of ecotourism: using tourism to support conservation The WWF attempts to minimize the environmental impacts of their trips by selecting commercial tour operators according to their reputation as environmentally friendly (Janet Fesler, World Wildlife Fund, personal communication, September 16, 1999).

Educational efforts to promote environmentally responsible tourism seem more promising than regulation for several reasons. The dispersed nature of the tourism industry makes integrated and effective regulation difficult. For example, the EPA regulates certain tourism-related activities such as transportation emissions, but the development of tourist infrastructure is regulated at the state and local level through planning and zoning laws. The fragmentation of the tourism industry in turn leads to diffuse impacts, which further complicates regulation efforts. In particular, it is difficult to regulate tourist activities in part because of enforcement and compliance problems. Tourists can be told that littering is illegal, or not to drop anchor in a sensitive coastal ecosystem, but it is hard to force them to comply, and to monitor whether or not they have complied. Educating tourists about the environmental implications of their actions may help increase compliance levels. Furthermore, tourists may be more receptive to educational efforts than to regulation.

Educational efforts aimed at industry sectors seem most effective when cost savings are emphasized. For example, groups such as the Green Hotels Association first emphasize the costs hotels can save through energy and water saving measures (Patricia Griffin, president of Green Hotels Association, personal communication, October 21, 1999). In addition to cost savings, marketing is also important for tourism-related industries. Tourism service providers are even more likely to participate in environmental management programs if they recognize the potential for positive media attention. Some hotels have found that their efforts to reduce their environmental impacts have resulted in an increase in business, as people become aware of their efforts. For example, the Sounders Hotel Group in Boston attracted more than $750,000 in new convention business because of their environmental efforts. Therefore, an effective educational program geared toward tourism service providers such as hotels should emphasize the potential economic and marketing benefits of environmental stewardship. Environmental awareness has had an important impact on the tourism industry, but, as with all other sectors, economic motives are still primary.

5

Green Policy of Tourism Industry in Maldives

Introduction

The aim of this paper is to assess the impact of tourism on the environment of Maldives and explore the environmental management practices in the tourism industry of Maldives. First, the emergence, growth and present status of tourism development in the Maldives is outlined. Then the environmental impacts of tourism are discussed. Next, the environmental management practices are outlined. The relevant legislation, institutional structure, tourism planning, standards and controls are also presented.

Tourism Development in the Maldives

The Republic of Maldives is a small island, developing state consisting of 26 coral atolls dominated by the sea and is situated in the Indian Ocean, south-west of India. In total, these atolls contain about 1,190 very small islands of which only 200 are inhabited. The capital of the Maldives is Male', an island by itself, and the Male' International Airport also has an island (Hulhule) to itself.

Tourism development in the Maldives is based on the principle of isolation of tourists from the bulk of the indigenous population and the physical configuration of tourism development is an unusual one. In the Maldives, the "tourism industry" is synonymous with "resort islands" and each resort occupies a separate island and is totally self-contained. This isolation is practical because of the availability of a large number of uninhabited islands that can be developed into tourist resort islands.

According to a tourist opinion survey in 1991 conducted by the Ministry of Tourism, the main attractions in order of priority are white sandy beaches, opportunities for snorkeling and scuba diving among coral reefs and spectacular marine life, sunny weather, clear lagoons and scenic peaceful environments. The expectation is one of a "Robinson Crusoe" existence without any problems where the "Art of Doing Nothing" is practiced in a relaxing atmosphere.

Tourism History

Maldivian tourism entered the international scene only in the early 1 970s. Tourism commenced with the opening of two resorts in 1972 and about 1,000 tourists visited the islands. Until then the Maldives was virtually unknown to the tourist travel trade. By the late 1970, tour operators, notably from West Germany and Italy, started to feature the islands within their programs and international tourism had become an important source of income for the Maldives.

The first decade (1972-1982) in the development of the Maldives tourism industry evolved essentially in an unplanned laissez faire manner. Hulhule Airport was the basic and only gateway entry to the Maldives and the natural hub for tourism development.

Thus the first two resorts to be developed were Kurumba and Bandos both on islands in close proximity to Hulhule Airport and Male'. In 1973, along with three other resorts, Club Med established itself on Farukolhufushi island, also only 20 minutes by boat from Hulhule Airport.

Tourism in Maldives originated from excursions from Sri Lanka and because of the reputation of Maldives as a diving destination. Tour operators identified the ideal combination of packaging the culturally-orientated product of Sri Lanka with the unique island paradise holiday of the Maldives. During the 1972-1980 period the market changed from the more limited and specialized divers' market to the much bigger mainstream market for beach holidays.

With the growing importance of the mainstream market for sand, sea and sun holidays, the tour operators found that the market base was sufficient for introducing the Maldives as a separate destination.

With the completion of the runway at Hulbule's International Airport in 1981, direct charters from Europe, using wide bodied planes, flew in tourists. The expansion of air travel assisted by various promotional and other concessional fares on scheduled services, together with the rapid growth of charters, has helped the growth and development of the Maldives as a tourist destination.

In the beginning the facilities provided for tourists were basic. The room was furnished with just a bed and the essential cooling fan. Food with no exotic flavors was served by local people with no formal training, and scuba diving and island hopping were the only recreation facilities besides sun bathing and swimming. At present, a diverse range of facilities are offered at different resorts. At the luxurious end of the spectrum, public spaces have expensively tiled finished floors, vast varnished and carved timber frame roofs, elaborate light fittings and plush furniture, impressive reception areas, international cuisine, swimming pools, fountains, piped music and a lush landscape incorporating many ornamental imported species.

Tourism Indicators

Two resorts with a bed capacity of 280 opened in North Male' atoll in 1972. By the end of the first decade (1972-1982), 44 resorts became operational and bed capacity rose to just under 4,000. With the spatial policy shift towards opening of An Atoll, together with consolidation and upgrading of existing resorts, the next decade (1982-1992) saw the addition of 36 new resorts with over a doubling of bed spaces to reach a total of almost 8,500. By 1995, there were 74 resorts in operation in the Maldives.

During the year of inception of tourism in the Maldives, 1972, only 1097 tourists visited the Maldives. The number of annual tourist arrivals (reaching over 300,000 in 1995) now exceeds the total indigenous population of about 244,000. Europe is the leading generating market followed by the Asian market. Germany and

Italy are the two main suppliers of tourists and in 1994, shared 40 percent of the total tourist arrivals to the Maldives.

In the late 1970s, international tourism became an important source of income for the Maldives. The readiness of the Maldives to develop its tourist sector can only be understood in terms of its very limited economic possibilities, especially the absence of local raw materials to diversify into exports of manufactures. At 17 percent of gross domestic product, which provides over 25 percent of the government revenue and contributes around 60 percent of the country's foreign exchange earnings, tourism is the second largest contributor to the economy and it is increasing in importance yearly.

Tourism and the Environment

Tourism depends on environmental quality more than any other activity and a central precept that has been preached in tourism is not to kill the goose that lays the golden eggs. Yet, in general, it is characterized by rapid, short-term development which more often than not damages the very environment the tourists come to enjoy and simply moves off elsewhere. Without careful attention to the balance between the volume and type of tourist activity, and the sensitivity and carrying capacities of the resources being developed, tourism projects can be not only environmentally harmful but also economically self-defeating.

Tourism in the Maldives exists solely due to the physical and geographic features of the coral islands. The beauty of the underwater world at the reefs, clean water in the lagoons, white and pristine sandy beaches, a rich island vegetation and ideal tropical climate which form a virtual paradise that attracts tourists from Europe and Australasia.

Environmental Impacts of Tourism

The first proper evaluation of tourism in the Maldives was carried out in 1983 after 10 years of tourism development. It was revealed that the pollution of the sea with garbage, piles of waste found in the resorts often close to the tourist cottages, the picking of corals, the use of spearguns were features present that did not fit into the tourists' image of the Maldives. In 1991, after almost two decades of tourism development in the Maldives, the perception of impacts has changed. According to the present perceptions, the islands offer uncommon visual beauty unspoiled by human settlement, virtually unsurpassed marine environment and the strongest of all, unspoiled, under populated tiny tropical islands replete with natural beauty and abundant sea life.

The Environmental Protocol prepared in 1992 by the Ministry of Planning and Environment to determine the carrying capacity constraints in the tourism sector concluded that the natural resources of the Maldives are in a sufficiently pristine state, and of such high aesthetic quality, that a period exists in which environmental deterioration can occur without an adverse effect on tourism. However, concern was expressed that the duration of this period cannot be predicted and with increasing environmental pressures, rising environmental sensitivity, and without compensatory environmental management, adverse effects may be felt sooner than later.

According to a survey carried-out in August 1995 involving the management of 47 resorts, beach erosion was identified to be the major existing environmental problem facing the resorts. The highly dynamic Maldivian beaches erode and build in response to wave action associated with storms, the tidal cycle, and the monsoons.

The results of a survey carried out in 1992 showed that 12.8 percent of the total shoreline of 32 resorts surveyed consists of seawalls and groynes and is not sandy. The same survey also showed that 12 of the 32 resorts surveyed (38 percent) had offshore breakwaters to protect the beach. The maintenance of natural beach is of paramount importance to attract clients to the resorts and the construction of artificial structures designed to control and limit beach erosion are not only unsightly but also expensive.

Rubbish on beach is the next environmental problem identified by the resort management. Rubbish on beach mainly results from waste dumped at sea irresponsibly by neighboring resorts and inhabited islands that get washed ashore onto islands with the current and to some extent from the messy habits of certain tourists. The resort management is quite emotive on this issue as this is one issue that will reflect very badly on the image of the resort environment.

Solid Waste

Solid waste disposal is one of the most obvious impacts of tourist resort operation and one of the easiest environmental management problems to deal with and thus has been addressed in a number of reports on tourism development in the Maldives. The pollution of the sea with garbage and piles of waste found in the resorts often close to the tourist cottages were identified in 1983 among features that was not aesthetically pleasing. In 1985 the Department of Tourism reported that the disposal of non-biodegradable waste was then a serious problem and that there was need for education to increase environmental awareness, and for the use of re-cycling technology.

In the new Tourism Master Plan solid waste is identified as a major issue for resort islands and it is stated that at current tourism levels, problems are probably more aesthetic than environmental. The plan also points out that while solid waste itself may not currently pose a serious environmental threat, its impact in conjunction (e.g., synergistically) with the effects of other human activities should be considered.

Sewage Disposal

In 1980 only two resorts were reported as discharging saltwater flushed toilets to the open sea. In a survey of methods of sewage disposal reported from 34 resorts in 1992, 23 resorts disposed sewage into the ground while 11 discharged sewage to the sea.

A survey in 1993 revealed that at 67 percent of tourist resorts sewage effluent is piped into septic tanks, and the untreated sludge is dealt with by natural processes and soil absorption. At 33 percent of the resorts analyzed, septic tanks and sea out falls were the reported practices. Measures to protect the environment in cases of direct sewage discharge include the siting of outfall pipes 100 m from the island and 30m below mean sea level.

Sewage disposal has both health implications and environmental consequences. Aquifer contamination by faecal coliform bacteria or the contamination of bathing waters could give rise to health problems. Since a very small percentage of resorts pump sewage into the sea and even so, these resorts have a very small population it might be concluded that the current levels of sewage emission into the coastal waters of the resorts do not pose very serious problems to human health. The capacity constraints survey carried out in 1992 showed that the sewage discharges from resorts are relatively small and the observed effects were limited. Even though the volume of waste matter disposed is quite small, nutrients from sewage could build up over time, especially if the process of discharge is not managed well. However, volumes of water and rates of water exchange are large and in view of the productive fisheries, the atolls are probably already subject to relatively high nutrient input from upwellings as oceanic currents hit them.

Groundwater

There is an increasing move away from using ground-water as a resource in tourist resorts. Drinking water in tourist resort comes from rainwater which is collected on roofs and stored in large tanks and is now supplemented by desalinated water and imported bottled mineral water. There has also been a move away from the system in which groundwater was used for showering and flushing toilets to one in which saltwater is used for flushing with the wastewater pumped out to sea and desalinated water used for showering.

Groundwater quality deterioration could be caused through increasing abstraction of groundwater which depletes the already thin freshwater lends; salt water intrusion into the freshwater aquifer; and contamination of groundwater from sewage discharges. In addition to sewage, groundwater can also be contaminated through the use of contaminated soils; the excessive use of fertilizers; the use of pesticides; and inappropriate solid and liquid waste disposal.

An analysis of groundwater quality and pollution in tourist resorts, based on the results of Maldives Water and Sanitation Authority Surveys and consultants' opinions showed that groundwater quality in the resorts is deteriorating. However, the capacity constraints study in 1992 concluded that whilst there is some evidence that groundwater quality has deteriorated on some resorts through tourism, the deterioration is not significant and is unlikely to be irreversible. The study also suggested a number of factors mitigating any possible deterioration and they are:

1. The sources of pollution are relatively benign though more and more pesticides arc being used and rubbish buried on islands.
2. High rainfall backed up by evidence that salinity vary widely on many of the islands between the wet and dry season indicates that flushing rates, and oxidation, of contaminants are likely to be rapid.
3. Before upgrading, resorts traditionally used groundwater flushing for toilets and for showering, this minimizes the historic loss of groundwater.
4. The contaminant adsorption properties of coralline soils are generally extremely limited. One advantage of this is that any contaminants should be flushed out eventually. This is good for the state of the ground-water but not so good for adjacent lagoon waters.

Coral Reefs

On tourist resort islands reef damage has been caused by scuba divers, and by snorkelers and bathers walking out across the reef flat. The greatest threat at present almost certainly arises from snorkelers and bathers, from both inadvertent breakage and deliberate removal of coral and coral fauna for souvenirs. A study at Kurumba Village has assessed the effects of snorkelers on the reef flat/crest at depths up to about 1.5 m. Results indicate breakage of 18 percent of all Arcopora corals/month. Hence most or all coral colonies of this genus stand to get broken each year, suggesting a significant effect from snorkelers.

The present evidence on reef degradation from sewage in the Maldives is inconclusive. The Environment Protocol reported that none of the 32 resorts surveyed in 1992, and none of the 70 dive base operators on 41 resorts, identified sewage as a problem causing reef deterioration. Direct and indirect damage to reefs is also caused by divers and tourists' demands. However, the greatest impact to reefs in the Maldives has originated from coral mining for construction purposes.

Island Vegetation

The image of a palm fringed sandy beach and lush tropical

vegetation is integral to the perception of, and satisfaction, with Maldives as a tourist designation. At present there is no requirement to survey and consider the vegetation of an island as part of the planning approval process prior to resort development. In the construction process trees and shrubs are cut down and coastal vegetation is removed. Exotic ornamental and fast growing species are imported to replace the vegetation removed and for new resort gardens. The introduction of exotic species not only reduces the ability of the island to recover to its natural state but also the exotic species may overcome local ones directly or through the introduction of pests.

There is also the matter of maintaining the natural perception of the island for marketing purposes. Whilst the palm is the most important vegetation feature on an island, there are local plants that have historic and cultural importance and so have marketing value which imported exotics do not have.

Soil and fertilizer have largely been imported to improve the growth prospects of exotic imports. These imports are very much on trial and error basis and there is little doubt that many soils and a variety of fertilizers have been tried. This process detracts from efforts to use local vegetation which is already adapted to local conditions, and so should not have to be sustained artificially. Imports may also introduce soil associated pests and diseases for which local plants have limited resistance.

Environmental Management

National Legislation

The Department of Tourism and Foreign Investment was organized in 1978 and made responsible for supervision, co-ordination and maintaining standards of tourist services in the country. To develop and regulate tourism, and simultaneously to strengthen the institutional framework for administering and monitoring the industry, this department was renamed the Department of Tourism in November 1982 and made solely responsible for tourism management. In 1984, the Tourism Advisory Board was established as a consultative body affiliated to the tourism authority. The tourism sector was given elevated status in 1988 with the establishment of the Ministry of Tourism, according to the designating law 3/68 1 under 1/69 J as at 1993, to provide ways to develop the tourism industry in the Maldives, to plan methods of income generation through tourism, to provide guidelines, and to administer the industry.

The Ministry of Planning and Environment was established in 1988. This Ministry is responsible for the formulation of policies on environment, environmental guidance to other development sectors, the implementation of environmental impact assessment and the designation of protected areas.

Policy and Planning

During the first decade of tourism development, there was no specifically planned development; rather, tourism took place according to individual private sector initiatives in locations that offered market advantages principally related to the access opportunities offered by Hulhule Airport. This essentially informal development managed to generate almost 3,500 bed spaces of international quality and the industry was achieving enviable occupancy rates of up to 80 percent in the high season.

The first formal initiative to plan, in an integrated way, the future development of the tourism industry in the Maldives, came when the Department of Tourism and Foreign Investment commissioned Dangroup International in November 1980 to carry out a Maldives Tourism Development Plan. This long-range (10 years), tourism development plan was prepared for the Maldives in May 1983 and some, but not all, of its recommendations were considered feasible for implementation.

The tourism plan provided some ideas for development. However, to date, most of the tourism planning and management has resulted from government initiatives, based on its evaluation of the best forms and standards of development. Many of the government's present approaches and standards have evolved through the monitoring of the earlier phases of development to determine what is most suitable. Approaches and standards have been refined—and some abandoned—based on the experience gained from previous types of development.

By government policy, the resorts are located on uninhabited islands, in order to reduce any possible socio-cultural impacts.

Also most islands are too small to contain both resorts and traditional villages. These islands are owned by the government and it can allocate them for resort use as needed.

The resort developer receives a long-term lease and pays an annual rent that is calculated individually for each island. The resorts must supply their own infrastructure of electric power, water supply, sewage and solid waste disposal, boat dock and recreation facilities. They must also provide housing and related facilities for the resort employees. The families of the resort employees remain on their home islands, often some distance away.

The government policy has been to expand tourism for its economic benefits, but in a systematic manner of staged development. In the late 1980s, Kaafu Atoll was considered saturated with resort development. This decision was made within the framework of maintaining high environmental standards for the existing resorts, and retaining sufficient land for village and urban expansion and recreation parks.

All new resort development was then programmed to take place in Alif Atoll, which is accessible by sea and air from the international airport. In parallel the government policy turned to encourage expansion and upgrading of existing resorts to higher standards, including meeting present environmental quality standards. This upgrading was considered necessary to maintain the viability and competitiveness of these resorts and to maintain all tourism development at a reasonably high level, catering to quality tourist markets. As an inducement to achieve these objectives, resort leases were extended from 10 to 21 years and much of this upgrading has been accomplished.

The Third National Development Plan (1991-1993) recommended the development of a ten-year zoning plan (1991-2000). Under strategies and policies to achieve the main objectives of tourism development, the NDP (1991-1993) included a proposal to assess environmental impacts of resort developments and operations, and further strengthen measures taken to protect and conserve the environment and natural setting for tourism, and to adopt remedial measures on environmental degradation.

The issues that are examined in the new Tourism Master Plan draft include new markets, priority markets, air travel and other transportation issues, tourism infrastructure development, legal aspects, human resource development, gender situation, socio-cultural aspects and environmental impacts.

Environmental Impact Assessment

The Environmental Protection and Preservation Act of Maldives (4/93) provided the basic framework for the Environmental Impact Assessment (EIA) process in the Maldives and under Article 5 (1) of the Act, an impact assessment study shall be submitted to the Ministry of Planning, Human Resources and Environment (MPHRE) before implementing any activity that may have an impact on the environment. According to the EIA guidelines issued by MPHRE all new resort developments require an EIA study before approval for development can be made.

Carrying Capacity Limits

As an important basis for deciding the number of rooms and extent of resort facility development allowed on each resort island, the government has established carrying capacity standards. These are based on several factors. The cutting of trees is controlled so that the natural appearance and facade of the island are maintained and no buildings are allowed to appear above the tree tops. The maximum area of the island to be occupied by buildings is 20 percent, with two story buildings allowed to conserve land area if there is sufficient vegetation to conceal these buildings from the ocean view.

To preserve the tourists perceptions and image of beach orientation, all guest rooms should be facing the beach, with a minimum of 5 meters of linear beach available in front of each room. Only 68 percent of the beach length can be allocated to guest rooms as 20 percent has to be allocated to public use and 12 percent left as open space.

Construction on reef flat and lagoon are discouraged; however, as over water bungalows are very popular among tourists, they are permitted provided that equal open space is left on the land for each building developed on the lagoon.

Architectural and Design Controls

The design of resort buildings is controlled so that they are well integrated into the island environment, take advantage of the tropical climate and use local building materials to the extent possible, such as thatch roofs.

Previously many buildings were constructed from coral mined from the reefs. However, the use of coral is now restricted and use of imported materials is now encouraged, although these are expensive by local standards. Coral and sand mining from resorts and their house reefs is strictly prohibited.

Hard engineering solutions for dynamic coastlines are discouraged and construction of solid jetties and groynes are controlled. Design of boat piers and jetties should be in such a way that they do not obstruct the original flow of currents or disrupt the wave climate within the lagoon.

Biodiversity Conservation

To protect and preserve marine biodiversity a number of measures have been prescribed. Spear, poison and dynamite fishing are strictly prohibited. Net and trap fishing are controlled and confined to certain areas. Removal of shells, juvenile lobsters and lobsters ready to lay eggs are strictly prohibited.

The catching of turtles is strictly prohibited and trade in all turtle products is banned. The commercial exploitation and export of a number of other species is also banned. Resort operators also voluntarily prohibit the catching of reef fish from the house reef or tourist resorts. Fifteen important dive sites have been declared as protected areas in 1994, where fishing, anchoring, removal of coral and other destructive activities are prohibited.

The Ministry of Tourism recognizes the importance of vegetation in maintaining the natural beauty of the islands and there are a number of regulations which aim to secure this resource. These include a limit of 20 percent of the islands for building, the requirement that no buildings be put up that disrupt the natural facade of the island, that there be a minimum setback limit of 5 meters from the vegetation line of the island, and that no buildings should appear above the tree tops.

Waste Disposal

According to the regulations issued by the Ministry of Tourism, garbage from tourist resorts should be disposed off in a manner that would not cause any damage to the environment. All garbage disposed into the sea should be done as far away into the sea as necessary in order to ensure that it does not get washed onto any islands with the current. Tourist resorts are required to have incinerators and compactors adequate in size to burn all flammable materials and crush all the cans respectively. Those who lack these facilities are not allowed to operate. Plastic or polythene bags should not be thrown into the sea and such material should be burnt. Those who contravene these regulations are subject to fines and penalties.

Two airlines have joined in the effort to keep Maldives clean by arranging for waste to be carried back to Europe. Under this program all tourists who fly in to the Maldives in these airlines arc given a bag and asked to bring to the airport, all the waste they produce during their stay in the Maldives when they depart. The airlines carry the waste to the original destination for recycling free of charge.

Under sewage and exereta disposal the tourism book of regulation specifies that the sewage system should be prepared such that pollution of water supplies, beaches and other areas are prevented; nuisance, ugly sights, and unpleasant odors do not occur, human wastes do not come into contact with people, animal and food; and breeding of flies and mosquitoes will be prevented.

Conclusion

Tourism in the Maldives began in 1972 and it then evoke the image of a lost paradise. The tourism industry of the Maldives is dependent entirely on environmental quality and since it established itself in the tourism market it has maintained its strong position in a rapidly growing market. A few critics in the 1980s proclaimed that environmental pollution had begun to rear its ugly head in the Maldives. However, the natural resources of the Maldives are still in a sufficiently pristine state and of very high aesthetic quality and environmental concerns are few.

Environmentally unsound practices in solid waste and sewage

disposal pose the most serious threat from tourism to the delicately balanced coral reef ecosystem of the Maldives. Though solid waste is a cause of environmental concern, at current level it is more of an aesthetic problem. In the past the portion of waste and garbage which could not be burned was dumped into the sea. This practice is now prohibited by law and waste incinerators and crushers have to be used in all resorts. Sewage effluent is discharged into the sea by the resorts. However, their discharges from resorts are very small and the evidence on reef degradation from sewage discharges is inconclusive. Some of the resorts are turning to the latest technology in sewage treatment using UV radiation to produce virtually pure water.

The Maldives has developed a very suitable form of tourism, appropriate for the small island environment. The present form of tourism development has not generated any serious environmental impacts. This has been accomplished through careful management. The government has developed appropriate policies, legislation and plans and instituted mechanisms to apply strict standards and regulations.

6

Tourism and the Environment Issues in Coastal India

When Goa joined the Indian Union in December 1961, its only large industry was the export of its rich ores of iron and manganese. Goans depended on indigenous fish and coconuts for their vital nutritional requirements. The popularity of milk and vegetables amongst local inhabitants was low, and most of their dietary and other consumer items were imported. Before 1961, Goa had very little "development" in the modern sense of the term. With rich coastal biodiversity and abundant natural resources, the quality of life and the social fabric was good. Its main assets were its genial and peace loving people, a tranquil and unspoiled environment, and an absence of population pressure.

Tourism was adopted as a key sector for Goa's development, not only for the well-established reasons of increasing income and employment but also for its potential to generate non-manual employment in a state with an increasingly educated work force and limited industrial growth.

Fearing industrial pollution, the planners and decision-makers opted for tourism as an avenue to earn the state's income over increased industrial development in addition to mining. Except at academic levels, very little awareness and understanding existed back then among planners about the processes of the life support systems of the coastal environment and the interactive roles played by each component. This paper highlights the issues and the implications of tourism on the coastal marine and the socio-economic environment of Goa.

Nature and Growth of Tourism in Goa

Most of the tourism in Goa is concentrated in the coastal stretches of Bardez, Salcete, Tiswadi and Marmagao. Over 90 percent of domestic tourists and over 99 percent of the international tourists frequent these areas.

Consequently, beach tourism is the only type that is avidly encouraged by policymakers and other concerned parties alike. Goa is visited by two types of tourists with distinct needs which this state satisfies. The first is the domestic tourists, who comprise 80 percent of all tourists.

These people come in search of the culture that is "different" from the rest of India, as the Goan image holds a degree of mysticism, a sense of freedom and unconventional" dress style. The second is the international tourists who visit Goa purely for the natural environment—sun and beaches. Within the category of international tourists are there are two sub-categories: backpackers and charter tourists.

Although both visit Goa for the beaches, they stay away from each other. The backpackers are not found in areas of charter tourists; they prefer to mingle and live with the local communities. Whereas, the charter tourists tend to stay in the luxury starred hotels. Domestic and international tourists also differ in terms of the areas they frequent. For the domestic tourist, the beaches hold limited appeal, so domestic tourists remain away from the places frequented by the international tourists.

The timings of visits are clearly different for the domestic and the international tourists.

In previous decades, a clear off season for all tourists could be identified, today this is not so for domestic tourists, who come throughout the year albeit in larger numbers in the non-monsoon months. Conversely, international tourists avoid the monsoon months, as for them the use of the beach is the prime attraction to come to Goa.

Table 1 gives the share of domestic and international tourists over the last 15 years. The bulk of tourists coming to Goa are domestic, and this trend has grown considerably in the last few years.

Table 1. Share of Domestic and International Tourists of Goa

Year	*Total tourists*	*Share of domestic (%)*	*Share of international l(%)*
1981	439,015	93.33	6.67
1982	477,165	94.13	5.87
1983	530,015	93.67	6.33
1984	669,992	90.71	9.29
1985	775,212	88.05	11.95
1986	834,081	88.31	11.69
1987	861,448	89.02	10.98
1988	854,935	89.11	10.89
1989	862,443	89.40	10.60
1990	881,323	88.16	11.84
1991	835,067	90.63	9.37
1992	896,010	86.45	13.55
1993	969,234	82.39	17.61
1994	1,059,595	80.16	19.84
1995	1,107,705	79.31	20.69
1996	1,150,000	78.26	21.74

Source: India, Government of Goa, Department of Tourism. Personal Communications.

The various factors that have contributed to this rise in domestic tourism are:

- increased disposable income of the middle class,
- increased urbanization and stress of living in cities and towns,
- increased ownership of cars, which is making domestic tourism more attractive, especially among the upper-middle and middle classes,
- improved employment benefits, such as the leave travel concession,

- development of inexpensive mass transport and improved connections to various places of tourist interest,
- increased number of cheap accommodations and resorts,
- greater advertising targeted at domestic tourists both by the central and the state governments, as well as the tourist industry, and
- development of time sharing of holiday accommodations, that is being targeted at the middle class.

According to official tourism statistics, while the period of 1981-86 saw an increase in domestic and international tourists, the period of 1986-91 saw a slow down in growth rates for domestic tourists and a fall in growth rates for international tourists (Table 2).

Table 2. Growth of Tourism in Goa
Average Annual Growth Rates (%)

Period	Domestic	International
1981/82-86/87	7.98	27.20
1986/87-1991/92	2.75	-1.34
1991/92-95/96	3.90	31.00

Source: India, Government of Goa, Department of Tourism. Personal Communications.

Tourist arrivals in Goa have increased over the last five years with a higher rate of growth of international tourists than domestic tourists. Goa's growing importance on the Indian tourist map for international tourists can be seen from Table 3. While in the early 1980s, the share of international tourist that came to Goa was less than 3 percent, by the mid-1990's, the share has increased to over 10 percent.

In the earlier years, the international tourist was one in search of alternative lifestyles and mingling with local communities; however, in more recent years, a considerable homogenization of the traveler has occurred in terms of package tourism. In the 1980s, the domestic tourist came from the middle class and from the adjoining states; however, now domestic tourists that come to Goa are diversifying, as the place attracting a number of the rich young elites from more distant states. In response to these changes, the tourism industry in Goa has evolved into a curious mix of low-budget tourism and up-market hotel development, a mix that is marked with tensions and potential conflicts over the appropriation of resources.

Table 3. International Tourist Arrivals in India

Year	*Tourist arrivals in India (millions)*	*Share of Goa in total tourist arrivals in India (%)*
1981	1.26	2.4
1982	1.29	2.3
1983	1.30	2.3
1984	1.21	4.9
1985	1.26	7.1
1986	1.45	6.2
1987	1.48	6.4
1988	1.59	5.9
1989	1.74	5.2
1990	1.71	5.9
1991	1.68	7.8
1992	1.87	6.4
1993	1.82	9.3
1994	1.87	11.2
1995	2.10	10.9

Source. Center for Monitoring the Indian Economy. 1995. Basic Statistics of the Indian Economy; and India, Government of Goa, Department of Tourism. Personal Communications.

Impacts of Tourism in Goa

Tourism development among policy-makers tends to be discussed in terms of the factors that are of concern to the national and the state governments. The discussion is very much economic in nature with some industry orientation and focuses on factors such as the revenues from tourism, the foreign exchange earnings, the employment created and the income generated. The focus has always been on the implications of tourism development on the economy of Goa and on the relations among the various components of its tourism industry. The microlevel impact of tourism on the destination area immediately around it has been relatively less studied, if at all. The impacts of such a large-scale, diversely interactive activity as tourism should be more inclusive of all components. Tourists travel to and from their destinations, are accommodated, fed and entertained. All these activities require extensive infrastructural networks and support services that may not remain limited to the geographical positions of a tourist's movements. Moreover, the effects result very much from the interactions among the tourists and the agents in the destination area.

Economic Aspects

The foreign exchange earning potential of the tourism industry is one of the main attractions for its support by national governments, while state governments are more concerned with its contribution to local income, taxes and employment. On an average, earnings in foreign exchange for the last three years were US$43-57 millions. It is estimated that tourism contributes to around 13.7 percent of Net State Domestic Product; 7 percent of employment and 7 percent to state tax revenues. The money spent by domestic and international tourists is received by different segments of the industry which provide the supporting goods and services.

Tourist receipts can be classified into five categories: accommodation and food, shopping, internal travel, entertainment and miscellaneous items. Table 4 provides an overview of the distribution of expenditures among the five categories for international and domestic tourists.

Moreover, in 1992, about 90 percent of the domestic tourists who came to Goa spent less than US$35 per capita per day. Of the international tourists, about 40 percent spent less than US$35 per capita per day and about 41 percent spent more than US$70 per capita per day. As mentioned earlier, however, this trend is changing today (Table 5). In the last few years indications are that the domestic tourist coming to Goa is increasingly from the more affluent segments of society, and the international tourist have increasingly been more of the inexpensive charter packages.

Table 4. Distribution of Expenditures for International and Domestic Tourists

Category	*International Tourists (%)*	*Domestic Tourists (%)*
Accommodations and food	53.95	58.20
Shopping	24.84	26.70
Internal transport	13.63	10.40
Entertainment	2.61	1.80
Miscellaneous expenses	4.97	2.90
Average length of stay	9 days	5 days
Total amount spent per visit	US$590	US$110

Source: Kirloskar Consultants Ltd., 1994. Report on Study of Tourism Industry in Goa. December.

These expenditures form the direct output of the industry. However, the industry buys goods and services from other sectors of the economy. This additional output produced through inter-industry spending is the indirect output of the industry and is normally estimated using multipliers. It is not quite clear how much tourism is actually benefiting the Goan economy as a whole because a large part of the goods required to support the tourism industry is brought from outside the state.

Tourism: Food and Agriculture

Food and beverages comprise the largest component of the expenditure of domestic tourists (40 percent) and second largest component of the expenditures (accommodations being the largest), of the international tourist (20.5 percent). Increasing the amount of local food used in the tourism industry is a way of increasing backward linkages from tourism, involving the local community and therefore, moving toward more diversified and sustainable development. Yet, policymakers have not focused on strengthening the economic linkages between tourism and the food sector. The hotel food supply chain has not been studied in Goa and local surplus production from agriculture and fishing could be potentially integrated into this chain as an additional means to generate local income. However, a careful balance must be struck between producing for tourists' requirements and ensuring food supply at reasonable prices to the locals.

Regional Imbalances

As previously mentioned, most of the tourism development in Goa is concentrated in the four coastal stretches of Bardez, Salcete, Tiswadi and Marmagao. These areas are, similarly, the most developed regions of Goa, accounting for approximately 66 percent of Goa's Gross State Domestic Product (GSDP). They have dense settlements and are more developed in terms of infrastructural support services. About 70 percent of small-scale units, 78.5 percent of the capital investment in small industry and over 68 percent of the employment in this sector are found here. Historically, the region developed relatively faster than the rest of the state due to its coastal location, which provided easy access for sea trade and was attractive for settlement. There are a number of interesting locations with tourism potential exist in the hinterland; however, very little has been done to develop them. Hence, there is a considerable imbalance between the coastal and the hinterland regions in infrastructural and other indicators of economic development.

Investment in the Tourist Industry

Since tourism's acceptance as the primary avenue through which to develop, it has grown in scope to be comparable with mining, the only other industry in Goa. State expenditures on the tourism industry has doubled over a period of 10 years. Expenditures amounted to approximately Rs.15 million in 1986-87, and they grew to approximately Rs.30 million by 1996-97.

Private investment also increased. If the investment per room by hotel category, which was estimated by Kirloskar Consultants 1994, investment in the hotel industry has risen from Rs.2.08 billion to Rs.3.25 billion in 1996, an increase of Rs.1.19 billion in just 2 years. If the type of hotels that have been built over the last two years is analyzed, investment in starred hotels increased by 39.5 percent during this period while that in other hotels has gone up by 47.5 percent. Tourism studies suggest that the financial performance of the hotel industry is poor compared to several other industries in the state although no evidence has been presented to back this claim'.

Table 5: Expenditures of the State on Tourism per Plan

Annual	*Plan Actual expenditures (Rs. Millions)*
1992-93	22.96
1993-94	25.93
1994-95	27.01
1995-96	29.25
1996-97	30.00
EIGHT PLAN (1992-97)	135.15

Source: India, Government of Goa, Department of Town and Country Planning and Department of Statistics and Evaluation Department. Personal Communications.

From the statistics available and through observation, local participation in the tourism industry is high in terms of the number of small hotels and paying guest accommodations, yet the bulk of economic investment is concentrated in just a few hotels. Thus, using just the accommodation sector as a proxy for the tourism industry as a whole in 1996, almost half of all investment in the sector was in the hands of just four large hotels; the largest hotels together controlled 69 percent of all investment, and the balance was made up by smaller hotels.

Seasonality of Income and Employment

The industry peaks and troughs: October-February being the good months and June-August being the lean months due to the monsoon. This seasonality requires the tourism industry to respond by adjusting the output in terms of the services it provides which affects hotels, restaurants and their employees. Because of the search and initial training costs that the employer faces, and because of the need to cater to sudden spurts of demand, a hiring and firing policy is not cost-effective to an employer'. The first reaction of employers is to keep labor, but reduce the work hours, a situation akin to holding inventories of labor in excess of demand. This strategy is supported by employing unskilled labor during the peak season, who are then laid off during the off season as the costs of hiring and firing unskilled labor are not high. A sample survey indicates that the highest seasonality of income (in terms of lower off season earnings) and the highest seasonality of employment (in terms of hours worked per week) are experienced by the smaller hotels. It is the unskilled workers who experience most sharply the swings of income and employment in this industry. This is a social cost of the industry to which hitherto scant attention has been paid.

Social Aspects Shifts in Population and Traditional Occupations

In the tourist belts of Calangute-Candolim in Bardez, a shift in the composition of the resident population has occurred to include a large number of migrants from the states of Karnataka, Rajasthan and Kashmir due to potential employment in the tourism industry. Most of these people are engaged in selling artisanal pieces, handicrafts and garments. It cannot be denied that tourism has also given a boost to local art and handicrafts; however, the commercialisation of such arts and crafts has resulted in a certain deterioration in their quality as they are being manufactured for bulk sale. At another level, Goan cultural practices are being used as tourist attractions, such as Carnival and Shigmo, which have been given a certain orientation to suit the demand of tourists. Much of the spontaneity of these practices has been lost'.

Moreover, some of the villages along the coasts have become very tourist-oriented and thus, shifted away from their traditional occupations. A couple of decades ago, these villages were predominantly fishing-or agricultural-oriented. Tourism has increased land prices and encouraged locals to sell their land, thereby sharply increasing the competition for land in the tourist belt. It can be argued that tourism has accelerated the decline of agriculture in Goa, by providing a viable alternative for the lateral transfer of investment capital, land, and labor by the locals. In the tourist belt, land conversion from agriculture to non-agriculture uses has occurred'. In the fishery sector, while fishermen do not always compete with tourists for shore space, there are instances on the Goan coasts where traditional fishing operations have been constrained by lack of shore space. In some areas, fishing ports and the houses of fishermen have been displaced by resort development.

Economic forces are driving social forces here. On the one hand, expectations of higher returns, from the sale of land to builders and/or from hiring out houses to tourists rather than from actively engaging in agriculture or fishing are creating incentives for shifting occupations. On the other hand, social forces are at work in the sense that tourism provides locals with an opportunity to keep their women at home rather than have them till the soil or sell fish in the market. This is perceived as a movement upwards for the locals, and a factor that cannot be ignored in the dynamics of the intersectoral movement of land and labor. Often large tourism development projects require the displacement of some of the original inhabitants of the area. Some of those displaced by present projects, chose to invest their compensations in capital assets, e.g., taxis, and have become to a degree upwardly mobile in an economic sense. However, there are others who due to their initial circumstances are unable to move along the same path, and instead become marginalized, having to replace self-employment for menial jobs in the very resorts that have displaced them. The issue of income distribution needs to be examined.

Impacts on the Goans' Sense of Community

One of the impacts of tourism on the Goan community is the "creeping expropriation" felt by the locals. This feeling of being pushed out arises from the fact that starred hotels have effectively gained control over beach resources, which locals have used for generations, and are selling access to them at a price. The area that is available to them as commons is increasingly reduced and overpopulated, causing the locals to avoid the beaches as a whole.

Consequently, the growth of tourism in Goa has been accompanied by strong anti-tourism activism". Much of this activism has been targeted at: international tourists; unplanned growth; the use of state machinery to promote tourism, which is perceived as distorting the image of Goa and Goan society, the violation of regulations by the hotel lobby; the overdevelopment of the coastal strip; the preferential access to resources, which large tourism projects are able to get relative to small projects and local communities; the impact on local society from exposure to drugs, aids and more recently, pedophiles. The bottom-line is that there has been little involvement of the public in the policy decision-making process resulting in a strong sense of alienation about decisions that are affecting the lives of the local community.

Environmental Aspects

Coastal zone environment is particularly fragile and can be divided into two areas: the marine part and the land part. For the purpose of this discussion, coastal waters, bays, backwaters, creeks, tidal inlets, and estuaries are considered as components of the marine part of the coastal zone. The sandy beaches along with two dunes (one which runs along the seashore, and another that runs parallel but about 100 to 500 meters away from the seashore) and their vegetation are considered components of the land part. In between these dunes there lies a sandy plain, which acts as a buffer zone between the main land and the sea.

Impacts to the Marine Part of the Coastal Zone

The marine part of the coastal zone provides many functions and in the present context are:

- To support marine flora including subtidal varieties, such as mangroves. The mangrove ecosystem itself serves as a habitat for diverse types of species of birds and marine biota, in addition as the protection of the coastline from erosion, tides and storms.
- To support a wide variety of marine organisms including mammals. The marine organisms among themselves form a very intricate, well-established food chain starting with the chemical constituents of sea water called nutrients.
- To function as a natural thermostat which balances the climate on thc subregional, regional and global scales.
- To disperse riverine load effectively in near-shore regions.

Most of the above functions are interactive in nature. In the coastal current movement, the most important force is the tidal cycle, which drives the sea water along the shoreline, bays, creeks and upstream through the mouths of rivers and estuaries. Other important forces are the near shore and riverine, or estuarine currents. All these currents carry natural sediment load and any other marine discharge, resulting from manmade activities, and deposits them at a site defined by an equation containing parameters, such as current velocity, counter currents, topography of the seabed or riverbed and other oceanographic factors. The transportation capacity of the currents has to be understood in terms of its effect on marine biota. For example, a rise of a few degrees in temperature of a sea water body would adversely effect species occurrence and predominance among biota, which in turn could influence other life forms. Also, a sudden appearance or disappearance of a species due to anthropogenic factors may cause stress in other species. Given the interactiveness and complexities of the coastal environment, any developmental activity should to be preceded by the Environmental Impact Assessment studies to forestall environmental degradation.

The following impacts on the marine part of the coastal zone have been observed while surveying the ecosensitive coastal areas of Goa. They have been represented in a flowchart in the Annex. The work was carried out by National Institute of Oceanography on request from the Ministry of Environment and Forests, Government of India, in August/September, 1 1996.

- *Loss of mangroves:* Thick mangroves on the outskirts of Panaji, at Sao Pedro near Old Goa, around Talpona backwaters and at innumerable other locations are being reclaimed. In addition to the biological impacts of the loss of mangroves, the tidal waters could flood the surrounding coastal areas causing erosion and thus opening the estuarine banks to storm surges.
- *Reduced fish catch and species:* A steady decrease in the total annual fish catch has been observed in Goa. The catch has declined from 105.44 thousand tones in 1993-94 to 101.90 in 1994-95 and in 1995-96, to 87.82 thousand tones. More specifically, at Sancoale-Chicalim Bay, the decrease in production of certain varieties of shellfish and crabs, both local delicacies, is believed to be due to the land reclamation of mangrove swamps and to the construction of roads to

the Sao Jacinto Island and at Talpona. More generally, one or more of the following factors may be responsible for the reduction in fish catch:

a. Unscientific fishing practices: These can include the use of nets with a mesh size smaller than permissible during spawning periods and the fishing beyond sustainable yields. These practices are pursued due to high demand for fresh seafood in the market.

b. Loss of spawning grounds: Reasons for this could be mangrove deforestation, land reclamations and siltation. Short-term economic gains from the development of these areas is obviously preferred over the long-term benefits of the conservation of ecology.

c. Introduction of anthropogenic material: Any disturbance at any step in the marine food web may inadvertently affect other species. The introduction of untreated sewage and waste to the environment would give rise to toxic algal blooms wiping out many species. Increased turbidity and sedimentation can also affect the benthic communities.

- Erosion: Dispersion of sediment load at any given point depends upon a number of parameters related to marine currents. Any activity which causes disturbances in these parameters, could alter the sites of deposition and result in erosion, accretion or siltation and changes in the ecology of that area, such as land reclamations, the extraction of sand or the construction of jetties. Consequently, there are a large number of eases where coastal stretches have been subjected to the forces of erosion. Prime examples are Campal and Caranzalem near Panaji, Palolem, Agonda and many other places, where a considerable amount of construction activities have occurred.
- Accretion/siltation: Accretion and siltation is occurring. An island is in the process of formation upstream of the mouth of River Talpona. Due to sand bar formation at the mouth itself, which has been more pronounced in the last few years, the river is navigable only during high tides.

In addition, local fishermen have noted siltation in the river bed. All these observations suggest disturbances in the natural sediment load dispersion patterns in the River Talpona.

Impacts to the Land Part of the Coastal Zone

The land part of the coastal zone mainly comprises sandy areas along with the dunes and its vegetation cover. This part provides the following functions:

- To protect the coast from the forces of the oceans,
- To replenish the sand on the beach that is carried away by the sea,
- To gather the sand that is blown landward by the wind with the help of dunes and its vegetation, and
- To serve as habitats for numerous organisms, including turtles.

Sandy areas are also used for tourism development:

- To mix the sand with cement for construction purposes, and
- To develop the land.

All along the coastline of Goa, for example, between Chapora and Sinquerim in Bardez, Caranzalem and Miramar in Panaji, Salcete Coast in Central Goa and in Galgibaga, Talpona, Palolem in South Goa, there has been a boom in construction activities, most of which are for tourism or for associated purposes. To make space for and to use them as a component of cement for construction, sand is being extracted in substantial amounts. When the environmental functions are weighed against the economic services that sand performs, the fact that the former are not priced, tilts the demand in favor of the economic user-groups. There is need to quantify and monitor such sand losses and their ecological impacts.

The following impacts have been observed on the coastal stretches of Goa due to development activities:

- *Loss of sand dunes:* Sand dunes have borne the brunt of construction activities along the coastal stretches of Goa.

Anjuna and Baga-Calangute-Candolim stretches in North Goa, and Salcete beaches comprising Betalbatim, Colva, Varca, Cavelossim and Mobor in central Goa, were the first beaches to lose their dunes. Our survey showed South Goa to be the next in line as in Galgibaga, two dunes, 1 0 meters high, have already been flattened into plateaus at half the heights to make way for construction.

- *Endangered species:* Four species of turtles have been reported to frequent the beaches at Morjim, Miramar, Bogmalo and Palolem, covering almost the entire stretch of the Goan Coast. The "Save The Turtles" campaign of the Goa Foundation, a local Non-Governmental Organization, carried jointly with the Forest Department of the Government of Goa, reported that the number of sea-turtles visiting their nesting sites on different beaches in Goa particularly in Morjim, is steadily decreasing.
- *Tidal ingress:* The ceaseless mining of sand and sand-dunes have effectively razed gentle slopes of sand which stop the tides from rushing further on the shore. The consequent tidal ingress has reduced the area of beach at different places, such as Miramar in Panaji, Baga-Calangute-Candolim-Sinquerim stretch and Anjuna in Bardez, and in Salcete and Mormugao on the north and central coasts of Goa.

Impacts of Recreational Activities

Recreational facilities affecting the coastal environment are generally, but not limited to, those related to upscale tourist activities. These are:

- *Swimming pools:* The water for this is invariably drawn from subsurface aquifers. The withdrawal of large amounts of ground water in a limited area can be detrimental to thc water table of the region, particularly since it is a source of drinking water. Additionally, some parties owning wells with a good underground stream of fresh water sell their water at Rs.100 (US$2.5) per 500 liter tank to fill these swimming pools. Consequently, the groundwater levels in some coastal areas is decreasing and is frequently accompanied with salt water intrusions. The manifestation of sea water intrusions in the form of salt water in wells along the coastal belt from Chapora to Aguada has been observed in coastal aquifer studies.

- *Water sports:* Motor boats used in shallow coastal waters continuously disturb the habitats of endangered species and other marine life. Moreover, they tend to degrade water quality by the discharge of oil and grease.
- *Beach driving:* Tourists regularly drive on the beaches during low tide. Concrete ramps have even been constructed to take the vehicles on the beaches such as at Palolem.
- *Beach accommodations:* In the initial states of tourism in Goa, beach shacks became popular due to their small numbers, economical rates and simple decor; however, after several decades, these structures crowd the shorelines without any comfortable space among them, and they lack deferentially toilet facilities and proper refuse collection, all of which often result in waste invariably find its place in the coastal waters.
- *Sanitation:* Goa lacks modem treatment and disposal systems for both sewage and garbage. Even the internationally famous beach stretch of Baga-Calangute Sinquerim, does not have rudimentary toilet facilities. Tourists, locals, shop owners and the hordes of migrant laborers, who are employed by construction companies along the beaches, have no other opt ion than to use the beaches to answer the call of the nature.
- *Beach litter:* Plastics are among the very serious problems in a number of Goa's beaches, and an action plan is urgently needed to mitigate the problem". Both the last mentioned problems could be solved through improved enforcement of regulations and infrastructual improvements.

Impacts of Expanded Transport

Even though tourists in Goa are almost exclusively accommodated in coastal areas, they arrive and depart Goa by some kind of transportation operating in other areas of the state. While the air and sea travel would cause negligible damage to the environment in broad terms, motor vehicles cause air pollution by their uncontrolled exhaust fumes.

Also, the alignment of the Konkan Railway has broad reaching environmental impacts. The laying of the tracks for the railway in Goa, especially through wetlands and tidal marshes at Maxem and between Bali and Mayem along with numerous bridges on the Mandovi-Zuari estuarine fronts, has been done without proper hydrodynamic and geomor-phological studies. The gigantic embankments, several kilometers long, supporting the rail lines along the lowlands of Goa have lead to substantial alterations in physical, chemical, biological and geomorphological setups. Blocking, diminuting or increasing the tidal flow has resulted in a major redistribution of sediments giving rise to erosion/deposition or deposition/erosion with conspicuous changes in shorelines or near-shore realms.

Mangrove swamps have been destroyed; tidal regimes disrupted; paddy fields flooded, and the embankments are sinking due to soft underlying strata 32. A comprehensive analysis of the environmental impacts of the Konkan Railway alignment is needed to study such questions as the following. Is the siltation taking place in the backwaters and estuarine regions of Canacona in South Goa due to river runoffs carrying haphazardly dumped material from the digging out of the railroad? To what extent has the Konkan Railway Alignment through ecosensitive areas contributed to the environmental degradation of estuarine/coastal areas of Goa? In board terms, factors other than tourism could be responsible for the observations made above, but the contributions of the tourism industry in all these situation should be identified given the criticality of the coastal environment demands.

Tourism Policy

In the wake of the report, "Our Common Future", by United Nation's Commission on Environment and Development in 1983, India passed its own Environment Protection Act in 1986. This was followed by a Notification in February 1991, inviting the governments of India's coastal states and union territories to prepare

Coastal Zone Management Plans for their respective territories. The much publicized Rio Summit in June 1992, along with Indian environmental norms, started a land race for coastal development regardless of the laws, regulations and conventions in vogue. The land race got started probably because the coastal resource users experienced inertia in the implementation of various legislation on the part of the authorities.

It seems increasingly clear that (i) despite several important pronouncements and regulatory mechanisms in place, local planning does not always adhere to guidelines and regulations and (ii) where it does adhere, planning and development regulations have been observed in the breach. Thus, the Government of Goa, in October 1988, published its Regional Development Plan, anticipating, among other activities, the growth of tourism by 2001 A.D. In this plan, a strategy is outlined:

"[The] location of new beach resorts should be considered not only from point of view of land availability but also from the consideration of beach resource ecology, based on the Environmental Assessment Studies. Further, spreading thinly on all available sandy beach stretches from Tlerekhol/Arambol in the north to Betul/Agonda in the south is not advisable from the standpoint of conservation of resources both natural and man-made. Instead, it is suggested that beach-head developments at certain selected centers should be encouraged."

Despite these admirable commitments toward conservation and the protection of the coastal environment and ecology, the Regional Development Plan for Goa 2001 A.D. does not contain any reference to the "no development zone" of 200/500 meters from the high-tide line along the seashores, which had been much debated around the country in the early 1980s; nor does it mention the Environment Protection Act of 1986 of the Government of India. Moreover, the Coastal Zone Management Plans, prepared by the Department of Town and Country Planning of Goa in 1995 and 1996 for approval by the Central Government, actually recommend tourism-related development for almost the entire length of the Goan coastline, barring only a few places, which contradicts the Department's own guidelines.

The current policies and relaxed enforcement thereof have led to the haphazard and uncontrolled growth of townships. Places like Calangute and Candolim in Bardez and Colva in Salcete have become over commercialized and haphazard in their development pattern. These areas have a number of unauthorized constructions, which have paid little heed to local planning rules, infrastructural supports or aesthetics. During the 1980s and the early 1990s, the lure of catering to tourists especially, international tourists and the hope of making rapid profits have led to considerable investment in resorts and apartments. Today there are signs of over investment, this is spreading a price war. When a certain location is to be developed as a prominent tourist area requiring extensive infrastructural and other support services, it gets developed as a small township. This increases its real estate value manifold, inducing other sectors of the society to set up business and residences in these areas as well. A quick look at the developments along the coasts of Goa and the future plans for it, reveals that:

i)these follow the ideas submitted in the CZM plan of Goa (which is yet to be formally approved) rather than its Regional Development plan; and,

ii)the tourists are almost exclusively accommodated along the 105 km stretch of the coastline while little effort has been made to adhere to the regional plans of creating other types of tourism besides beach tourism.

One successful example of regulated tourism development is Seychelles, an island nation in the Indian Ocean. It spared its beaches from concretization and allowed resorts to come almost entirely amongst the coconut groves just behind the sandy stretches, taking care of the coastal marine environment. This policy, unfortunately, is not in place in Goa where constructions are allowed as 'close to the waterline as possible.

Conclusions

Although tourism is concentrated along the coastal zone in Goa, it has had a number of positive benefits in terms of increased incomes, increased employment, added avenues for upward mobility for locals, increased revenue and increased foreign exchange earnings. However, there are also some socio-economic and environmental impacts associated with these benefits that need to be highlighted. These impacts have arisen as a result of the trajectory that tourism has followed in Goa and can be summed up as follows:

1. The growth of coastal tourism has been rapid and uncontrolled.
2. The seasonal nature of tourism has led to swings in employment and income most markedly in the small sector and to the unskilled worker.
3. There has been no clear nor firm policy relating to tourism; most decisions have been on a purely ad hoc basis, except for a marked predisposition to upmarket tourism. The policy initiatives that have been introduced are not attentive to local concerns. This has led to some disaffection among locals toward tourists that needs to be studied.
4. There has been a marked spatial concentration of tourism development along the coast, which is leading to heavy demand for resources in these places.

7

Green Impact Assessment in Hospitality Industry

New control procedures have been required which identify those impacts, which a project might have on the human environment, in the short term *and* in the long term, near the project site *and* remote from it and in terms of the direct physical and objective impacts *and* induced social and cultural impacts.

With increasing industrialisation in the ECE countries the scope and scale of new plans, new technologies and new projects has also increased. At the same time it has become clearer that the level of human and social well-being depends as much on the quality of the environment in which people find themselves as on the economic fruits of these new plans, technologies and projects It is perhaps in part the combination of these two factors, namely the some what subjective area of the environmental basis of human well-being and the shear size and potential impact of modern industrial and social projects, which has led many governments to consider whether in fact additional control of projects is not required, over and above that which already exists through the usual planning procedures and pollution control legislation.

Such an approach implies a much closer involvement of people in the planning process, since it is people who are ultimately affected by environmental changes. Hence as a country systematically evaluates plans or projects for their effect on the environment by instituting, a more open planning process involving those institutions, professionals and even orderary citizens who are concerned about environmental quality, it is involved in

Environmental Impact Assessment whether officially labelled as such or not.

And just because of the fact that EIA is essentially a dimension of the planning process rather than a specific product (such as Environmental Impact Statement), the best way of understanding it better is by sharing experiences of those cases of where it has been applied, rather than attempting to establish right rules for drawing up such statements.

Definition of Environmental Impact Assessment

EIA in its simplest terms is the assessment *before any decision* is taken of the *future impact* of the consequences of that decision for the quality of the total human environment on which man largely depends for *his well-being.*

EIA is thus highly *specific* in terms of a particular decision or project rather than general for all decisions or any projects and it is highly specific in terms of targets which are impacted on rather than general for "all society".

EIA is thus *future* oriented in that it seats out to know what are the long term effects in one place, what are the consequences of diffusion of impacts away from the initial site, what are the induced effects through the food chains, through modifications of natural habitats, through disturbance of natural, physical and ecological equilibria and even, or even most important, the induced impact on man of these change in his environment.

EIA is finally *multi-faceted and human oriented* and essentially seeks to know what will be the consequence of economic decisions for those aspects of human and social development which depend not only on the purely economic, but also on the quality of man's interactions with the natural and man-made physical environment.

EIA is thus different from but complementary to the two classical tools for environmental protection, i.e. land use planning and pollution control. Indeed Environmental Impact Assessment is essentially a means of completing environmental protection procedures, which started in most countries with laws on land use planning and on pollution control.

Land use planning broadly aims at the best possible use of *resources*—particularly land, water, air, energy and raw materials.

Thus land use planning sets out guidelines for protection of the land as a resource in the form of general requirements for a given type of activity, e.g. industrial, agricultural, etc., but normally does not enter into specific questions beyond those of conformity to codes for layout, use of utilities, etc. In other words, land use planning tends to define what and where a potential source of impact is, but not how it might impact on a given target.

Similarly, pollution control broadly aims at protecting natural and the human population from damage or disease induced by elements introduced into the environment by man and particularly by his *technology*.

Pollution control is concerned with what a given activity may contribute to the environment and also to some extent with how targets in general will respond to that level of pollution. But once again this tends to look at environmental protection in general terms and primarily from the point of view of the source, rather than from that of the impact of a specific target group, i.e. from the view point of the target with all the problems of synergistic effects or the real human consequences of any damage. Environmental impact assessment deals with these same factors but in terms of the specific case of a single project and in terms of the subjective and political process of how this project should maximise the net contribution to human well-being, locally as well as nationally.

Hence while land planning is essentially concerned with the introduction of resource constraints into the planning process and pollution control is essentially concerned with the introduction of technological selection into the planning process, environmental impact assessment essentially introduces people into the planning process through their concern for the quality of that environment on which their well-being depends.

In addition land use planning or pollution control can not consider the indefitely variable situations which one finds in the real world and which are due to differences in topography climate, ecology development patterns, technology, etc. They must necessarily reflect a macroscopic approach to environmental protecting. Environmental impact assessment, however, recognises that a local situation might have a different balance of costs and benefits from that which occurs at the national level and that as a result of specific project-environment interactions, a design process and a political process has to be entered into which will result in mutually acceptable costs and benefits being generated by the project and born both by the developer and by the local community.

So EIA is specified to the case under consideration and it specifically concerned with the target, i.e. the "who" which is impacted on by the "what" from the "where".

Thus, in looking at environmental impact assessment in different countries it is interesting to examine to what extent it is a political process by which acceptable projects are generated by interaction between promoters and the public and to what extent it builds on and completes and the public and to what extent it builds on and completes existing land use planning and pollution control proce-dures.

Because EIA is an evolutionary rather than a revolutionary stage of environmental protection it should grow from and be integral with existing procedures, institutions and laws governing land use planning and pollution standards. It is thus inherent in and implicit in legislation and procedures in almost all countries, but when made explicit it completes the legislative system., i.e.

One consequence of this integrated view of environmental protection is :

(a) that environmental impact assessment could be (and in some cases is) carried out through existing planning and pollution control procedures without being formalised and hence.

(b) All countries have experiences to relate provided that land use planning and pollution controls are both project specific and target specific, i.e.

Approaches to EIA in Different Countries

As a result of the information submitted to the Secretariat by member government on the status of EIA in their countries an analysis way carried out. This shown perhaps that most approaches to EIA can be exemplified as to whether they tend to be based on

Informal Procedures, i.e. and open planning dimension of existing procedures of Formal i.e., founded by and originated from a legislative base which intended to integrate economic, social and human development. Secondly, there are other approaches by which the EIA is either carried out Explicitly, i.e., separate from the planning process and producing for example some separate Environmental Impact Assessment or Implicity, i.e. as an integral part of the planning process with emphasis on the planning process rather than the environmental product.

The informal and indeed implicit approach is characterized by the situation in the U.K. Here traditional planning has always involved the extensive use of public hearings with evidence being admitted the extensive use of public hearings with evidence being admitted from a wide cross-section of society. For major projects such as the Third London Airport and evidence submitted amounts to a veritable Impact Statement! Yet, the process is informal and implicit in the British approach to decision making. Even the setting of effluent standards in the U.K. is a matter of local consultation by carrying out a mini-EIA based on ecological, economic and technological inputs. Countries such as the Netherlands have also tended in the past to favour informal and implicit approaches.

Other countries have tended to favour more formal approaches to the question of integration economic, social and human well-being, but still without calling for explicit or separate Impact Statement. Thus in the USSR the planning process includes ecological and social factors. In Poland all planning applications have to outline the predicted impacts on the environment. In Hungary impacts have to be determined at the project formulation stage. In Czechoslovakia impact assessment of projects includes building into in planning an outline of the measures required to ensure rational and effective management of the environment. In Bulgaria environmental concerns are being built with operational planning and indeed a Bulgarian industrial region is being used to assess the CMEA methodology for "Economic and Non-Economic Evaluation of Man's Impact on the Environment."

Outside the CMEA region, other countries exhibit this same characteristic of a formalised but implicit approach, e.g. Norway,

Finland, France and Belgium to some extent. The informal but explicit approach is perhaps characterised by Austria where, while there is no legal basis for impact assessment, consultation of all ministries, institutions and even the public for any project likely to cause pollution or nuisance is required by law.

Finally and perhaps most recently and even more, a future trend for many countries is the formal legal basis for carrying out explicit impact assessments of plans or projects. Here the clear examples are Sweden and the U.S.A., both of which passed laws in 1969, requiring environmental impact assessment of major projects by a process which is separate from and independent of the normal project licensing process. Germany, Canada and Denmark have a similar approach which tends to place emphasis on Impact Statements or Impact Reports from an Assessment Panel.

However, whether a country's approach to EIA is implicit or explicit, formal or informal it remains very characteristic of the cultural, social and political environment of the country concerned. Hence it is not so much important to consider how EIA practices can be imported from one country to another but how one country can learn from the existing institutions and processes according to certain principles.

These principles can best be elucidated and adopted, not by a series of rules, but by considering case which show successes and failures in taking into account the environmental impact of planning or project decisions.

A particular the seminar should show how EIA is a process by which those whose lives are going to be affected by a project become involved in the planning of that project at an early stage, so that it can be designed with maximum development value and minimum impact on the environmental basis of human well-being and optimum ration of benefits to costs and so that the implementation of the project can proceed without conflict and with maximum commitment by the community

However, the actual form which EIA takes will be determined by the social, cultural and political environment of the country concerned. And this latter point is what the national case studies should bring out.

Guidelines for Rapporteurs

The rapporteurs should condense considerably the impact studies prepared nationally in order to make them presentable to the seminar. In order to provide both a focus for the preparation of the presentations and a common reference point between the different reports, it is suggested that the presentation of cases should show:

I. To what extent the EIA process is an *Integrated* approach to and integrating force;in, development planning.

II. How EIA can *create* better projects which contribute more to social and human well-fare through a better environment.

III. How EIA is *comprehensive* in both the range of impacts it considers and the implications of these impacts for human well-being.

IV. How EIA builds on existing planning and control processes in an *evolutionary* manner.

V. How EIA is capable of dealing with projects or plans whose environmental impact has a *global* reach and which crosses political and administrative boundaries.

VI. To what extent EIA involves and encourages public *participation* in planning and

VII. How post project *monitoring* of plans and projects is helped by and integrated with EIA.

EIA as a Continuous Integrated, Inter-disciplinary and Oriented Process

Here the keyword is *integration*—integration of EIA into the planning process from the very beginning, integration of those who are professionally concerned with the areas which might be impacted on, into the assessment and planning process and integration of both economic and non-economic scientific disciplines in planning.

Integration implies (for example) :

(1) That the project planners identify as a matter of routine and at the very start of a project, the "target" areas that

are likely to be impacted on e.g. a particular area of farmland, a river, a historical site, a rare species of animal, a unique ecosystem or an aspect of health of the local human population. In this they will be aided by a checklist of potential targets which could be affected by the project or plan.

(2) That the planners (who are obviously concerned primarily with economic and technical questions and thus know best the project-based origin of the impacts rather than the destination and effect of the impact) bring in professionals who understand the "target" areas in general and who can study and appreciate the significance of the actual "target areas in particular. Thus they might be agriculturalists, aquatic biologists bad hydrologists, archeololists, aquatic biologists and hydrologists, archeologists, ecologists and zoologists, environmental health experts, etc.. In this process the planners and "environmental" experts might be aided by an Impact Matrix, such as the Leopold matrix, in which the various activities are listed which will ensue from decision, whether concerned with the construction phase, the operating phase or the movement of materials, people and energy in and out of the project area. On the other axis of the martix all the environmental components are added which will, or could be modified by the impact of various project activities. The dialogur of planners and "environmentalists" at this stage not only enables one to focus in on important impacts (which can then be studied in depth) but also reveals more critical project activities and environmental components at risk than either group would have identified working separately.

(3) This early identification of impacts enables.

   (a) the planners to identify relevant issues and to modify their plans at minimum cost and delay so as to avoid major impacts.

   (b) the environmentalists to study in depth a limited number of impact areas which are likely to be of major significance.

(4) Another aspect of this early or preliminary impact assessment in that it should be carried out before the "Point-of-no-Return", i.e. the point in a plan or a project at which so much economic and political commitment has been made that it is not possible to stop or turn back. It has to be remembered, of course, that "decisions" do not in fact occur a one point in time. They are really a series of commitments—often spread over several years.

(5) Once the "decision" is made in the light of potential impacts, the EIA becomes an integral part of the decision implementation process. At this stage in many case the involvement of professional "environmental" experts will be supplemented by those, who know the local scene best and whose support is needed to get the project or plan implemented. These groups might be the local farmers, fishermen, local historians, naturalists or academics, local doctors and even local citizicns. The involvement of these "local" experts will often reveal further local impact areas for which minor project modifications will be appropriate. The exact nature of such involvement or integration of the plan with the people whose lives will be affected by the plan will depend on the social, cultural and political setting. It might be in the form of direct consultations or of more formalised public hearings or of the extremely formalist Joint Planning Committee on which project planner, "environmental" experts and representatives of local interest groups sit and which plans the detail of the project. Examples of this later approach are to be found in the planning of a molybdenum mine in Colorado and of an oil terminal in the Shetland.

(6) One important dimension of environment is that it is extremely diversified local and specific, hence, the better the integration of the local experts and the local community, the better is the assessment and the better is the plan.

EIA as a Creative Process of Selecting Better Alternating Projects

Clearly EIA is a rather pointless exercise if it only identifies negative impacts and then does nothing about minimising them, or even converting them into positive impacts either by modifying the projects or by substituting it with an alternative project with a lower impact. Hence another key of EIA is the creative *generation,* evaluation and selection of alternatives i.e. EIA as part of the design process.

Case studies could be analysed to show how the process of EIA leads to significant modifications of the plan or project how the alternative were evaluated and if possible what were the environmental and economic consequences of the alternative projects.

Alternative might involve:

(1) The formalized requirement that planners either come up with alternative which will be evaluated in parallel for impact or better still an iterative process by which the planners and "environmental" experts should propose alternatives in the light of the impacts which have been revealed as has often happened in the case of highway projects.

(2) Any approach to evaluating alternatives, should involve some from of Cost-Benefit analysis. However, the validity of allocating economic values to noneconomic, but nevertheless socially important and highly subjective, environmental factors is disputable. Nevertheless, Cost/Benefit analysis is a powerful discipline for both planner and "environmental" expert, as well as being a useful method for displaying the alternatives to the various groups concerned with the project. In this, Cost/Benefit analysis plays a key-role in heading off conflicts based on one group feeling that injustice has been done, since clearly if one social group receives all the economic benefits of a reject and another has but bear all the environmental costs, conflict is inevitable. Hence, one criterion in selecting alternatives is that the balance of Costs/Benefits of different social groups, e.g. those living near an area to be stripmined and those living in a distant city receiving the electric power, should be established, i.e. EIA should be a Positive Sum Game.

In the end the acceptable alternative is not that which is acceptable to the expect analyst, but that which is acceptable to the people whose lives are going to be affected. Hence, experts should consult the people either directly or through a process of public hearings of referenda.

(3) Proper consideration of alternatives therefore, implies that the EIA process is both stage-wide—with each stage further refining the assessment, discarding less essential impacts and paying more attention to critical areas and involving a wide group—and iterative—with the alternatives being generated and fed back into the preliminary screening process until the "right" plan or project emerges.

(4) As the ultimate refinement of integrated planning and EIA with the generation of alternatives, the "right" projects which emerge are essentially those which fit into the environment like a hand into a glove and indeed have been tailored to or generated by that environment as being totally appropriate, through the involvement of local and concerned people in a planning process which is open, flexible and people oriented.

EIA as a Comprehensive Process of Evaluating long Term and Secondary Effects

If existing land use planning and pollution control legislation cannot cope with real if scenarios of impact with space and time limited to the here and now, they certainly cannot cope with the *comprehensive* scenario involving secondary and tertiary consequences perhaps for many decades into the future as, for example illustrate such indirect and long term dimensions of EIA. A comprehensive approach to EIA involves :

(a) relating the sources of impact with the destination of the impact, e.g., diffusion or transport of air or water pollution.

(b) grouping the various targets susceptible to impact of a given type, e.g. all plants sensitive to SO_2.

(c) setting out the reactions which could take place between components of the non-living physical environment in space and in time, e.g. CO_2 emission—selective change in atmospheric transparency to radiation—climatic change.

(d) setting out the links between different living organisms and transmitted impacts, e.g., increased concentration of bio-accumulative and biotodic substances in the food chain.

(e) setting out the ecological relations, e.g. defore-station–erosion–loss of soil or water retention—loss of soil fertility—impact on human society.

- Focussing particularly on the indirect effects and the long term effects, because it is just these effects which are most easily overlooked by the planner, by environmental experts and by the local people.
- Stressing likely irreversible effects, e.g. causing death, destroying a species, or a monument or work of art, tipping the climatic balance, creating a desert or new source of ionising radiation or poisoning the oceans, since in a highly stressed ecosystem an irreversible impact could entrain a series of vents which would result in an eco-logical (and human) catastrophe.
- Taking into account the ultimate impact on people and on the quality of human life and hence subjecting the whole assessment to the value system of those involved. Thus there is a requirement for the planners to display the results of the assessment, point out the probability of impact, to educate the concerned public of its implications and in turn to be educated by the people in the value system they use in evaluating the human impact of the given plan or project and their willingness or not to accept a certain level of risk.

EIA as an Ovulating of Existing Processes, Legislation and Institutions

Since EIA builds on existing licensing, planning and control procedures and is integrated with existing agencies, ministries, commissions, it is of particular interest to examine cases which show this *evolutionary* character, i.e. :

(1) How existing legislation copes with environmental impact assessments.

(2) How existing EIA procedures cope with environmental impact assessment.

(3) How EIA legislation builds on existing legislation.

(4) How new institutions to handle EIA build on existing installations etc. (sec section 3 above).

EIA as a means of Dealing with Tarns-boundary Pollution Problems

Because EIA deals with specific problems rather than general general and because it deals with them in a very comprehensive way, it is a powerful tool for dealing with *global* environmental problems, i.e., those which cannot be confined to national or other political boundaries. Thus EIA can look at the impact of a given project on flora, fauna, land and water for as far as the wind will carry a detectable pollution from the site, even if that is in another country. Similarly it can consider the impact of a project in an entire watershed or river basin which might encompass many countries as is the case of the Rhine or the Danube. Land use planning and pollution control legislation being nationally based are impotent in such cases and if applied are likely to lead to sitting pollution industries on coasts, on the last stretch of a river before it leaves the country or by building high stacks.

Hence EIA is a powerful tool for dealing with air pollution problems in general and trans-boundary pollution problems in particular, whether due to water borne pollution as with the Rhine, or the Great Lakes, or airborne pollution as with Scandinavian's "Acid Rain" or certain projects along the US/Canadian border.

Other global problems are those involving impact on the global atmosphere, or the climate, or the regime of the oceans by releasing certain chemicals, burning certain fuels, using particular forms of transport, destroying major feats or diverting major rivers.

Cases which highlight this specifically *global* character of the correct programmes by France, Grermany and Switzerland for constructing nuclear power plants on the Rhine.

All cases should be analysed to bring out :

(1) the integration of local, regional, national and international impacts,

(2) the involvement of local, regional, national and international institutions and teams,

(3) the avoidance of conflict and the obtaining of international consensus and agreement for the implementation of plans or projects with global impact.

EIA as a Means of Obtaining Public Participation in Planning

Public *participation* in planning is desirable because in a society with an increasing level of education it is demanded more and more, it is important because in environmental matters the people often have better local knowledge than the planners an finally necessary because it is the people who will have to live with the consequences of the project and indeed whose collaboration is vital in the smooth implementing the project.

In almost all the above sections the role of public participation has been stressed but it would be worthwhile for the rapporteurs to show how in each case the use of EIA encouraged public participation in a constructive and orderly way, how the participation process was carried out and the consequences of it.

EIA as a Foundation for Post-project Monitoring

Finally the case studies should be presented is such a way as to show how the use of EIA and the orderly way in which potential targets were identified and potential impacts predicted helped to *monitor* actual targets and actual impacts after the project was implemented.

While such case of project monitoring might not be generally available it is very important to emphasise this aspect of EIA since post-project monitoring :

(a) is the only user way of protecting people and the environment on which their well-being depends, from negative impacts of a project and

(b) is the best way of checking up on the validity of the various EIA methodologies which are used and hence to develop one which does accurately assess future environmental impacts.

8

Analyzing Impacts on Environment in Hospitality Sector of European Countries

Introduction

The 29th Century and the second millennium are soon coming to an end and the start of the third millennium is just at the doorsteps. Progress has not only been achieved in the field of technology but also in Mans quest to attain an improved social standing. The Industrial Revolution was a determining factor in this attainment ushering in the development of travel activity. During the second half of this century tourism has become one of the most important economic and social phenomena of our age. No one can deny that the significant growth in this sector has characterised and influenced our life-styles and has changed the economies of many countries.

Travelling for tourism purposes is constantly becoming an important element in our lives. For some travel has become a need and people are taking more than one annual holiday. Both international and domestic tourism have increased and will continue to increase as technology improves and destinations become more accessible both in transportation terms as well as in terms of price. The World Tourism Organisation (WTO) forecasts a travel boom in the 21 Century. International travel increased from 25 million in 1950 to 625 million in 1998, an average annual growth of 7%.' Although the annual rate of increase in international tourist arrivals will decrease to an average of 4% per annum,

WTO's Vision 2020 estimates that international tourist arrivals will reach 1.56 billion by 2020. This is 2.5 times the figure recorded in 1998. Receipts from international tourism (excluding transport) are projected to increase more than threefold between 1995 and 2020 to reach US$ 2 trillion. Notwithstanding this current level of tourism activity, it is forecast that only 7% of the world population will participate in tourism activity by 2020 (current estimates are around 3%). Thus there remains a large market which is as yet untapped. Europeans still hold the highest level of participation in international tourism at 14% of the population (or one in seven) as against one in hundred South Asians: Moreover, the World Tourism Organisation estimates that the domestic tourism markets account for 10 times as many travellers as international tourists and in terms of receipts is 5 times greater.

Europe will, therefore, still retain its importance as the prime international tourismgenerating continent and will also remain the most visited destination in terms of absolute numbers, even though its share of international tourism will decrease.

Aims and Structure of the Report

The Group of Specialists on Tourism: Analyzing Impacts on Environment has agreed to the up-dating of the report 'Tourism: Analyzing Impacts on Environment in European Countries' which was prepared in 1995. The first report gave a brief overview of tourism development in most of the Council of Europe's member countries, highlighting the problems caused by tourism development and what actions are being taken in seeking to achieve a more sustainable approach to tourism development.

This report aims to identify actions, which have given, or might give, positive results in achieving a more sustainable and environment-friendly tourism development, in the context of the implementation of the recommendations on sustainable tourism development principles formulated by the Council of Europe and adopted by the Committee of Ministers.

The report will be structured in the following manner:

1. Overview of sustainable tourism development in the nineties;
2. Tourism development and the Environment in Europe;

3. Evaluation of those courses of action aimed at achieving sustainable tourism development.

Methodology

Apart from desk research, a questionnaire has been sent to the member countries. The information requested will provide details with regard to:

- Current trends in tourism development
- Structure and organisation of tourism
- Relationship between the Tourism sector and Environment and Planning sectors
- Actions taken by both Tourism: Analyzing Impacts on Environment agencies towards implementing and putting into practice sustainable tourism development principles
- Indication of results achieved and possibly how have these been measured
- Implementation of the Council of Europe's recommendations on sustainable tourism development

Responses were received from 21 countries. The next section will briefly highlight important international events with regard to sustainable development over the last decade.

Tourism and Sustainable Development

The nineties were characterised by a number of important international events with regard to tourism and sustainable development. It is not the scope of this section to mention all such events but only to highlight some of the most important ones.

The United Nations 1992 conference in Rio de Janeiro set the stage for many subsequent conferences/seminars and meetings on the Environment and particularly on sustainable development. The Rio conference, which produced the well-known Agenda 21 document, was a precursor to future developments in the field of sustainable development.

The European Union with its 5th Programme on Sustainable Development proposed the need to revise the pattern of world development and to support the introduction of tourism as one of the key sectors to be considered.

The first ministerial conference on tourism within sustainable development was held in Hyeres-Les-Palmiers (France) in 1993. During this conference an Euro-Mediter-ranean Declaration on Tourism within Sustainable Development was adopted and signed by all the Ministers of Tourism of the countries bordering the Mediterranean.

This was followed by the preparation of the Mediterranean Tourism Charter which was adopted by the Ministers for Tourism in Casablanca (Morocco) in 1995.

Another important conference was the United Nations Global Conference on the Sustainable Development of Small Island Developing States (Barbados, 1994). This conference addressed various issues which are determining to Small Island States in seeking to achieve sustainable development (e.g. Climate Change and Sea Level Rise, Natural and Environmental Disasters, Management of Wastes, Coastal and marine Resources, Freshwater Resources and Tourism).

Another important milestone was the UNESCO world conference on sustainable tourism (Lanzarote, 1995). An 18-point Charter for Sustainable Tourism was adopted and has provided a basis for many countries in formulating a tourism policy based on sustainable development principles.

The World Tourism Organisation's (WTO) report 'Agenda 21 for the Travel & Tourism Industry: Towards Environmentally Sustainable Development' sought to translate Agenda 2 actions for tourism. This document provided a basis for WTO members to address those issues, which in their own country are impairing the possibility of achieving a more sustainable form of tourism development.

The work of the Council of Europe in this regard has also given positive input towards encouraging a greater awareness amongst its member countries on the importance of developing a sustainable tourism sector and encouraging action particularly at the national levels. Through the work of the Group of Specialists on Tourism: Analyzing Impacts on Environment within the Directorate of Environment and Local Authorities the following general recommendations were drafted and approved by the Committee of Ministers.

- Recommendation No. R (94) 7 on a General Policy for Sustainable and Environment-Friendly Tourism Development;
- Recommendation No. R (95) 10 on a Sustainable Tourist development Policy in Protected Areas;
- Recommendation No. R (97) 9 on a Policy for the Development of Sustainable Environment-Friendly Tourism in Coastal Areas;
- Recommendation No. R (99) 16 on the Development of Environmental Management Training for those involved in the tourism sector, including future professionals.

The work has not only been limited to the production of these documents but has included a series of colloquys and seminars and assistance to various East European countries through pilot projects seeking to apply sustainable development principles.

Tourism: Analyzing Impacts on Environment in Europe

Europe (10,490,000 kim2) occupies 7% of the earth's surface and has a population close to 800 million. Europe consists of 46 countries. Apart from a great territorial diversity (3 climate zones and II bio-geographic zones), it has a pronounced economic inequality between the richest regions in the north and west (25% of the population with GNP of US$ 24,000 per capita) and the poorer regions of the northeast and southeast (53% of the population with a GNP of US$ 2,000-3,000 per capita). The land surface also differs widely from a high 3.8 million km2 in Russia (excluding the Asiatic part) to a low 0.44 km2 at the Vatican City.

In 1998 Europe received 373 million tourists or 60% of international tourism and has generated US$ 226 billion in revenue. In addition, approximately 3 billion domestic trips were taken by Europeans during the same year. However, tourism is unequally distributed amongst the regions of Europe. 87% of the revenue is concentrated in 12 countries and the other 34 countries only receive the remaining 13%4 WTO estimates that 717 million tourists will visit Europe in 2020.

However, the average annual increase in international tourist arrivals to Europe over the next 25 years in expected to be only 4.6% per annum. In the East Asia/Pacific region growth is estimated at 17.6% per annum, the Americas at 6.3% per annum, African at 11% per annum, the Middle East at 15.7% per annum and South Asia at 15% per annum. Thus Europe is losing its market share which will decrease to 45% by the years 2020. This trend may be reversed of other European countries enter the international trouis markets, particularly those in Eastern Europe.

The following are annual tourist arrivals and receipts for the European countries which responded to the questionnaire.

Country	*International Tourist Auriculas for 1998 in millions*	*Receipts for 19998 in (US# million)*
Croatia	5.4	2726.3
Czech Republic	16.325	3,509
Cyprus	2.2	1,860
Estonia	2.9	700
France	70	29,700
Germany	16.511	15,859
Greece	10.919	5,186
Hungary	15.0	2,568
Ireland	5.5	3,400
Italy	3.4	30.427
Latvia	0.242	211
Former Yugoslav Republic Macedoina	0.156	15
Malta	1.182	668
Netherlands	9.1	5749
Norway	3.5 (1997)	5,800 (1997)
Poland	18.8	8,000
Romania	2.96	Na
Slovakia	15.8	488
Sweden	2.57	4107
Switzerland	11.5 (1997)	8,394 (1997)
United Kingdom	25	21,233
Ukraine	2.6 (1997)	290 (1997)

Source : WTO, Tourism Market Trends (1999 ed.), Europe and country contributions

It is very difficult to find clear and reliable data on tourism's impacts on the environment. Some of this information can be obtained through estimates e.g. tourist/resident ration, water consumption, sewage production, waste generation. Nonetheless, any impacts on the environment will certainly have implications on the tourism section. The Buropean Environment Agency has certainly have implication on the tourism section. The European Environment Agency has produced a second report of Europe's environment—'Europe's Environment: The Second Assessment'. This report was a key input to the June 1998 Environment for Europe Conference in Aarhas. This report provides information about the state of the enshrinement and trends in 12 environmental problem areas and, moreover, identifies the main socio-economic driving forces exerting pressure on the European Environment. The report's conclusions indicate that although some pressures on the environment have been reduced, yet, this has not resulted in the expected level of improvement in the state and quality of the environment of Europe.

The report has indicated that the main sectors impacting on Europe's environment are transport, energy, industry and agriculture. Touris is, therefore not considered as one of the major activities impacting negatively on the environment. However, this differs between areas, particularly the Mediterranean coastal areas which have been dominated by tourism development. Nonetheless, some level of impact attributed to the transport sector may well be as a result of tourism activity. Passenger transport by car has increased by 46% and those transported by air increased by 67% since 1985 (EU countries only).

Bio-diversity is also under threat with a growing number of species in decline. Up to half of the known vertebrate species are under threat. More than one-third of the bird species in Europe are in decline as a result of damage being caused to their habitats particularly by intensification of agriculture and forestry, increasing infrastructure development, water abstraction and pollution. Recreational use, including tourism, is one of the activities, which is impacting negatively on sand dunes. Various initiatives and the enactment of specific leagislation for the protection of species and habitats, in most countries, has led to the protection of considerable land and sea areas and, thus conserving a number of species and habitats. At the European level, the implementation of the Nature 2000 network of designated sites in the EU, and the EMERALD network under the Bern convention in the rest of Europe, are the currently most important initiatives.

The expansion of tourism development in coastal areas has been one of the main activities which has led to an over-exploitation of water resources thus resulting in soil salinisation. This has effected 4 million hectares, primarily in the Mediterranean and Eastern European countries.

Tourism and Transportation

Tourism is dependent on transportation. The various modes of transport are necessary to encourage travel. The improvements in transport through the ages assisted the development of tourism to reach the levels we know today. However, transport has also led to adverse environmental problems particularly as a result of carbon dioxide emissions, road building, noise pollution and sea-water pollution. Between 1985 and 1995 passenger transport by car increased by 46% (in passenger km) for European Union countries only, while the number of passengers tranported by air grew by 67%. The transport sector in 1995 was the largest contributor to NOx emission (60%). As a result of improvement in vehicle emission standards and fuel quality, emissions of the various gases has been decreasing. It is difficult to apportion the transport related impacts resulting from tourism activity, however, considering that many travel by car, tourism may be contributing very much to CO_2 emissions since road transport accounts for 80% of such emissions. Air transport accounts for 15% of such emissions in EU countries." The development of transport related infrastructure-roads, termini, marinas, etc.-have also significant adverse impacts especially if these result in cuts through ecosystems and spoils the view of natural scenery and historic monuments.

Car and air transport are major polluters when compared to rail or inland waterway means of transport. The social and environmental costs in Germany of road transport alone have been put at 2.5% of GDP12. In terms of energy consumption, generally speaking, road and air transport are the highest consumers in Western Europe as against Central and Eastern European countries. Worldwide air transport accounts for about 15% of energy use by transport. Transport is a less important contributor to CO2 emissions in Central and Eastern Europe than in Western Europe.'

Although most of the emissions from road transport are experienced within urban areas such emissions are having an indirect effect over rural areas and protected areas as a result of acid rain. Air travel is related very much to tourism activity and is a prime contributor to NOx and CO_2 emissions. A report by the International Air Transport Association in 1992 indicated that the share of NOx produced by aviation may increase because newer aircraft have more efficient engines with higher combustion temperatures and hence tend to produce more NOx.14 The average altitude is also increasing thus raising the altitude at which such emissions occur. This may increase the effect on global warming.

It has been estimated that the road network takes up about 1.3% of the total land area of the EU whist the railway network covers 0.03%.15 In the EU it is planned to construct 12,000 km of new motorway by 2002.

The FNNPE report refers to the adverse impacts caused by the use of car for recreation in protected areas. Day trippers arriving in areas like Hohe Tauern (Austria) and Ojcow (Poland) cause traffic congestion, congestion of car parking space and litter problems. 90% of day trippers in the former locality arrive by car.'6 Exhaust from private cars and coaches of visitors to ski resorts have led to dashed trees and to wildlife damage. Transport pollution resulting from alpine tourism in Switzerland has produced 136,000 tonnes/year of carbon monoxide in 1987.17 In Mediterranean resorts (e.g. Southern Spain, Algarve) there has been pressure to construct trunk roads through protected or unspoiled areas and traffic congestion on coastal roads.'

Actions to Achieve Sustainable Tourism Development

The report 'Tourism: Analyzing Impacts on Environment in European Countries' (1995) had identified a number of initiatives and courses of action with regard to sustainable tourism development.

Planning

1. Zoning of nature areas and visitor management measures;
2. Tourism legislation to encourage awareness
3. Preparation of land-use plans and designation
4. Preparation of tourism plans at national,
5. Establishment of specific construction
6. Joint public and private sector tourism planning initiatives;
7. Rehabilitation of degraded areas and introduction of measures to prevent further erosion and degradation of the environment resources;
8. Preparation of management plans for tourism and recreational areas.

Economic

1. Introduction of taxes, grants and other financial incentives to encourage appropriate tourism development and activity;
2. Introduction of fiscal and other control measures to direct private investment towards environment conscious investments and to prevent environment degradation by imposing fines on polluters;

Have these actions produced the results expected? How have these been measured'? Has collaboration between Environment Protection Agencies and Tourism Agencies increased'? What type of studies and legislation have been 'prepared to integrate environment considerations with tourism development demands? These are only a few of the questions that this report will seek to answer through the responses given y each country which are presented in the following section.

Country by Country Responses to Questonnaire

This section of the report will present the responses given to the questonnaire by each of the 21 countries.

Tourism's Positive and Negative Impacts

In the first question countries were asked to highlight the main impacts currently being experienced as a result of tourism development.

Country	Positive impacts	Negative impacts
Croatia		
Czech Republic		
Cyprus		
Estonia		
France		
Germany		
Greece		
Hungary		
Ireland		
Italy		
Latvia		
Former Yugoslav Republic of Macedonia		
Malta		
Netherlands		
Norway		
Poland		
Romania		
Slovakia		
Switzerland		
United Kindgom		
Ukraine		

Tourism Policies, Legislation and Plans to Achieve Sustainable Tourism Development

The achievement of sustainable tourism development needs careful direction and commitment. This is assisted by the formulation of specific policies, the enactment of legislation and the drafting of plans.

Country	Policies/Legisliation/Plans
Croatia	• The Declaration on the Protection of Environment in the Republic of Croatia (1992) contains measures to protect the environment and preserve the attrac-tiveness of the landscape. • The Croatian State has prepared and adopted a National Island Development Programme and the Law of Islands with tourism given an important role. Their main task is to stimulate sustainable economic activities and a demographic renewal along with environmental protection. • The Strategy for the Development of Croatian Tourism (1993 and 1998) encourages the improvement of the quality of supply and to ensure sustainable development. • Based on the Strategy, a Master Plan for Tourism Development as well as Strategic Marketing Plans for some counties (foreseen in all counties) were developed at both national and regional levels. Other documents dealing with sustainable tourism development include: Tourism and Area Study, Colf as an Element of the Development Strategy of Croatian Tourism, Programme for the Development of Tourism in Rural Areas, Programme for Development of Small and Medium Tourism Businesses.
Czech Republic	• The Protection of Nature and the Land-scape and other Acts/Decrees regulate various activities (e.g. construction of facilities, etc.) affecting environmental protection • In June 1998 the State programme for nature and landscape preservation was approved, supporting sustainable tourism development. The Ministry of the • Environment and the Ministry of Local Development is to prepare a system of classification for tourism development which

will be compatible with the natural environment and the sustainable use of the landscape.

- Ministry for Local Development prepared a State policy for tourism which includes cooperation of various players, legislation, financial and tax conditions and the establishment of a Committee for Tourism (with representatives of various sectors) to advise the minister.

Cyprus

- The Cyprus Tourism Organisation (CTO) together with other tourism stakeholders is working on plans towards the development of special interest tourism, namely conference and incentives, athletic, nau-tical, health, nature, religious, cultural and agrotourism.
- The CTO is developing a strategic plan for tourism development until the year 2010 in its efforts to reposition Cyprus as an attractive tourism destination. This plan aims to enhance sustainable tourism development, maximise tourism's contribution to the economy and secure the viability of investments in tourism.
- Legislation is constantly reviewed to ensure that tourism development satisfies essential aspects of sustainability. The development of marinas and golf courses follow a process requiring the participation and consent of the Local Authority and the people. All programmes and plans must be supported by environment impact studies which are discussed with local communities. A comprehensive Environmental Law will soon be finalised and approved.

Estonia

- The National Tourism Master Plan 1995-2000 is the main plan for sustainable tourism development.
- Several strategic plans addressing sustainable tourism development issues are being formulated, particularly the National Tourism Development Plan (until 2010), including an Operational Plan (until 2003), and the

Environmental Action Plan (until 20 It)) recommending the formulation of a National Strategy for Recreational Areas and Ecotourism.

France

- The law on the sustainable management and development of the territory (1999) directs the State and other agencies' role in sustainable development. Regions formulate policies along the direction of the regional schemes.
- Agreements between State and regions will encourage, as from 2000, common actions on sustainable development including tourism (e.g. use of public transport in cities). Developments aim to value regions for their tourism and ecological potential (e.g. management of the Loire and Lake Bourget).
- A specific policy on cycling has been formulated setting up a national network of green cycling routes.

Germany

- German authorities, in co-operation with all stakeholders in the tourism sector, apply and promote a range of initiatives which include:

a) Information strategies, co-operation projects with major travel operators;

b) Green hotel management and green camping sites;

c) Voluntary commitment of the leisure industry to develop environmental design;

d) Environmental declaration (voluntary commitment) of the German tourism industry;

e) Development of tourism environmental quality labels (on regional level);

f) Promotion of the application of environmental management schemes (EMAS II) for tourism facilities.

- Participation in international programs and activities aimed at promoting sustainable tourism (Commission for Sustainable

Development, Baltic 2 I, implementation of the Convention on Biodiversity — Council of Euronet

Greece

- Specific planning policies regarding the carrying capacity of congested areas coupled with visitor management projects and land use planning tend to control the potential damage of such impacts.
- Current tourism policy in Greece is to upgrade the quality of the tourist services, improve infrastructure, better spatial spread of tourism facilities, effective human resources management, diversification of the tourist product and lengthening of season.
- Physical planning and regulations-location of tourist facilities, environmental impact assessments, building regulations, land use regulations in coastal areas and relevant EU directives/policies.
- Management plans—vocational training for local residents, establishment of specific agencies, visitors' management projects.
- Economic incentives-grants for investment in non saturated regions, upgrading of facilities to introduce environmental protection measures.
- Public awareness programmes-local and national campaigns and eco-labels e.g. Blue Flag
- Various relevant legislation is in place primarily to control infrastructural development in natural and cultural environments, emphasis on strategic.

Hungar

- No specific legislation placing tourism on an equal footing with other economic sectors. Nevertheless, a conceptual framework has already been formulated and the development of the first draft bill is underway. Recent legislation concerning tourism has been aimed at establishing industry standards, guaranteeing minimum quality standards and regulating passenger safety

- Other relevant legislation:

a) Environment Protection Act

b) Nature Protection Act

c) Act on Forestry

d) Act on Hunting

e) Act on Fishing

f) Act on Historical Monuments

g) Act on Regulation of Traffic on Waterways

h) Act on the Development and Preservation of the Built Environment

- The following Acts have a direct bearing on the problem of integrated planning of sustainable tourism development:

1. Act XXL/1996 on Sue Development and Regional Planning
2. Government Decree 184/1996 (XII. Il) on regulating the co-ordination/approval of site development concepts/programmes and regional plans
3. KTM (Ministry of Environment Protection and Regional Development) Decree18/1998 (VI. 25) on the requirements of site development concepts/programmes and regional plans.

Ireland

- Board Failte and the Department of Tourism and Trade will issue guidelines on good environmental management to the tourist accommodation sector.
- A national policy for the sustainable use of the coastal zone based on the national Coastal Zone Management strategy completed in 1997.
- Planning and Development legislation will require planning authorities to incorporate sustainable tourism development considerations in development plans.

- New legislation is being prepared along lines recommended in Strengthening the Protection of the Architectural Heritage (1996) and a package of administrative and financial measures will create a fully effective framework for protecting the built heritage.
- Tourism Development Plan 1994: Developing Sustainable Tourism —set out how the Irish Tourist Board must put in place a tourism product strong enough to achieve the targets set along the lines of sustainable development.
- A National Biodiversity Plan was published in 1997.

Italy

- The Multiregional Tourism Programme and the National Sustainable Development Plan have been produced to comply with Italy's Agenda 21 commitments and the Ministry of the Environments three-year plan for the protection of the environment. This includes:

a) cleaning up areas which have suffered particular environmental degradation and pollution,

b) eliminating situations of serious environmental risk, particularly industrial risk, c) safeguarding and maximising national heritage, particularly protected areas and promotion, activation and;

d) developing environmental management services (e.g. waste water treatment facilities, solid urban waste recycling and treatment.

- Tourism development follows the policy guidelines determined by the European Union, WTO, WTTC, Hague Tourism Declaration. Agenda 21, Agenda 21 for Baltic Sea Region Tourism Sector (Baltic 21) and other internationally recognised documents. At the same time Latvia continues to develop its own legal base and national policy for sustainable tourism development as well as to strengthen its institutional system.

- Tourism Development Concept of Latvia (1997) determines the national policy guidelines and development principles, as well as policy instruments, long-term goals and the resources for achievement of these.
- The Tourism Law (1998) defines national tourism policy and its implementation, conformity assessment of tourist accommodation establishments, the protection of tourists' interests and security as well as international co-operation.

Former Yugoslav Republic of Macedonia

- The general tourism policy has identified a few objectives: total tourist product improvement in Macedonia, stationary tourist supply, improvement in the lake areas, as well as, the creation and development of the new tourist product (based on the rich cultural and natural heritage).

Malta

- The Ministry of Tourism, in conjunction with the National Tourism Organisation —Malta, have finalised an Economic Impact Study and a Carrying Capacity Assessment Study for the Maltese Islands is underway, providing the basis for the formulation of a long term tourism strategy based on sustainable development principles.
- As part of the Structure Plan Review process the Planning Authority is preparing a Tourism Topic Study which will address the main tourism issues relating to land-use and provide the basis to formulate tourism land-use related.
- The Travel and Tourism Services Act (1999) setting up the Malta Tourism Authority giving tourism planning a more important role.
- A subject study on yachting development in the Maltese Islands has also been prepared to guide development of marina projects.

	• A policy paper on golf course development has also been prepared to guide development proposals in this field.
Netherlands	• National Policy Plan on Recreation 'Kiezen voor Recreatie' • Policy Agenda on environment, recreation and tourism • Policy Plan on environment and economy — relates to tourism in general terms • Netherlands Biodiversity strategy • International Nature Management — focuses on outgoing tourism • General policy agenda of the Ministry of Agriculture Nature Management and Fisheries—includes focus on awareness, sustainable transport, coastal zones and yachting. • A Policy Agenda on Environment, recreation and tourism with 12 different projects and the 'Initiative group on Outgoing Tourism, Environment and Nature' with several projects by its members (tourist sector, NGOs. government and transportation sector) • General legislation on spatial planning and nature conservation
Norway	• A report prepared by a working group appointed by the Ministry of Industry (responsible for tourism) provides guidelines for the future work in this sector. The Norwegian Association of Tourist Industries (RBL) has on the basis of these guidelines developed a strategy and a plan for implementation directed at their members in the accommodation and catering sectors. • A separate environment foundation (GRIP-senter) working on promoting 'green practices' in industry, has developed more detailed guidelines and tools aimed at different levels of the tourism industry.

Poland

- Investors in tourism have to abide by spatial planning policies and physical management plans, environmental law, etc. In some provinces there are 100m protection zones around lakes where building is restricted. Some lakes and rivers are protected as zones of silence, where the use of motorboats and other noise emitting sea-craft is prohibited. There are nature reserves where access is limited or restricted.

Romania

- Tourism policies, legislation and plans include aspects relating to the economic and social sustainability of tourism, however, the National Tourism Authority does not have any policies, legislation and plans concerning environmental issues. This is the responsibility of the Ministry for Water. Forests and Environmental Protection that apply Law No. 137/1995 on environmental protection.

Slovakia

- The report 'Tourism development in Slovakia' approved by Government provides the basis for the strategy, targets and measures for tourism development.
- Legislative measures include a number of environment-related laws. These are:

1. Act 17/1992 on Environment
2. Act 127/1994 on Environment Impact Assessment
3. Act 287/1992 on Protection of Nature and Landscape
4. Act 50/1876 on Spatial Planning and Building Regulation

Sweden

- The Swedish Tourism Authority (STA) in collaboration with the Swedish Environmental Protection Agency and the Swedish Travel and Tourism Industry formulated a strategic sustainable tourism development plan. Local networking is an important element in this plan.

Switzerland	• No response
United Kingdom	• Devolution of tourism promotion and development policy to Scotland, Wales and Northern Ireland. • Strategic Body for Tourism in England to be created. • Competitiveness White Paper to reinforce the commitment to reduce burdensome regulations. • White Paper on Integrated Transport Policy. • UK Government produced a new strategy for Tourism in England in 1999 and similar strategies have been produced in recent years for Scotland. Wales and Northern Ireland. • Strategy for Sustainable Tourism being developed. • Local Agenda 21 being developed in line with UK commitment to UN Agenda 21.
Ukraine	• The Environmental Protection Law (1991). the Nature and Conservation Fund (1992), the Establishment and Regulation of Special Economic Free Zones (1992). including recreation and tourism and the Tourism Law (1995) • The 'State programme for Tourism Development up to 2005' and two regional programmes — 'Sustainable Tourism Development in the Black Sea Coastal Zone of Ukraine' and the 'Environmentally sound tourism and business action plan for the Carpathian region of Ukraine' (1995,1996).

Organisation of Tourism

Another important determinant for sustainable tourism development is the manner in which the various tourism related functions are carried out within each country. A well-organised setup is necessary and this requires a strong interaction between the private sector and the public sector as well as the participation of other important key players particularly the local residents.

Country	*Organisation set-up*
Croatia	• The Ministry of Tourism is responsible for overseeing the development of tourism in the country. The Ministry includes a Department for Tourism Development and within this Department there is a Section for Area Development and Environmental Protection in Tourism. The Ministry has tourist offices (independent or within an Economy Office) in all 20 counties and the City of Zagreb, which implement tourism policy on a local and regional level. • A system of Tourism Boards has been established for the purposes of strengthening and promoting tourism and especially for raising awareness about environmental protection and its importance. The Croatian National Tourism Board, with its Main Office, covers the entire country. Several institutes and university faculties are involved in professional activities regarding tourism development.
Czech Republic	• The Ministry for Local Development is responsible for tourism. The Czech Centre for Tourism provides technical support to this ministry. The Committee for Tourism should be established as an advisory body of the Minister for Local Development. (In a preparatory committee there is also a representative of the Ministry for the Environment). • Administrations of National Parks and Administrations of Protected Landscape Areas are state administration bodies on their territories with responsibility to manage all activities (and also tourism) in conformity with the protection of nature and landscape. • In Prague and other towns the various administrations/municipalities are responsible for tourism and the environment.

	• Castles are managed by Institutes for Historical Monuments (under the Ministery for Culture), or by community administrations or by private owners. There are also professional associations (Federation of Businessmen in Tourism, National Federation of Hotels and Restaurants) and an NGO Club of Czech tourists.
Cyprus	• The CTO (a semi-governmental organisation responsible to the Ministry of Commerce, Industry and Tourism) is responsible for the formulation of tourism development policies and programmes.
	• Other key Ministries include the Ministry of Finance and the Planning Bureau, the Ministry of the Interior and the Town Planning and Housing Department and the Ministry of Agriculture, Natural Resources and the Environment and the Environment Service and the Ministry of Communications and Public Works. This ensures that tourism development programmes are developed within the framework of a national development programme.
	• The main private sector bodies include the Cyprus Hoteliers' Association, the Cyprus Hotel Managers' Association, the Travel Agents' Association, the Tourist Guides' Association and the Recreation Facilities Establishments Owners' Association. These bodies participate in government committees to discuss problems and formulate policies for tourism development in the future.
Estonia	• The Ministry of Economic Affairs and Estonian Tourist Board at national level are responsible for tourism. At the local level County Governments, Local Authorities and the Tourist Information Offices of the Estonian Tourist Board are the responsible agencies.
	• The private sector organisations include the

Estonian Association of Travel Agents, the Estonian Hotel and Restaurants Association, the Estonian Ecotourism Association and the Association of Estonian Guides. These are the main organisations involved in the decision making process.

France

- The Ministry of Tourism together with a Directorate for Tourism and the regional tourism agencies give the general direction for tourism and related legislation. Three organisations relate to the Ministry — Maison de Ia. France (marketing), Laitance Frailness de l'tngéniérie touristique (product development) and L'Observatoire national du tourisme (statistics).
- Regions and towns are active in the promotion and development of tourism in their localities.
- Private sector agencies include the small family run hotels and restaurants, professional organisations (e.g. les Relais et Châteaux), the hotel chains, tour operators and the rural gites

Germany

- Authorities responsible for tourist development are the Ministry for Economy with regard to tourism aspects and the Ministry for Environment where environmental issues are concerned.
- The other key players include the national and international tour operators, major carriers, local and regional authorities and various private sector associations (e.g. the German Travel Agents' and Tour Ope-rators' Association, the German Tourist Board and the German Hotel Association)

Greece

- Tourism policy is established by the Ministry of Development since there is a specific General Secretariat in this Ministry in charge of the tourism sector. The Ministry is assisted by the Greek National Tourism Organization (GNTO) which is also responsible for licensing and classifying tourist accommodation development.

The GNTO is also in the process of privatising most of the developments falling within their responsibility-marinas, hotels, spas and other properties. The GNTO is also responsible for the marketing of the country.

- Public investment is directed towards tourism infrastructure whilst funding from national resources and EU Structural Funds (e.g. Community Support Framework and LEADER programme) go to support investment in alternative forms of tourism.
- Investment grants are provided through the Ministry of National Economy and partly by EU funds.
- Competent regional and local authorities monitor and control tourism industry activities particularly with regard to their impacts on the environment in general.

Hungary

- At the national level the following bodies are responsible for tourism:

1. Ministry of Economics—Deputy State Secretary for Tourism
2. The National Tourism Committee includes all major professional organisations and representatives of other ministries responsible for the development of the industry.
3. Magyar Turizmus is the promotional arm of the Ministry of Economics.
4. The private sector associations include the Hungarian Hotel Association, the

   Association of Hungarian Travel Agencies, the Association of Tourist Guides, and the National Organisation of Rural Tourism.

- Local-government agencies have the responsibility of co-ordinating tourist activities including marketing. A Regional Tourism Committee, established in 1998, covering the entire country was established to perform marketing activities at regional level and carries out decentralised management functions.

- The Government's regional development programme promotes the establishment of small-region tourist organisations. Such organisations are involved in agro-and rural tourism while there are some excellent initiatives in the area of eco-tourism.

Ireland

- The Department of Tourism, Sport and Recreation sets out the national tourism policy for Ireland which are communicated to the Irish Tourist Board (Bord Failte) through policy instruments such as the Operational Programmes for Tourism and other policy guidelines.
- Bord Failte (Irish Tourist Board) is responsible for the promotion and development of tourist traffic and product development.
- Regional Tourism Authorities, local authorities and other local official bodies operate at the regional and local levels.
- The private sector includes the tourism product providers, travel agents, air and sea carriers and overseas distributors of tourist products.

Italy

- Central and regional government both promote Italy abroad and central, regional and local government all promote Italy domestically. The Department of Tourism is within the Presidency of the Council of Ministers.
- ENIT (Italian Tourist Board) is the agency that promotes Italy overseas.

Latvia

- The national tourism policy is the responsibility of the Ministry of Environmental Protection and Regional Development. The main tasks include the following:

1. To work out and implement the National Tourism Development Programme;
2. to work out drafts of laws and regulations:

3. to represent the interests of the State in the field of tourism;
4. to co-ordinate the elaboration of regional programs and international projects of tourism development;

- The Latvian Tourism Development Agency (LTDA) was established for the implementation of the national tourism development policy. The main tasks of the LTDA are related to marketing and promotion, market research and tourism database development.
- Local governments are responsible for the preparation of development plans and spatial plans, determining in them perspectives for tourism development, promote tourism in their localities, preservation of the tourism resources and promote cultural and educational work in the filed of tourism.
- The Latvian Tourism Advisory Council promotes co-operation between ministries, local governments, tourism enterprises and public organizations, involved in implementation of tourism policy integrating tourism in overall development.
- The private sector and NGOs provide and maintain high quality standards of tourism services and contribute to marketing and advertising. Different professional and regional tourism associations are operating in Latvia.

Former Yugoslav Republic of Macedonia

- The tourist-catering enterprises and other economic and non-economic subjects, taking part in the tourist trade.
- The Ministry of Economy formulates legislation and measures in order to create the conditions for tourism development.
- The Ministry of Tourism is responsible for setting the policy framework of the tourism industry.

- The Malta Tourism Authority (MTA) advises the Ministry on tourism development. The Authority which will be composed of four Directorates – Marketing and Promotion, Product Planning and Development, Enforcement and Support Services, Human Resource Utilisation and Training.
- The private sector is strongly represented in all Government agencies and has a major role in the formulation of development policies affecting 'he industry. These include, primarily, The Malta Hotels and Restaurants Association and the Federation of Associations of Tourism and Travel Agencies.
- The Planning Authority is responsible for land use planning and environmental issues concerning tourism development. The Environment Protection Department is concerned with the protection of environmental resources from tourist development.
- NGOs also participate actively in tourism issues. Friends of the Earth (Malta) have been organised various seminars and produced publications on aspects of sustainable development.

Netherlands

- Responsibility for sustainable tourism development at national level falls within the:

  1. Ministry of Economic Affairs

  2. Ministry of Agriculture, Nature Management and Fisheries

  3. Ministry of Housing. Spatial Planning and Environment
- Other ministries have a minor role particularly the Ministry of Development Cooperation where projects are concerned and the Ministry of Transport and Water Management where infrastructure and air transport sectors are concerned.

- At the local level provincial and local governments are responsible for tourism planning whereas management of recreational and nature areas is the responsibility sometimes of Local government, independent bodies or nature organisations.
- The business community is also involved both in planning at the local level as well as in policy formulation processes.

Norway

- The Ministry of Industry and Trade is responsible for the development of the tourist industry. Other relevant ministries include the Ministry of the Environment, the Ministry of Transport, the Ministry of Local Government and Regional Development and the Ministry of Agriculture.
- The State Industrial and Regional Development Fund (SNE) has a range of resources at its disposal for the strengthening and development of trade and industry, including product development in tourism, in outlying districts. Direct assistance in the form of subsidies, loans and start-up grants is available to support these policy aims.
- The Norwegian Tourist Board co-ordinates the marketing of Norway overseas.
- The private sector is also actively involved in tourism development.

Poland

- The State office for Sport and Tourism is responsible for the formulation of tourism policy. The Polish Tourist Information Centres abroad deal with marketing activity.
- Provincial governments are responsible for assisting in the promotion of tourism businesses and hotels. Provincial self-governments, county and community local governments are dealing with the promotion of tourism at the local level.
- Private tourism companies and other organisations (e.g. the Polish Tourist Association) need government assistance.

Romania	• The National Tourism Authority is the public sector body responsible for the regulation of and the strategic development of tourism. • The Tourism Promotion Office is the authority responsible for promotion and control in the tourism sector. • Other important institutions include the National Centre for the training of tourism professionals and the Centre for the permanent training of tourism professionals in the most important tourist regions and various private sector bodies
Slovakia	• Ministry of Economy. Section for Tourism is responsible for state policy on tourism, development, legislation, creation of favourable conditions for entrepreneurs and international co-operation at government level. Marketing is the responsibility of the Slovak Agency for Tourism (NTO). • Private/professional agencies include: 4. Slovak Association of Hotels and Restaurants 5. Slovak Association of Tour Operators and Travel Agents 6. Slovak Association of Tourism Information Offices 7. Slovak Association of Country and Agro-tourism 8. LA VEX. association of ski-lifts operators • Other specialist organisations include the Slovak Guarantee and Development Bank (provides financial support for tourism entrepreneurs), the Institute of Education for Business and Tourism (provides vocational training and training and certification of tourist guides) and Ustav Turizmu (a consulting company for economy, marketing and development of tourism). • The absence of local and regional tourism associations poses a serious problem to the

development and promotion of tourism in Slovakia. It has had negative impacts on co-operation, marketing, development strategy, unprofitable leisure activities and other issues at local and regional level.

Sweden	• The Ministry of Industry is responsible for tourism policy and development. The Swedish Tourism Authority formulates strategies in collaboration with agencies at national, regional and local levels, including research and training. Marketing is carried Switzerland out by the Swedish Travel and Tourism Council. owned on a 50/50 basis between Government and the industry. Regional and local agencies are involved in marketing and product development
Switzerland	• No response
United Kingdom	• The British Tourist Authority (BTA) is the lead agency for promoting international tourism to Britain. However, each country has its own tourist board — Scottish Tourist Board, Wales Tourist Board and Northern Ireland Tourist Board. In England the Regional Tourist Boards (RTBs) work with the new Regional Development Agencies (RDAs) to ensure co-ordination of development policies. Similar arrangements apply in the other countries. • In Scotland the Scottish Tourism Co-ordinating Group (STGC) brings together the main relevant private sector bodies under the Chairmanship of the Minister for Tourism.
Ukraine	• At national level the State Committee for Tourism of Ukraine is responsible for tourism development. • Agencies such as Intourist, Crimtour, Odes-Tourist and other operate at a regional level. • The management of resorts and recreation areas and development in such areas is the responsibility of the Ministry of Health

	Protection of the Ukraine and the State Committee for Urban Development and Architecture. The management of conservation areas (including tourism and recreation zones) is fulfilled by the Ministry of Environment and Nuclear Safety of Ukraine and the relevant departments at regional levels.

Tourism Development, Environment Protection and Socio-economic Development

Tourism is multifaceted and the interests are wide-ranging and often conflicting. Seeking the balance becomes difficult and the decision making process often becomes a forum of power struggles to influence the decisions taken. What structures, mechanisms and frameworks have been adopted or are in place to ensure the integration of tourism development issues with environmental protection and socioeconomic development?

Country	*Integration of tourism, environmental and socio-economic issues*
Croatia	• The Land-Use Strategy (1998) and Land-Use Programme (1999), contain a separate chapter on tourism. The Ministry of Tourism participated in the preparation of these documents, which contain the basic principles found in the Strategy of Croatian Tourism Development and other development documents. • Based on the above programmes. Area Plans of a lower order are developed (county, city, municipality, and detailed Area Plans), designating tourism zones and implementation procedures. Tourism Development Programmes, prepared for individual areas, also give attention to socio-economic and demographic elements and environmental protection regulations. The public is consulted during the preparation process. • In compliance with law, environmental impact studies are conducted for all operations on the

sea and for larger operations on land. Tourism representatives participate in committees that review these studies. All studies must undergo a public review.

Czech Republic

- Since 1990, development of tourism was operated on a market economy — i.e. without an appropriate state policy. But of course development was regulated on the basis of other laws and privatisation was supported. State nature conservancy faced a Cyprus Estonia France Germany Greece similar situation during the preparation of the Act on the Protection of Nature and the Landscape. Other important Acts include the Building Act and EtA Act. Building of facilities is managed by building offices and offices for environment of the state administration. In national parks and protected landscape areas administrations have the power to manage building activities or to prohibit them.

Cyprus

- All tourism development projects must be supported by environmental impact assessments, and be compatible with the development plan for a particular area, prior to their approval. Public participation and public hearings are organised in cases where objections or diverse opinions are expressed. All planning issues are co-ordinated by the Planning Bureau so that all plans and decisions are compatible and in harmony with the overall development policies of the government.

Estonia

- The socio-economic, cultural-social and environmental goals of tourism development have been defined in the tourism strategy 2002. Increasing the environmental awareness, environmentally sustainable development, support for the conservation of the natural and cultural heritage are more concrete aims under the environmental goals.

France

- In certain regions, directives on territory management plan and co-ordinate the State's orientation with regard to socio-economic development and environmental protection.

- The 1992 tourism legislation has set out tourism development guidelines, including environment protection measures, which guide regions and departments.

Germany

- In particular areas with structural problems (decrease in industrial and agricultural production), tourism is regarded as an opportunity to create new jobs. Therefore, domestic tourism development is supported by the federal government and regional authorities. Along with the promotion of tourism, there are initiatives to educate tourists and raise sensitivity for the environment.

Greece

- Tourist development, environmental protection as well as the socio-economic development are taken into consideration during the various planning stages. Coordination is taking place mainly through the physical planning system at the national and regional level and is completed in the implementation of projects at the local levels.
- The integration of socio-economic and environmental concerns is carried out in all studies and projects currently being carried out. Such integration occurs at the public participation and consultation levels, through the carrying out of environmental impact assessments for a specific area or Specific Environmental Studies or Physical Planning Studies for larger areas.
- The European Union's 5′ Action Plan for the Environment (1992-2000) is the basis for the integration of environmental and socio-economic issues in tourism development. This is achieved through-

1. exchange of experiences during seminars, conferences, etc.;

2. encouraging sustainable tourism developments e.g. preservation of traditional settlements and careful development of mountain and rural tourism;
3. informing and creating awareness amongst the general public through leaflets, exhibitions, etc.;
4. public participation in land use planning and development;
5. strict legal framework concerning tourism developments especially accommodation developments, including EIA;
6. environmental training for tourism personnel;
7. diversification of tourism and development of alternative forms of tourism (rural, mountain, conference, etc.);
8. co-ordination of actions with various NGO's and associations promoting ecotourism.

Hungary

- The Regional Tourist Committees have the task of creating integrated planning. Monitoring the environmental, social, and economic impacts brought about by tourism and taking the necessary decisions and interventions.

Ireland

- Planning Authorities and other agencies make provision in their development plans for sustainable tourism to avoid over-development. Bord Failte will consider the implementation of a managed network of scenic landscapes by 1999. Together with the Department of Tourism and Trade, it will issue guidelines on good environmental management to the tourist accommodation sector.
- The Department of Arts, Culture and the Gaeltacht will implement good environmental management, including energy conservation, in historic properties and other tourist attractions under its care and formulate codes of conduct and practice to foster a greater awareness of the potential impact of tourist behaviour on sensitive areas and sites.

Italy	• Issues in this regard are addressed as follows by considering: 1. The relationship between enjoyment of the specific monuments and the locality as a whole and the need of conservation, the cost of environmental management and the relative cost and benefit ratio of the different urban development policies in relation to the number of tourists and residents, tourism and tourism-related businesses and non-tourism businesses. 2. The environmental component of tourism activities with due regard to the variable ecological pressure of the tourism business cycle and the potential for making them more eco-efficient. 3. The ecological characteristics of the physical tourism products (not only accommodation establishments and tourist attractions, but also the urban areas as a whole).
Latvia	• Regulations on Spatial Plans defines the order of spatial planning. Local governments determine areas important for recreation and tourism, and deal with these objects as required in the Law 'On objects of education, culture and science and national sport bases of national significance". • Law on Spatial Development Planning is to provide for the creation of a spatial development planning system, being able to promote sustainable development for all levels and fields. • Law on Assisted Regions offers local governments funding for tourism development. Currently 25 tourism development projects are financed by the Regional Development Foundation
Former Yugoslav Republic of Macedonia	• The project proposal "Sustainable Tourism Development on the Lakes and Mountain Areas and Heritage Protection", proposed by

	the consulting company "Ecotourism Ltd." from Great Britain, with the possible financing by the European Union.
Malta	• The preparation of the Carrying Capacity Study for the Maltese Islands (Malta Tourism Authority) and the Tourism Subject Study (Planning Authority) address the land-use related issues on tourism development and will provide the strategic framework for tourism land-use policy formulation in the Structure Plan review. The Ministry of Tourism is to embark on a long-term tourism strategy which will involve the participation of all stake-holders. • The Malta Tourism Authority has geared up to address tourism development issues in an integrated and co-ordinated manner giving importance to conservation issues. • The Planning Authority's public consultation procedures ensure that the wider public and particularly local councils participate in the discussions and consultations over all projects, and particularly, large scale developments.
Netherlands	• No response
Norway	• Generally speaking, conflicts as a result of tourism development rarely occur in Norway. Nonetheless, in certain parts of the country, particularly the southeast. Pressure for development on the coastal zone is very strong. The Ministry of Environment is responsible for the Planning and Building Act, which regulates land-use planning processes. Such processes also ensure the participation of those concerned at local level, including environmental groups.
Poland	• Tourism investment and development have to abide by the comprehensive physical plan prepared by or for local government and approved by the provincial government authority responsible for environmental protection.

and poverty alleviation (World Resources Institute et al. 2005; NACSO 2006). Eco-tourism, premised on stunning wildlife and scenery, has attracted an international, 'up market' clientele to Namibia and generated revenues, employment and additional benefits for participating conservancy communities.

Community-based conservation is based on the idea that if conservation and development can be simultaneously achieved, the interests of both are served (Berkes 2004). Community conservation stresses the role of local residents in decision-making for natural resources (Adams and Hulme 2001). Communitybased conservation has been practiced in many forms, but in the broadest sense includes conservation by, for, and with the local community. The co-existence of people and nature, as distinct from protectionism and the segregation of people and nature, is its central characteristic (Western and Wright 1994). Recent commons scholarship stresses that local levels of collective action are necessarily linked to higher levels of social and political organization in a globalized world. Indeed, Namibia's conservancies have many and increasing cross-scale and cross-level linkages, including important linkages with international tourism enterprises.

Centrally and internationally conceived approaches in community-based conservation emerged in the 1980s in Southern Africa to buttress national parks as wildlife reserves, and better conserve wildlife as an economic development alternative to agriculture in semi-arid regions (Adams and Hulme 2001). These have been termed community-based natural resource management or CBNRM (Fabricius et al. 2004). CBNRM has featured the devolution of certain bundles of wildlife use rights to local communities, premised on making wildlife pay, with benefits exceeding the costs of living with wildlife such as crop and property damage. The central theory is that benefits from wildlife for local and indigenous peoples will promote conservation.

The revenue and resource sharing devolution to communities under CBNRM was led by Zimbabwe and Namibia in Southern Africa and was a direct outgrowth of wildlife management on the private land estates in both countries preceding independence. In the 1970s, Zimbabwean legislation was passed that conferred strong proprietor rights over wildlife to private, white landowners. This same type of legislation was passed in Namibia in the 1970s under

Romania	• The Ministry of Water, Forests and Protection of the Environment has included in its Directorate for Directives, Implementation and Authorisatiom responsibility for Tourism: Analyzing Impacts on Environment issues.
Slovakia	• In Slovakia, co-ordination in this respect has only recently been operating effectively. Tourism developers are beginning to understand that a healthy environment is vital for the success of their tourism development in the future. On the other hand. Especially in mountain villages and sub-regions are there examples where tourism and agriculture operate together, thus keeping the population in the area and maintaining the quality of the existing landscape. Although there are some examples of successful practice in this regard, the system still needs improvement to function more effectively.
Sweden	• This aspect is addressed by the local spatial planning process and the regional planning process for economic development. Strategies from the Swedish Tourism Authority are included in such plans.
Switzerland	• No response
United Kingdom	• Throughout the UK. local authorities have strong planning powers in order to match the needs of economic development and environmental protection. Cases where the national interest is involved, then central government can be 'called in' for a decision.
Ukraine	• Documents and recommendations with regard to planning foundations, norms and standards for tourism and recreation development provide guidelines for development in coastal areas, forests and the anthropogenic loading on natural eco-systems. These include;
	1. Recommendation on Designing of Resorts and their centres, Recreational and Tourist Zones in Settlements (I 988);

2. Planning Foundations for Development of Resorts and Recreational Regions (1990);
3. State Building Standards of Ukraine (1993).

Successful Measures in Attaining Sustainable Tourism Development

Sustainable development is a long term process and whether actions in this regard are successful or otherwise can only be ascertained in the long term. Nonetheless, specific actions can give indications, in the short and medium term, whether tourism policies and development is on the track towards achieving a more sustainable approach to tourism development.

Country	*Successful measures for sustainable tourism development*
Croatia	• Sustainable development principles in tourism are contained in various plans and regulations. Pilot projects included the 'Carrying Capacity Assessment for Tourism Activities on the Island of Vis' (LINEP/MAP), which used physical, cultural, social. Demographic and other factors to estimate the number of visitors allowed on the island according to sustainable development principles. Guidelines were drawn up for assessing tourism carrying capacity of Mediterranean coastal zones. Guidelines are used in the formulation and implementation of plans at all levels. Under the Programme of Technical Support for Environmental Protection in the Mediterranean, an Environmental Management Plan of the Cres-Losing archipelago was designed, which suggests protected areas and ways to integrally manage coastal zones. • The Croatian Government has adopted a National Island Development Programme and the Law on Islands, according to which an Island Sustainable Development Programme will be developed for each island or group of islands.

- In 1991, a coke plant in Bakar Bay was removed and its employees re-employed in other sectors. A plan for the development of the bay was prepared.

Czech Republic

- The provisions of Act No 114/1992 regulate development of tourism in a landscape.
- There are also possibilities to prepare and implement projects with the help of PHARE programm (mainly in trans-boundary national parks or protected landscape areas).

Cyprus

- Introduction of town planning measures and fiscal restrictions, to encourage desired development, has reduced construction along the coast. Tourist developments having all prerequisites of harmonisation with the environmental fabric of the area, enjoy the benefits of credit facilities and finance. However, unless projects are supported by objective and thorough [EAs, they are not accepted for consideration. All plans submitted to the Cyprus Tourist Board for approval are also supported by a full landscape analysis and a marketing study. 15% of the development site is designated for use as public open space.
- Legal and planning measures contributed towards better quality and more comprehensive developments, more successful in being in harmony with the surrounding environment (natural and cultural) and within the context of the overall development policies for the island.

Estonia

- Strategic plans covering sustainable tourism development are still being prepared. The National Tourism Development Plan covers the period up to 2010 with an Operational Plan up to 2003. The Environmental Action Plan covering the period up to 2010 recommends the formulation of a National Strategy for Recreational Areas and [co-tourism. The National Tourism Master Plan 1995-2000 has been the main guideline for regional and local planning and development within the context of sustainable tourism development.

France

- Legislation on the management and sustainable development of the land (1999).
- Economic measures and research have shown results but legislative and planning measures are still recent to show results. Economic support for Regional Nature Parks (35) e.g. Vosges du Nord and National Parks (7) and the rehabilitation of leading sites.(30) e.g. Dune du Pilat. Efforts to improve visitor management in the national parks (visitor centers, interpretive path ways, ecomuseums).
- Regional plans for land management, plans for green cycling routes, local agendas 21, quality plans for green tourism facilities. Research includes evaluation of tourism policies, national tourism, environment and land-use indicators. Impose sustainable tourism policies in towns preparing Local Agenda 21s.

Germany

- Competitions and networks among tourist sites and villages e.g. Environmentally Friendly Tourist Destination 1996, 'Sustainable Recreational Activities in Nature Parks' and 'Nature Conservation 21';
- Promotion of conferences, seminars, etc. on sustainable tourism development in cooperation with all stakeholders;
- Financial support to NGOs for the production of information brochures and handbooks, campaigns, etc. on sustainable tourism development.

Greece

- A number of specific areas have been designated as 'Areas of Controlled Tourism Development' and within these areas have been declared as "Saturated Tourist Areas". In these areas tourism development is to be controlled and current infrastructure upgraded.

- The Development Incentives Law enhances the modernization of operating tourism units, the conversion of traditional listed buildings into hotels as well as investments in environmental protection and the use of renewable energy sources.
- Awareness on environmental issues through the dissemination of leaflets, publications, etc., seminars and workshops with regard to protection of the biodiversity and sustainable tourist-n.
- Public investment in infrastructures, incentive policy, promotional campaigns in encouraging eco and nature based tourism. NGOs and the voluntary sector also participate.
- GNTO's national and regional marketing initiatives also seek to attract environmentally conscious tourists. Local efforts are also undertaken.
- A strategic plan for tourism development has been formulated by the GNTO in the framework of the "National Plan for Regional Development 2000-2006". This plan takes into account all relevant environmental concerns and supports actions favouring sustainable tourism development (water conservation, upgrading, renewable energy. etc.). Plan is elaborated with the participation of all stakeholders

Hungary

- The Lake Valence resort area is a prominent tourist attraction in the vicinity of Budapest. Serious attempts were made to create an infrastructure to protect the health of the lake in line with integrated tourism planning. The establishment of natural reserves was successful and development was permitted only where the required infrastructure was in place. With the regular dredging of a system of canals outside the reserve boundaries, the lake gained a new lease on life (a successful example of environmental rehabilitation). The development of an integrated environmental monitoring network is underway. Environmental impact and environmental load studies are being prepared.

Ireland

- Bord Failte's Tourism Development Plan for 1994– 1999 entitled 'Developing Sustainable Tourism' prompted a number of actions to achieve sustainable development. Land-use plans take account of sustainable tourism; a National Coastal Zone Management strategy study was completed in 1997; the Foreshore Acts prevent and penalise any damage to beaches, sand dunes and seashore ecosystems; research on the critical loads of specific tourist areas, including sensitive coastal or wilderness areas, will be commissioned; CERT, the national training agency. Together with the education sector will continue to provide training emphasising the sustainable use of resources and highlighting natural products.
- The national network of scenic landscapes embraced 25 areas of outstanding scenic beauty, which would be actively managed and selectively promoted. Comprehensive Area Management Plans are urgently required to ensure that these landscapes are protected and preserved from excesses of tourism. A demonstration project funded under the EU LIFE programme and carried out in collaboration with An Taishe (National Trust for Ireland), has tested this proposal in 3 pilot areas.

Italy

- The Environmental Plan for the Adriatic resort of Rimini is a model of how environmental planning can be a structural component of local development. The Plan has three objectives:

  1. Provide a basic tool for proper environmental policy;

  2. Provide a support tool for planning in general; and,

3. Provide the backdrop for ensuring that all planning decisions deliver quality growth.

- The result has been the definition of a series of priority projects in which water-related problems (treatment of effluent, groundwater pollution), maximisation of resources (wooded and green areas), restoration of ancient monuments, reduction of noise and atmospheric pollution all rank highly.

Latvia

- The Latvian Tourism Development Agency (LTDA) is a member of the project Via Baltica Touristica Steering Committee which is to develop and promote Via Baltica as a tourist route from Genriany to Finland and vice versa, thus connecting Western and Northern Europe via Baltic States and Poland. It's achievements so far are:
- training courses for entrepreneurs about Via Baltica Touristica development and their involvement in it;
- Seminar "Via Baltica Information System Project" (Riga, December 1998);
- Via Baltica tourism road signs system is being developed at present;
- Seminar on tourism investments;
- Pilot development programs for one region in each country are being developed. Bauska region in Latvia was chosen. These programs will be used further as examples for tourism development program elaboration for other regions on Via Baltica.

Former Yugoslav Republic of Macedonia

- No response.

Malta

- The Structure Plan policies significantly reduced the sprawl of tourism development into rural and coastal areas. The Structure Plan Monitoring

	report evaluates the success or otherwise of specific policies in the Structure Plan. • A policy paper on golf course development was also formulated by the Planning Authority providing guidelines, particularly, with regard to site selection. • A subject study on yacht marina development went into great detail to identify potential and appropriate sites for such development. • The Tourism Topic Study (2000) will provide a forum for the discussion of tourism land-use related issues, among key-players, with a view to formulating development strategies for future tourism development. • The Malta Tourism Authority's studies on the Economic Impact of Tourism and the Tourism Carrying Capacity will assist government in determining what should be the role of the tourism sector in the overall economy and also the Islands' capacity. It is intended that the new national Plan for Tourism is based on sustainable development principles.
Netherlands	• The National Monitoring Programme to assess the state of nature and the state of the environment. • Legislation on spatial planning and legislation on nature conservation provide a regulatory framework with regard to development of sustainable nature and ecotourism. • The tourist sector and consumer organisations have voluntarily adopted codes of practice standards or guidelines for directing tourist activity along sustainable development principles. • Awareness campaigns e.g. TV programmes, special events at zoos, general brochures on Tourism: Analyzing Impacts on Environment by tour operators aimed at tourists. A project

has commenced consisting of an inventory of nature data in several foreign destinations.

Norway

- The Ministry for the Environment has implemented a management plan for tourism and outdoor recreation in the Arctic archipelago of Svalbard (Spitz-bergen). The aim of the plan is to ensure that on the basis of an environmental framework the different forms of tourism be directed to zones where traffic can take place without jeopardizing the vulnerable natural environment. The archipelago is divided into different categories-nature reserves, national parks, outdoor recreation areas and tourism areas-with different levels of accessibility, regulation and facilities. This regime has been fairly successful in managing an increasing number of tourists to Svalbard. A recently published proposal for a new environment law for Svalbard will, when adopted, strengthen further the legal basis for such measures.

Poland

North eastern Poland is one of the last regions of Europe with untainted nature and exceptional landscape. The area is known as the 'Green Lungs of Poland'. As a result of an agreement reached by the administration and the local authorities, the area was defined and brought into force in 1988. Since that time, a number of organisational steps have been taken, such as the formation of the Programme Council and work on a 'Strategy for the Spatial Management of the Green Lungs of Poland' and 'Assumptions underlying the regional policy of the area named Green Lungs of Poland'. In this policy sustainable development is the main goal.

Romania

- Law no. 137/1995 contains a list of activities which are subject to environment impact assessments as part of the development process. These include, teleskis. Motor vehicle tracks and stadia with a capacity of 20,000 spectators or more. Unfortunately not all tourist activities are included.

Slovakia	• Restricted visiting time only for part of the year in sensitive natural areas (e.g. Vysoke Tatry, Mala Fatry). This has had a positive impact especially on the fauna; • Closing off areas for long-term periods (Belianske Tatry). This is applied only in exceptional cases: • Exhibition rooms at national parks; • Admission fees for visiting sensitive sites; • Keeping tourists on marked tourist paths/tracks; • Guided tours-some sites are open only for guided group/individuals e.g. High Tatra mountain region • Special circles with interpretation panels explaining value of protected areas and flora and fauna species.
Sweden	• Initiatives are being implemented in various areas (e.g. urban, mountains, islands, rivers and lakes) and with regard to activities (canoeing, fishing). These include the lake and river system in Vaermland and Dalsland for canoeing activity, the actions for the protection of the Stockholm archipelago, the cultural and natural environment in mid-Sweden coastal area and those in the Swedish mountains.
Switzerland	• No response • A consultative paper-Tourism: Towards Sustainability-has been distributed, and a strategy is being developed in line with Agenda 21.
United Kingdom	• An annual forum has been set up to assess the extent to which the tourism industry in England meets the principles of Agenda 21. Similar measures have been introduced in Scotland, Wales and Northern Ireland.
Ukraine	• The 'Lucomorie' project will be a model for sustainable tourism development in specially

selected local rural areas in the Black Sea coastal zone. The project aims to:

1. create environmentally sound complexes based on eco-tourism;
2. establish conditions for investment in projects with a guarantee of cash returns on investment from future profits;
3. generate 800 jobs for the local population;
4. promote recreational traditions jointly with new activities in conditions of modern tourism infrastructure.

- The income generated from special tourism activities (fishing, riding, hunting, etc.) is expected to be US$ 12-34 per day. The total number of tourists expected during the year would be around 150,000. This project is yet an idea and is finding sot-ne difficulty in implementation because of the current crisis in investment in tourism in Ukraine.

Implementation of Council of Europe Recommendations on Sustainable Tourism Development

The recommendations formulated by the Group of Specialists on Tourism: Analyzing Impacts on Environment within the Directorate for Environment and Local Authorities and approved by the Council of Ministers offered member countries a basis along which to develop and set out their tourism development policy.

Croatia	*Adoption of Council of Europe's principles*
Croatia	• The recommendations relating to sustainable tourism development formulated by the Council of Europe are implemented through regulations and plans on a national, regional as well as local level. Various examples have been given in previous sections. • Special attention is given to wastewater and solid waste disposal, as well as energy efficiency.

On a national level, ten Energy Programmes have been adopted whose goal is to research the possibilities of using renewable energy sources (solar, wind, water, biomass), to stimulate the usage of energy sources that do not harm the environment, as well as to stimulate rational energy consumption.

- A State Plan for the Protection of Water has been adopted and designed to fit the European Union regulations. The preparation of County Plans for the Protection of Water based on the State Plan, is currently underway. They contain specific information on : I) criteria for water protection; 2) who is responsible for implementing the Plan, and; 3) by what deadline. On a local level the local community plans and carries out wastewater drainage and provision of water.

Czech Republic

- The overall tourism policy which has been prepared for government is the new state policy for tourism and covers all players.
- Administrations of national parks and protected landscape areas manage tourism according to management plans, which solve problems in the same way as in Recommendation No (95)10.

Cyprus

- The Council of Europe's recommendations have been implemented to a significant degree in various legislation of the country and more effectively in the procedures followed in development related matters. Development taking place in rural areas and areas outside the development zone boundary is directed by National and Regional Plans. Local Plans and Area Schemes have been prepared and implemented controlling development in urban areas and particular areas within them.
- The participation of the public as well as the Local Authorities is safeguarded during the planning process. This is carried out at key stages

	during the process. No plan is implemented unless it bears the support of the local community. Environmental Impact Studies are a requisite for the approval of any development, promoted by the public or the private sector.
Estonia	• Not available
France	• Recommendations are included in the policy for the leading sites (R95) 10 and in the European Charter for sustainable tourism in protected areas which inspired the Local Agenda 21s and tourist-n policies in nature parks.
Germany	• Most principles are embedded in national legislation and as part of international agreements which include, Regulation on Environmental Impact Assessment; Nature Protection Act; Regulation on National Parks; Federal Legislation for Building and Spatial Planning; Federal Forest Act; Federal Water Act; Closed Substance Cycle and Waste Management Act. There is also the intention to introduce the principles in the Baltic 21 process as well.
Greece	• The recommendations have been taken into account during the formulation of tourism plans particularly in coastal zones and protected areas. In implementing projects such principles form the basis of the decision making process. • Various principles have been included in the outlines of various studies, as part of physical, urban and environmental planning and during seminars. • Principles have been entrenched in specific legislation (revision of Urban and Physical Legislation. Management Bodies, improvement of control and procedures of EIA).
Hungary	• At the national level: 1. Formulation of national tourism development strategy; 2. Legislation on tourism; government and ministerial decrees;

3. Ecological standards and economic regulations;
4. Government subsidy programmes;
5. Research and education;
6. Regional development policy;
7. Regulation of maintenance and access to world heritage sites.

- At the regional level:

1. Integrated planning;
2. Regional marketing policy;
3. Environmental, social and economic monitoring;
4. Product development policy;
5. Eco-certification systems;
6. Support for the preservation and rehabilitation of the natural and cultural heritage;
7. Education and training; introduction of ethical standards for the protection of the environment.

- At the local level:

1. Inventory and protection of natural and cultural heritage sites;
2. Raising local awareness for the protection of valuable resources;
3. Co-ordination of economic activities and communal responsibilities;
4. Reinvestment of revenues derived from the tourist industry;
5. Support local voluntary organisations set up for the protection of landmarks and natural resources;
6. Support events aimed at the preservation of the cultural heritage;
7. The authentic presentation of local tourist attractions;
8. Incentives to assist emerging local businesses active in the tourist industry.

Ireland

- An example of the high level of environmental awareness in the Irish tourism industry was the award, in 1995, of the inaugural EU Tourism and the Environment prize to Kinsale.
- *Bord Faile* is preparing a policy Statement on Sustainable Tourism. in consultation with the industry, to ensure that all the activities that it undertakes or supports thereafter are in keeping with the principles set out in the Statement.
- Bord Failte has identified some key tasks in its approach to sustainable tourism development:

1. To establish an effective mechanism to monitor market information on environmental and infrastructural obstacles to future tourism growth.
2. To develop a Sustainable Tourism Policy (STP) in association with IT IC. Department of the Environment and the Local Authorities.
3. The Environmental Unit within Bord Failte monitors planning applications, which may potentially result in strong adverse impacts on the environment.

- Other actions include:

1. Tidy Towns Competition;
2. A pilot project on tourism eco-labels was undertaken under the EU LIFE initiative, in 1995 and is now operating in four areas-West Donegal. West Mayo. Galway City/Connemara and the Brandon area of the Dingle Peninsula.
3. A pilot tax relief scheme for fifteen designated resort areas, which operated until 1998, was introduced to support the renewal and upgrading of tourist facilities and amenities.

Italy

- The private sector has a role to play through the Eco-labels and Eco-Audit programmes.
- The programmes for the Venice Lagoon and for the Upper Adriatic which began to show signs

of euthrophication in the late eighties, are quite crucial. Programmes in urban areas will tackle problems of rubbish disposal, traffic and industrial emissions and noise pollution. A key example is offered by the decision assumed by the local authorities in the Campania region to demolish a mega hotel development situated on the Amalfi coast and which was considered not eco-sustainable.

Latvia	• According to Rural Tourism Development program state subsidies are available for rural tourism development. The program is implemented by the MoEPRD in the cooperation with the Latviari Country Tourism Association (established in 1993, since 1996 a member of the Federation of the Rural Tourism Associations "Eurogites"). Rural tourism is included in Country Development Plan (SAPARD).
Former Yugoslav Republic of Macedonia	• No response.
Malta	• The conclusion of the Carrying Capacity study to identify the daily number of tourists the islands can take without creating extra pressures on the social and environmental fabric and the infrastructure. Other studies at local level are also to be carried out.
	• The Ministry of Tourism is still to prepare its tourism strategic plan which will be based on developing a sustainable tourism sector. The Planning Authority's Structure Plan Review will adopt the concept of sustainable development in the formulation of its policies.
	• Environmental Impact Assessments are carried out on large tourism projects or projects proposed in or near environmentally sensitive areas. However, the current regulations limit the requirement of an EIA to specific projects. It is envisaged to extend such an assessment to a wider range of tourist projects.

- The preparation of the Tourism Subject Study as part of Structure Plan Review has taken on board most of these principles.
- The scheduling process of the planning Authority is a process by which areas are graded in terms of ecological or scientific or historical/ architectural importance. This process conditions what type and level of development may be permitted in these areas.
- The Planning Authority has also prepared policy guidance with regard to controversial developments, as are golf courses and subject studies e.g. minerals extraction and yacht marinas

Netherlands

- Recommendations have been included in National Policy documents and Plans. Policies refer to awareness building, uses of sustainable forms of transport and the protection of coastal zones. Eco-tourism and nature-based tourism is an integral part of the National Policy Plan on Recreation and the Policy Agenda on Environment, Recreation and Tourism.
- There is no general code of practice standards or guidelines for the tourism industry with respect to sustainable tourism development, although some businesses and consumer organisations have developed their own specific guidelines.
- The definition of sustainable tourism development is not always clear and this i-nay often result in higher costs for the tour operator and the tourists.
- The Netherlands have agreed a bilateral 'treaty on sustainable development' with Costa Rica in which tourism is one of the topics. Such a treaty provides opportunities for exchange of experiences.

Norway

- Recommendations formed the basis of the report prepared by the Ministry of Industry and Trade, which drew up guidelines for further work in the field of sustainable tourism development. The recommendations are specifically mentioned in the report. This report deals with four main issues:

1. Environmental measures within the business itself (cleaner production, ceo-efficiency and waste handling);
2. Tourism and its use of the natural and cultural heritage;
3. Transport and environment; and,
4. Co-ordinated development of tourist destinations with regard to environmental requirements.

Poland
- No response

Romania
- Recommendation R(94)7 on general principles for sustainable development is implemented by the Ministry for Water, Forests and Environmental Protection through law No. 137/1995. With regard to the other recommendations these are the responsibility of the National Tourism Authority.

Slovakia
1. No permission is given to projects which cannot prove that they are environmentally, economically and financially feasible;
2. Tourism development is in principle totally self-sustaining whilst some projects benefit from grants and other financial support;
3. Tourism development is a gradual process planned in a few phases;
4. Tourism is a tool to support local communities in terms of job creation e.g. mountain areas;
5. There are some initial attempts to develop sot-ne kind of tourism as an alternative to mass tourist-n in recent years;
6. Support a pilot projects for sustainable tourism at national level;

7. Protected areas have developed a set of guidelines and rules which are to be accepted by tourists, set vice providers, developers, etc.; Sweden Switzerland United Kingdom.
8. Protected areas are divided into further zones with different levels of protection;
9. Tourists are directed along specifically way-marked paths;
10. Visitors to specific sensitive natural areas are limited during certain periods of the year particularly between November and the end of June.

- I-las not yet implemented policies with regard to :

1. a national strategy for sustainable and environmentally compatible tourism development;
2. environmental training for tourism professionals;
3. a long-term awareness campaign with regard to environmental issues among local communities, service providers, tourists, etc.

Sweden

- Strategic plans and strategies for the environment and planning acts are formulated along such principles. The industry has special plans and committees for environment and spatial planning. Knowledge of environmental and planning processes is important for agencies like the research institute at Mid-Sweden University, ETOUR, for the tourism sector at Karlstad University and the University of Agriculture in Uppsala.

Switzerland

- No response

United Kingdom

- Recommendations have been policy for a number of years. Such policies are implemented through the system of central and local physical planning which allows for national differences between the countries comprising the UK, as

	well as for regional differences e.g. between London and the Lake District and between Glasgow and the Highlands and the different Islands. The UK Government's new strategy-Tomorrow's Tourism-includes as one of its 15 action points that tourism is to be a blueprint of sustainable development. In 1998 the Government launched a major consultation exercise-Opportunities for Change-on sustainable development in the UK. Tourism formed part of this exercise and a supplementary consultation paper-Tourist-n: Towards Sustainability-was distributed to a wide range of organisations with an interest in tourism, asking for ideas on action to be taken in this respect.
Ukraine	• Very limited implementation since present national policy is passive towards tourism development. This will entail formulating a series of new laws and Decrees with regard to the Coastal Zone, resorts and the Protection and Use of the Historical and Cultural Heritage. • It would be necessary to draw up a framework for integrated planning and resource management and give preference to the development of small private tourist institutions. A statistics collection and monitoring system needs to be established with regard to the quality of the natural tourist resources.

Sustainable Tourism Development and Employment

The term sustainable development is still perceived as a concept which is totally pro-environment and sometimes it is criticised as stifling development opportunities. Sustainable development, as the term implies, encourages development but applying certain principles, which relate to social and environmental resource preservation and management. Therefore, as a form of economic development the principles of sustainable development should seek to offer long-term employment opportunities. Traditional forms of tourism development, particularly those based on mass tourism, have often resulted in job losses. Such situations are experienced during the low seasons when the inflow of tourists is not that high, and therefore, some jobs have to be lost. Sustainable development should seek to offer permanent employment opportunities, even though the seasonal nature of tourism places some constraints on attaining this goal.

Country	*Sustainable development and employment*
Croatia	• Some of the activities that affect employment include. 1. The reconstruction of accommodation facilities (hotels), as well as the enlargement of other tourism offers (sport. entertainment). 2. Improving infrastructure and improving the quality of the accommodation supply. 3. Construction of road infrastructure leading towards the most important tourist areas in Croatia is also underway.
Cyprus	• Apart from the accommodation and recreation/ entertainment sectors, other specific projects have had limited contribution to providing long-term employment opportunities or to safeguard existing employment. However, the development of yacht marinas and some comprehensive development currently under consideration will be a source of employment opportunities. • The creation of ancient areas parks (historic i-monuments) has also contributed towards the creation of specialised jobs. • Agro-tourism has opened up rural areas and created employment opportunities as a result of the attraction of and interest created by certain villages where hospitality and services are offered to the visitor. The programme for the revival of traditional arts and crafts boosted up employment in certain villages in spite of the small scale of such activities. Travel agencies

	and tourist guiding are expanding sectors in terms of employment opportunities.
Czech Republic	• Unemployment wasn't a hot problem in this country for many years. Now it will be possible to do something in this sphere with the help of the Regional development policy together with the policy for tourism development — prepared by the Ministry for Local Development. • In Prague, attractive historical towns, castles and some nature areas, there is a permanent flow of tourists, which provides many job opportunities. New tourism policy and regional policy must also seek to develop opportunities for other places which are very attractive, but still unknown to tourists.
Estonia	• No response
France	• In Regional Nature Parks substantial employment has been created in the tourism sector whilst in national parks and in mountain areas agro-tourism activities have maintained agricultural employment.
Germany	• The effects of sustainable tourism development, in relation to job creation, is difficult to measure. There is only the general assumption that tourist-n development in general leads to the creation of new jobs.
Greece	• A number of specific sustainable tourism project can directly and indirectly encourage employment opportunities for the local population, however, no figures are yet available on this matter. Greece has a high percentage of employment in traditional activities.
Hungary	• Over the past eight years tourism investors received support from the government through a variety of channels. Apart from centrally allocated funds, the labour department set aside special funds to support the creation of new jobs. In recent years the Hungarian tourist industry saw the addition of 1000 new jobs per

year on average (mainly in the hotel sector). Other tourist services, e.g. catering, are characteristically family operated businesses that added an additional 800-1000 new jobs over the sat-ne period.

Ireland

- Ireland's tourism strategy based on the principles of sustainable development has resulted in employment opportunities in various areas, particularly those related to activities in the countryside as well as coastal areas. The protection of such environments for enjoyment and recreational pursuits have sparked the development of activity based holidays-fishing. walking, trekking, equestrian pursuits, sailing, etc.
- The promotion of Irish goods and consumer services are important in maintaining jobs in this sector and encouraging others to seek such opportunities.
- The Scenic landscapes project which is intended to be a pilot project for other European countries, apart from ensuring the sustainability of the existing employment will also provide scope for further employment during the implementation of the programme. These would include animateurs who would assist in the consultation process between the various parties in the implementation of the project.
- Under the Operational Programme 1994 1999 for tourism development a pilot initiative on Tourism and the Environment has been established with a budget of ECU 3 million. 23 projects were approved and the pilot initiative is in the process of implementation. Projects supported included visitor management schemes, town centre management, new touring routes and application of best practice to environment restoration. Although it is not indicated how many jobs such projects will create certainly there will be demand for specific skills

and professions in the implementation of these projects.

- The Great Gardens Restoration project has resulted in the implementation of 20 projects which will involve the restoration of many large estates of the $_{18}$th century and will attract visitors to areas which traditionally did not attract overseas visitors.

Italy

- A number of initiatives have been taken in various areas and regions (e.g. the Adriatic Hydrographic Basin), in urban areas, in areas under risk and protected areas which certainly had an impact in the creation of new job opportunities.

Latvia

- Rural tourism diversifies employment possibilities, improves rural infrastructure and landscape, protects the environment and increases the rural population's income.
- In 1998 the government started to subsidize measures to support the development of non-traditional agricultural and competitive entrepreneurship, to promote the maintenance of population density in rural areas and the creation of new jobs, farmers' training and implementation of new technologies.

Former Yugoslav Republic of Macedonia

- No response.

- The current scenario being experienced in tourism employment is that demand exceeds supply. As a result of economies of scale, the lower category accommodation sector is rendering itself unseasonable resulting in the gradual shedding of a percentage of full-time employment, which however should be absorbed by other sectors of the industry.
- The improvement of the heritage product offers immense opportunities for job creation in the

	areas of management, marketing, conservation, etc. Work by NGOs in this field have provided opportunities for part-time employment and voluntary work.
Netherlands	• No response
Norway	• It is difficult to pinpoint specific sustainable tourism projects that have had led to the creation of employment opportunities. This is because the concept of sustainable development is a gradual process in existing businesses, hopefully resulting in a strengthening of their viability both in economic and social terms and partly because it is difficult to designate some businesses as being totally sustainable.
Poland	• In the area of the 'Green Lungs of Poland', central government established 4 national parks and the provincial authorities established sot-ne landscape parks. National and landscape parks resulted in employment for many people in the fields of nature protection, ecotourism, environmental education, etc. The provincial governments organised study courses in agro-tourism for the local farmers. Local governments organised a promotion campaign of the tourism attributes of the area and built facilities for environmental protection. Local people started to develop activities related to agrotourism, combined with the organisation of boat, bicycle or britzka rides. Some investors have also built accommodation and catering facilities.
Romania	• No specific projects were mentioned, however, it was indicated that the projects by the National Tourism Authority and those by the Ministry for Water, Forests and Environmental Protection are intended to create economic and social improvements, especially in employment creation.
Slovakia	• Village Zuberec sited under west part of High Tatra is an example of sustainable tourism

development at the local level. In the past development was concentrated into the most sensitive parts of the area-just below the main mountain range. Because tourism was successful there, the development is progressing. But, currently, the new facilities are built in proximity of the village, about 5 km from the sensitive natural area A new ski area was also constructed (ski lifts and snow making system). Accommodation facilities are also provided in the village, in private houses and rented buildings to keep the typical local character. This new development has been successful because the surrounding area is very attractive during both winter and summer. This project offered new employment opportunities for full- and part-time jobs. Families also earn some extra income which is very important for this region considering the high rate of unemployment.

- Another similar case are two neighbouring villages below the south side of Low Tatra-Bystre and Myto pod Dumbierom. The ski resort was modernised recently and a snow making system was installed. This ski resort encouraged the further development of accommodation facilities, restaurants and other leisure activities which give life to these villages and create more jobs and income. It has also resulted in positive impacts to the sensitive zone in the main range of Low Tatra (Chopok area) because it decreased the number of tourists visiting this site and spread visitors towards the modernised resort.

Sweden

- Specific tourism activities (fishing, canoeing, walking in the mountains, cultural activities) resulting from the market development of sustainable tourist-n products are creating jobs.

Switzerland

- No response

United Kinddom

- Employment opportunities were created as a result of the following projects-national Park related activities in England and Wales, Tourism

	Management programmes throughout Scotland in the last decade and through the Green Tourism Scheme for hotels in Scotland, which meet various green criteria.
Ukraine	• One of the current major problems in Ukraine is the development of rural tourism and farm tourism in agricultural areas and villages, in order to assist the regional economies and diversify sources of income at the regional and local levels. There are many examples of new private dwellings for tourists on the market which are practical and inexpensive comfortable accommodations and working places for the local population. Such 'bi-functional dwellings' are situated in the national parks and in villages near the Black Sea, Azov Sea and in the Carpathian. The greatest decrease in employment has been observed in tourist regions such as Crimea, Odessa, Tchernovtsy and others.

Environment Related Training in Tourism Study Courses

The provision of environmental training for professionals in the sphere of management and business studies has only recently gained importance. The importance of such training to tourism professionals has mainly been realised in the wake of sustainable development and the need to harmonise tourism development with environmental protection and conservation. A document has been prepared by Mrs. Anne Herberich for the Council of Europe entitled 'Environment Training for Tourism Professionals' (Nature and Environment Series No. 98). This document formed the basis for a recommendation which was adopted by the Committee of Ministers on 'the development of Environmental management training for those involved in the Tourism sector, including future tourism professionals (Recommendation No. R (99) 16).

Country	*Tourism: Analyzing Impacts on Environmental training*
Croatia	• Employers are responsible for providing training to tourism professionals environment related matters.

	• The ministries and state directorates, in co-operation with institutes and both interest groups (associations) organise workshops on environmental protection. These workshops aim to stimulate employers and decision-makers in the industry sector resolve environment related problems e.g. energy efficiency, effective waste disposal eco-management in tourism cleaner production, public participation in deciding about environment related matters, etc.
	• Individual companies (e.g. hotels) have designed solid waste management plan (reduction, sorting, recycling) and trained staff to carry out such programmes.
Czech Republic	• No training is currently provided
Cyprus	• Training takes place in the various tourism related fields, particularly in the form of workshops or seminars. These activities, however systematic, do not constitute par of a particular training programme. Recent training was provided in the area of Environmental Impact Assessment Techniques. This training was cotiducted with the assistance of UNEP and PAP/RAC in Split. Croatia.
Estonia	• Currently, a national curricula on tourism is being prepared, which will include a module relating to sustainable development. At the satne time a college is already running the draft curricula including the sustainable tourism development module. Pedagogical University has introduced a new programme on recreation and tourist-n. Several training centres are providing courses for rural tourism operators. nature tourist guides, etc. Under the PHARE National Tourist-n Development Programme in 1993-1998, some courses on sustainable tourism have been organised by the Estonia Tourist Board.

France	• Since 3 years Regional Nature Parks have organised environment training programmes for tourism professionals. Training in the hotel industry organise environmental training in the fields of energy saving, water management and the use of non polluting products.
Germany	• Tourism operators themselves provide training on issues like environment and sustainable development.
Greece	• Some universities offering special courses on tourism give environmental issues minor importance in their programmes. Recently, some universities have established faculties for tourism and leisure management.
Greece	• Various training programmes in this regard (environmental protection management of protected areas, sustainable tourism, specific guides) are financed by the GNTO or regional authorities. Specific training is also provided in relation to environmental legislation (impact assessment).
Hungary	• No response given.
Ireland	• CERT, the State Tourism Training Agency, provides training in hotel management, administration, servicing and catering.
	• Recruitment is carried out through the third level university colleges for specialised staff in subjects like accounting, marketing, statistical and public relations activities. Experienced personnel are also recruited from the travel trade to marketing offices abroad and also from advertising backgrounds. In particular Bord Failte is keeping fully abreast of all technological developments in the IT area and the future fibre optic improvements for access to markets will be of particular benefit to tourism.
Italy	• Modules on environment related matters are part of most of the tourism training programmes.

Lativia	• No response.
Former Yugoslav Republic of Macedonia	• Noresponse.
Malta	• The institute of Tourism Studies provides training in tourist-n and have recently introduced environmental management training modules to provide students with all environmental background. • The University of Malta provides a course leading to a degree in Tourism Management. The course includes modules relating to the planning of tourism development and environmental processes and issues. • Various seminars are organised during the year with the participation of people from the trade and such events provide a forum for the discussion of tourism-environment-planning related issues. Nonetheless, there is still more that needs to be dotle in this respect.
Netherlands	• The tourist-n training programmes are starting to include aspects relating to the principles of sustainable development and environmental management. For example the NIITV-tourism high school Breda. However, there are no specific programmes to educate policy makers in the concept and policy design of sustainable tourist-n.
Norway	• The Stavatger College of Hotel Management offers a one year course in Visitor Management. Sustainable tourist-n and use of resources forms art integral part of this course. The aim of the course is to give students theoretical knowledge Oil product development based on nature arid culture as resources for tourism. The curriculum includes basic training in Norwegian natural and cultural heritage, sustainable tourism development. project planning, management

and techniques in interpretation. The graduates are qualified for executive positions in private businesses and public administration.

Poland
- Those pursuing courses leading to graduating as tourist guides are given a special study course relating to environmental and nature conservation subjects.
- The provincial Agricultural Advisory centre organises special training courses to teach farmers how to operate in the agro-tourism business.
- Special training for tourist-n professionals was organised with the help of the EUPUARE TOURIN Programme.

Romania
- Environmental training is the responsibility of the Faculty of Geography (3 years training for tourism agents and other tourism sectors). Training is also provided by the Faculty of Economic Sciences.

Slovakia
- There is no special environmental training for tourism professionals.

Slweden
- Training is provided in all tourism courses at all levels (e.g. sot-ne post high school courses relate to different tourist-n related themes — fishing tourism course in Fors-haga, nature tourist-n course in Aelvda-len, cultural tourism course in Vadstena).
- University of Kalmar, University of Stockholm and other universities provide Tourism: Analyzing Impacts on Environmental education. Various research activities are also being carried out at ETOUR and Mid-Sweden University.

Switzerland
- No response

United Kingdom
- There has been a huge increase in the last decade in the provision of tourism related courses in British Universities and Colleges of Furtller Education. Indeed there are arguments that there is now over provision. In all of these institutions

which are involved in tourism training and education, the principles of sustainable tourism development are now taught.

Ukraine

- During 1995-1998 the following training workshops were organised:

1. Integrated Coastal Zone Management (TACIS);
2. Biobusiness-Carpathian region (World Bank-Ukraine);
3. Black Sea Sustainable Tourism (GEF-Ukraine);
4. Management and Conservation of the Northern-Western Black Sea Coast (EUCC-Ukraine);
5. Historical Towns of Ukraine; past and today (Council of Europe – Ukraine);
6. Tourism and Recreation development in Rural areas (USAID – Ukraine).

Conclusion

As indicated earlier on, it is only in the long term that the success and effectiveness of sustainable tourism development can be measured and possibly achieve results. However, it has been noticed that at the local and in some cases the regional levels various actions are being implemented and showing signs of success stories. However, it does not mean that such success can be implemented in all countries since the requirements of one country vary from another. Each country will have to find its own recipe. Certainly, the consciousness towards sustainable tourism development has increased, however, there is still the threat of short term interests in this sector which may undermine any efforts to implement sustainable tourism development principles. The concepts of prevention should strongly apply. Although a number of tools have been in use, e.g. environmental impact assessments, yet experience has shown that these studies did not always prove effective as a means to screen environment damaging projects.

Nonetheless, the principles of sustainable tourism development are gradually finding an important role in the tourism policy formulation, yet, in some cases, it has not proved effective in providing answers as to how destinations may move from a mass tourism oriented tourism policy to a more sustainable one. There needs to be a greater commitment at the political levels and this should filter down to all levels, although at the local level there seems to be more commitment to sustainable tourism development. It is hoped that this report provides countries with an insight to the successful experiences in other countries. Such experiences should be carefully monitored particularly since the success of sustainable tourism is long term and provide examples for other countries to evaluate and adapt to their own circumstances.

9

Tourism and Wildlife Conservation

Wildlife Tourism

Definition

Wildlife tourism can be broadly defined as trips to destinations with the main purpose of visit being to observe the local fauna. This therefore implies that wildlife tourism includes other niche markets such as bird watching and the exploration of marine life (such as whale watching).

As bird watching has grown to be a significant niche market in its own right, the definition of wildlife tourism has been restricted to trips to destinations with the main purpose of visit being to observe local fauna, excluding birdlife.

Estimate of Global Market Size

The global market size of wildlife tourism is estimated as being 12 million trips each year. Africa accounts for around one half of all these trips, with South Africa, Kenya, Tanzania and Botswana being the top destinations.

Some destinations rely heavily on wildlife tourism, but could survive without it (wildlife tourism contributes roughly $500 million to the Kenyan economy, or 14% of GDP). On the other hand, places such as the Galapagos islands rely almost exclusively on wildlife tourists (wildlife tourism contributes £60 million to the local economy).

Other destinations are enjoying increased influxes of visitors due to strong interest in certain mammals. For example there has been considerable growth in whale watching at Kaikoura in New Zealand and Puerto Piraminde in Argentinean Patagonia.

Potential for Growth

Interest in wildlife is growing considerably, in particular as its exposure in the international media increases. As with bird watching, the National Geographic channel and other renowned television channels have generated increased interest amongst consumers. There is still considerable potential for growth within this market, and it is expected to expand by between 8% and 10% per annum over the next decade. The age group that will most influence this growth will be the increasingly wealthy, healthy, and active 55+ age group.

Brief Profile of Consumers

Wildlife tourists are some of the most diverse of any niche market. They range from the experienced specialists who like to seek "virgin" places that remain relatively undiscovered, to the inexperienced tourist travelling on a package to one of Africa's well-known game reserves.

Across this spectrum, consumers vary considerably in age, gender, and socioeconomic grouping. Package tourists vary from budget travellers through to those staying in small exclusive lodges or tented camps.

However, specialists tend to be independent travellers, who are likely to stay in basic accommodation, and are generally very flexible with their travel arrangements.

Whilst the luxury-end of the package market tends to be the most demanding in terms of infrastructure and services, they also generate the greatest income. These consumers tend to be in the third-age group (50-65 years), often including the early retired.

Main Source Markets

The main source markets for wildlife tourism are:

- United States
- Europe (UK, Germany and Netherlands being the top 3 markets)
- Canada
- Australia.

Main Competing Destinations

Africa is the market leader and accounts for around one half of all wildlife tourism trips worldwide. The traditional wildlife destinations of South Africa, Kenya, Botswana and Tanzania receive the greatest volume of visitors. However, there are a number of emerging wildlife destinations which demonstrate the desire of consumers to seek out new destinations, in particular these are:

- Antarctica (whales, penguins and seals)
- Bolivia (New World's largest concentration of large animals such as the Giant River Otter and Jaguar)
- Finland (particularly Hiidenportti National Park for bears, wolves and lynx).

It's 2010, the Year of the Tiger, BUT, time is running out to conserve the wild tigers of Asia. 100 years ago, 100,00 tigers lived in habitats across Asia. Now, only about 3,000 of these magnificent animals survive. They have lost 40% of their remaining habitat in the past 10 years alone. Ecosystems, endangered species, biodiversity and loss of habitats are inextricably linked with the livelihoods of the poor. 'There will be no room left for tigers and other wildlife in Asia without a more responsible and sustainable program for economic growth and infrastructure development' The tiger may be only one species, but the tiger's plight highlights the biodiversity crisis in Asia'. said Robert

Zoellick, President, The World Bank Group

Keith and Steve introduced the delegates to contemporary case studies on Eco-tourism and wildlife conservation they are respectfully engaged in Namibia and Indonesia. While Eco-tourism is not a panacea for tiger conservation, it was generally agreed by delegates that properly planned and well managed, it should be one of the more beneficial tools to be applied. Keith's presentation was a case study of efforts undertaken in Namibia to provide incentives for local communities to live with wildlife, including predators.

The relevance of a Namibian case study is that the types of incentives in use may prove applicable for Tiger Range States.

The three core messages of this presentation include:

- Devolution of Rights over Wildlife and Tourism to Communities

- The parallel successes of Tourism Joint-Ventures (JV's) and Wildlife Recovery
- Impact at the Destination-Level.

'The devolution of rights over wildlife and tourism to local communities has created the "greatest African wildlife recovery story ever told" – and predators are an integral part of the story.' Keith Sproule Steve Noakes cited the experiences of Ecolodges Indonesia and the challenges facing the wild tiger habitat within Way Kambas National Park which have been identified by the local National parks staff, including:

- Protection flora-fauna & ecosystem of the Park-illegal poaching, illegal logging,
- Forest fire, encroachment, livestock invasion, etc.
- Law enforcement-effectiveness of coordination with local Government law agencies
- Human – elephant conflict mitigation: improvement strategy and facilities
- Area rehabilitation and reforestation of ex-forest fire, ex-settlement (deadly wells), ex-encroachment, etc.
- Building biodiversity research and database-information system, to develop more effective conservation strategy
- Effectiveness of management organization & human resources through education & training
- Community development and participation/involvement through improve education & awareness programs.

The 'bottom-line' of his presentation was 'Tourism not a panacea for wildlife conservation, poverty reduction & related MDG targets. But it can play an important part. It needs workable partnerships – government, private sector, community, conservation and development sectors.

Community Based Eco-tourism

Place – Power – Prognosis: Community-based Conservation, Partnerships and Eco-tourism Enterprise in Namibia

Private Eco-tourism enterprises, partnered with communal conservancies, are purported to be central to the success of Namibia's conservancies in achieving biodiversity conservation

the South African administration, prior to independence. There was strong political demand after independence in both Zimbabwe and Namibia to transfer the economic success of wildlife management on private lands to communal lands and relieve a racist divide in rights to use wildlife, where indigenous use of wildlife had been criminalized under colonial rule.

Design principles for long-enduring common property institutions at local levels have been recognized at varying levels of detail (Ostrom 1990; Agrawal 2002). These are norms and rules determining who is excluded from a particular resource use or area, and how participants deal with subtractability in ways that sustain collective agreement and mutually shared benefits. Namibia's wildlife is a common property resource for which excludability, or the control of access is difficult, given the mobile nature of wildlife, and where collective use involves subtractability, where each user is capable of subtracting from the welfare of others.

Under Namibia's CBNRM program, communal area residents form a common property institution called a conservancy and enjoy rights in wildlife and related tourism development devolved under national legislation. Conservancies are approved by and registered with the Ministry of Environment and Tourism. Registration requires a defined conservancy boundary, voluntary registered membership, a representative conservancy management committee, a constitution and a commitment to producing a benefits distribution plan.

Namibia's CBNRM program drew lessons from regional experience (Jones 2006 interview; Owen-Smith 2006 interview) especially Zimbabwe's Communal Areas Program for Indigenous Resources, Campfire.

There was a deliberate effort to avoid pre-determined administrative boundaries such as Campfire's use of rural district ward boundaries and ADMADE's use of nationally defined Game Management Area boundaries. Rather, Namibia's conservancies self-organized and negotiated their own boundaries, to help reinforce devolution of wildlife use rights and benefits to community level. Formal registration of conservancy members, and legal gazetting reinforced external recognition (Ostrom 1990), again a significant departure from both CAMPFIRE and ADMADE.

As well, the wildlife revenues and other benefits developed under conservancies were intended to accrue solely to the conservancies and were not to be shared with central or regional government, as they were under CAMPFIRE and ADMADE.

Institutional Linkages and Partnerships – An Evolution

The roots of Namibia's CBNRM program date back to 1982. The Namibian Wildlife Trust was concerned about severely depleted wildlife in northern Namibia. This conservation NGO deployed a conservationist to collaborate with four local headmen, who shared concern about the dramatic loss of wildlife in the region. The headmen appointed community game guards who were knowledgeable hunters and trackers from local communities. The aim was to stop poaching (Jacobsohn 2006 interview). The game guards monitored wildlife, reporting wildlife incidents and suspicious activities to the headmen, who in turn informed the government wildlife enforcement agency. The community game guards, in contrast to other CBNRM approaches emerging in Southern Africa were not enforcement personnel employed in salaried positions by the state.

By the late 1980s, wildlife populations had noticeably recovered and the community game guard program was considered a major contributing factor. This coalition of local conservation effort, featuring leadership and collaboration in a basic NGO and community partnership, spurred wider application. Increased demand for the program led to formation of a new Namibian NGO, Integrated Rural Development and Nature Conservation (IRDNC), to facilitate and support the development of CBNRM in the wider Kunene and Caprivi regions. IRDNC remains the leading NGO dedicated to CBNRM in Namibia.

The next stage in the evolution of Namibian CBNRM followed independence in 1990. The new black majority government extended rights in wildlife to communal area residents that previously had been granted only to white farmers on private lands by the colonial South African administration. IRDNC's leadership, based upon their knowledge and experience gained in the community game guard program, were engaged by the government to help design and conduct community surveys. This led to policy and legislation for a national CBNRM program under the *Nature Conservation Amendment Act, 1996.*

USAID provided donor assistance through the World Wildlife Fund (WWF US). USAID and WWF (US) have remained the main donors to CBNRM, although other international donors have come in. During this same period the Namibian Association of CBNRM Support Organizations (NACSO) was formed as a national umbrella organization for other NGOs supporting institutional development, natural resources management, business enterprises and livelihoods at the local conservancy level (Louis 2006 interview). Thus, we see a further evolution of cross-scale linkages and partnership formation that started locally in a remote part of northern Namibia, moved to national level, and in turn attracted and mediated international donor support. The national conservation NGOs, led by the IRDNC, filled various CBNRM facilitation and support roles, including technical support for annual game counts, wildlife monitoring and reporting, capacity-building in project planning and budgeting, and funding for salaries, vehicles, field offices and equipment at the local conservancy level. In a number of instances, NGOs have served as boundary or bridging organizations (Cash and Moser 2000; Cash et al. 2006; Berkes in press) linking international donor support to the local conservancy level.

The support and facilitation of local conservancies by national NGOs has centred on locally elected conservancy management committees and the community game guards, who remain the central feature of conservancy conservation efforts. Community game guards are now full-time staff monitoring wildlife on behalf of the conservancy management committees, with technical support from NGOs (Stuart-Hill et al. 2005). The accumulated evidence indicates that wildlife conservation has been achieved under CBNRM. Subject to ranges of natural variability, especially due to drought, overall wildlife numbers have recovered and increased since the 1980s. The national NGOs are headquartered in Windhoek and some have regional field stations or a regional mandate. NGO operations feature professional and technical staff cadres such as biologists, GIS technicians, social scientists and project managers, equipped with all-wheel drive vehicles, modern offices and sophisticated tools, including the latest in computing and remote sensing. Funding for this CBNRM network and establishment comes from the international donor community through multi-lateral and/or bilateral programmes.

Communal conservancy formation has increased exponentially over a relatively short period. There were only four conservancies in the late 1990s and over 50 by 2007 (Weaver 2007 interview). The first conservancies now regularly participate in regional forums to share experiences and develop planning and management skills with the support of NGOs. Thus, we see an emergence of both multiple crossscale and cross-level interactions (Cash et al. 2006). Social learning, knowledge sharing and trust have been emergent properties between certain conservancy and NGO partners, reflecting the greater duration of their interactions and experiences working together (Armitage et al. 2009; Berkes in press).

It is noteworthy that the evolution of CBNRM in Namibia has taken almost three decades. A growing network of national and regionally-based NGOs facilitating and supporting CBNRM has helped mediate and channel international donor support and purportedly offset competition among NGOs for donor funds. This network has also appropriated significant CBNRM funding from international donors to sustain itself. Partnerships between conservancies and Eco-tourism enterprises have played an increasing role in the last decade and I now focus attention on this particular aspect

Torra Conservancy and Eco-tourism Enterprise Partnership

The Torra Conservancy has received international recognition as a successful case of community-based conservation. Torra is premised on conserving and commercially exploiting the wildlife endemic to the spectacular and remote arid wild lands of the Kunene region. Wildlife move seasonally through the wider region that Torra shares with other conservancies, Skelton Coast Park and Etosha National Park. The Torra Conservancy was one of the first communal conservancies gazetted in June 1998, with 450 registered members drawn from Damara and Riemvasmaker, Herero and Owambo pastoral villages in the conservancy area (NACSO 2006). It achieved operational self-sufficiency in 2002 following support from international donors and national NGOs. Revenues from wildlife conservation cover the annual operating costs of the conservancy: staff salaries and other annual program operational expenses. The main revenue-generating enterprise is Damaraland Camp, an up-market, exclusive Eco-tourism resort (daily rates range from US$560–$670/person) owned and operated by

Wilderness Safaris, a South African tour company. Eco-tourism is environmentally responsible travel to relatively undisturbed areas in order to enjoy and appreciate natural and cultural features, while promoting conservation, low negative visitor impact, and beneficial socioeconomic involvement by local populations (Ceballos-Lascurain 1996). Damaraland Camp has fulfilled this concept, receiving international awards in recognition. The camp occupies an exclusive, wilderness site with dramatic scenery. It is accessible only by light aircraft or all-wheel drive vehicle. The main lodge and tented accommodations are luxuriously appointed, using natural materials that blend unobtrusively into the setting. Solar power and other 'green' practices for wastewater and solid waste management are featured. The camp offers local natural and cultural history tours delivered by local village members hired and trained from the conservancy membership.

Wilderness Safaris pays an annual land rent and monthly bed levies to Torra and employs over 20 conservancy members full-time. Training and employment for conservancy members has also been achieved in some 40 additional jobs in the wider Wilderness Safari lodge network. Damaraland Camp's annual income contribution to the conservancy has grown steadily from ~N$50,000 in 1997 to over N$300,000 in 2005 (Wilderness Safaris 2005). The conservancy has earned well in excess of N$2,000,000 from the camp since its inception ($1 US equalled about $7.5 N in this period). Damaraland Camp has been the single largest contributor to conservancy revenues and the single largest employer (Wilderness Safaris 2005). Indeed, up-scale Eco-tourism lodges generated over N$7.6 million for all of Namibia's conservancies in 2005, amounting to nearly 56% of overall conservancy income (NACSO 2006).

A key feature of the partnership between Wilderness Safaris and Torra Conservancy is the land tenure arrangement for the Damaraland Camp. Wilderness Safaris was first introduced to the community by IRDNC. IRDNC acted as a broker and facilitated 'role playing' with a local community committee to prepare them for negotiations with Wilderness Safaris.

Wilderness Safaris negotiated a lease for the Damaraland Camp (Salole 2003) on communal lands that form part of the Torra Conservancy.

Wilderness Safaris assumed 100% financing and risk for Damaraland Camp under an initial 10 year joint venture agreement with the Torra Conservancy which has been extended. An end goal was 100% ownership of Damaraland Camp by the conservancy. This has not progressed and there is little prospect for this in the foreseeable future. Reportedly, the significant capital re-investments required to maintain an exclusive and remote operation like the Damaraland Camp have exceeded the conservancy's fiscal capacity to attain outright ownership or even a strong equity position in the development.

The Torra Conservancy case illustrates a substantive partnership between the local community level and an international tourism enterprise. The conservancy has made an exclusive and attractive site available for the Eco-tourism development. Local conservancy members have been trained and hired to run the operation, bringing their local knowledge and culture into the Eco-tourism product and activities. The international partner has invested its capital to develop the property and applied its expertise, global reach and resources to promote and attract international tourist patronage, generating significant local wages and revenues for those privileged with jobs and the conservancy management committee. These features draw on the respective strengths of the partners (Berkes 2007). However, partnership arrangements have also perversely served to limit empowerment and benefits at the local community level. Further discussion follows to elaborate on these observations.

Benefits of Sustainable Eco-tourism

Increasing awareness of the problems of mass tourism is leading many holidaymakers to seek more responsible and sustainable forms of tourism. One of the most common forms of sustainable tourism is Eco-tourism, the term most commonly used to describe any form of holiday or recreation in natural surroundings. The Eco-tourism Society also adds the concept of social responsibility in its definition of Eco-tourism as:

> *"Purposeful travel to natural areas to understand the culture and natural history of the environment, taking care not to alter the integrity of the ecosystem, while producing economic opportunities that make the conservation of natural resources beneficial to local people. "*

Thus, Eco-tourism is a form of tourism to relatively undisturbed natural areas for the main purposes of admiring them and learning more about their habitats. Eco-tourism also seeks to reduce its impacts on the area visited. It also contributes to the conservation of natural areas and the sustainable development of adjacent areas and communities, generating further awareness among resident and nearby populations and visitors.

Although a relatively new part of the tourism industry, Eco-tourism has spread rapidly throughout the world. The most popular Eco-tourism destinations are spread relatively evenly throughout the world and include sites in Central and South America, Canada and the USA, Antarctica and Australia.

Another important Eco-tourism destination is Africa. For example, Kenya employs 55,000 people in its wildlife tourism industry alone. The Kenya Wildlife Service recorded $24 million of revenues from wildlife tourism in 1990. For 1995, it was $54 million with 25% of earnings paid to communities in areas adjacent to parks and reserves.

A recent study of Amboseli National Park in Kenya determined that each lion there was worth $27,000 and each elephant herd as much as $610,000 in tourist revenue per year.

Case Studies of Rainforest Eco-tourism

One of the major attractions in Eco-tourism is the rainforest. The benefits and problems of Eco-tourism can be analysed through case studies of rainforest Eco-tourism in Rwanda and Brazil.

Do Rainforests Benefit From Eco-tourism?

Income from tourism must reach the people who will ultimately decide the forest's future if Eco-tourism is going to be influential in saving rainforests. Unfortunately, too often the money generated does not benefit these people.

All to often it goes to the North, where the tourists originated, giving little economic protection to the forests. Profits leak back to the North through tour companies, plane tickets, foreign-owned accommodation and use of non-local supplies. As a result, the World Bank estimates that only 45% of worldwide revenues from tourism remains in the host country.

The percentage is often lower in the South. A study of the

Annapurna region of Nepal, a popular Eco-tourism destination, found that only 10 cents of every dollar spent stayed in the local economy-and that much of that small amount ended up in the large cities or in the hands of the wealthy elite.

Tourist dollars should help to improve management of conservation areas on which the tourism is based. However, the money from tourism often does not end up with the agencies that manage these areas. In Costa Rica, for example, the park service does not earn enough money from its entrance fees to manage and protect its numerous parks. Only 25% of its budget comes from fees. The other three quarters must come from donations.

Tourists often resent paying large sums of money on entrance fees. Although these fees are only a small portion of the money spent on a trip they can be the most important dollars spent in protecting the resource because they go directly toward protecting the site.

Can Eco-tourism Harm the Rainforest?

Despite many scientific advances, we know very little about rainforest ecology. Thus, it is difficult to know how many people can visit a rainforest in a day without disrupting the forest ecology. There is some evidence that just the presence of travellers walking on trails through the forest changes the behaviour of animals in the forest.

A major impact on the forest are the pressures caused by accommodating the physical needs and comforts of tourists; impacts of providing wood for fuel, accommodation and access routes, together with the problems caused by tourists' rubbish, put a large stress on the environment. For example, litter has been strewn along the trails of popular Himalayan tourist routes, and the alpine forest decimated by trekkers looking for fuel to heat their food and bath water.

Only a limited number of people can visit an area before that area is adversely affected. However, deciding that number is often very difficult.

Case Study: Manuel Antonio National Park, Costa Rica

In Costa Rica, Manuel Antonio National Park is a victim of its own popularity. It is a popular tourist spot for both international and Costa Rican tourists who come to see its beautiful beaches and natural scenery. It is also the home of one of the last surviving populations of spider monkeys in the country.

The popularity of the park has led developers to build many hotels in the area. This excessive building in the area combined with high visitation in the park has threatened the monkey population as well as other wildlife.

While half of the park has been closed to tourists, it is necessary to severely restrict visitors to the rest of the park, and even to enlarge it, if a viable ecosystem is to be maintained. However, there is opposition to any further restriction to local land use and access to the park by the local tourist industry.

Costa Rica is one of the few countries that has a national policy to promote Eco-tourism as a non-consumptive use of their rich rainforests. Costa Rica has the difficult task of trying to foster its tourist industry while limiting the number of visitors to sensitive environments. However, the enormous success of the industry has overwhelmed the forest and prompted a call for a comprehensive study into methods to manage and limit tourist impact on the forest.

Does Eco-tourism Affect The People of the Rainforest?

The pressures of Eco-tourism go beyond the natural world. Eco-tourism can also disrupt local people and their social structures. Indeed, it is difficult to bring the benefits of tourism to traditional people without disrupting their way of life.

Ecotourists bring their modern material comforts, such as preserved foods, cameras, razors and so on, with them. These can often be unimagined luxuries for local people who cannot pay for them without major changes in their lifestyles.

The local use of the forest for firewood, meat and agriculture can sometimes conflict with tourists' wishes to keep the land pristine. To protect the tourist industry, regulations are sometimes made that prevent locals from using these forest resources. With their livelihood eroded and often without the skills to work in the tourism industry, local people can be left with no alternative income. There have been many cases where the original inhabitants of an area are pushed out so outsiders can move in to try to profit from tourism. Careful planning is needed to attract enough tourists to make money and still maintain the unspoiled forest and indigenous communities within them. Opening an area to tourists without such planning can quickly destroy the forests upon which the tourism is based. Alta Floresta is one example of a tourist project that has been planned with care.

Case Study: Alta Floresta, Brazil

Alta Floresta, a town in the Brazilian highlands, is the home of an innovative research centre and Eco-tourism centre. The research centre was set up to study sustainable ways of using the forest and to help people in the area benefit from the changes that come from Eco-tourism.

The project emphasises community involvement through schools, hospitals and training programs. Local people are trained in sustainable farming practices and the harvesting of non-timber forest products. Instead of being forced out of the economy, they are trained to work in the tourist centre and lodge, thus becoming an integral part of the whole project. The tourist centre also educates travellers on the biology of the rainforest and causes of its destruction.

Eco-tourism Development and Management

Tourism is the world's largest industry. It accounts for more than 10% of total employment, 11% of global GDP, and total tourist trips are predicted to increase to 1.6 billion by 2020. As such, it has a major and increasing impact on both people and nature.

Effects can be negative as well as positive. Inappropriate tourism development and practice can degrade habitats and landscapes, deplete natural resources, and generate waste and pollution. In contrast, responsible tourism can help to generate awareness of and support for conservation and local culture, and create economic opportunities for countries and communities. WWF is taking action to reduce negative impacts, and to encourage responsible tourism that enhances not only the quality of life, but also natural and cultural resources in destinations.

The Purpose of these Guidelines

These guidelines identify some general principles, and highlight some practical considerations for community-based Eco-tourism. They seek to provide a reference point for field project staff, and to encourage a consistent approach. However, prevailing conditions and levels of knowledge about Eco-tourism vary considerably between countries and projects, and this will dictate how the guidelines are interpreted and used at a local level.

The guidelines are not intended to be a detailed 'how to' manual, but rather stand as a collection of issues and topics to be considered and addressed. In some countries, such as Brazil, WWF has been involved in the development of specific policies and good practice manuals for Eco-tourism which relate to local circumstances and go into more detail.

Although the guidelines are primarily intended for use within WWF, they may also be of value to partner organisations and other agencies, and demonstrate to a wider audience, WWF's interest and approach in this field. They are based on experience obtained from WWF projects, and from published literature and case studies. A list of helpful reference sources is also included. Throughout the text, information on individual WWF Eco-tourism projects is provided in boxes. Though these are only referenced where their content is relevant to a specific point, the information contained in them complements the guidelines as a whole.

In total, twelve guidelines are presented. These have been grouped into four sections that relate to different stages of community-based Eco-tourism initiatives. These are:

A. Considering whether Eco-tourism is an appropriate option;

B. Planning Eco-tourism with communities and other stakeholders;

C. Developing viable community-based Eco-tourism projects;

D. Strengthening benefits to the community and the environment.

Although this is a broadly sequential ordering, all the issues raised by the guidelines should be considered together to obtain a comprehensive picture.

What is Community-based Eco-tourism?

Eco-tourism is a frequently debated term. Sometimes it is used simply to identify a form of tourism where the motivation of visitors, and the sales pitch to them, centres on the observation of nature. Increasingly, this general sector of the market is called 'nature tourism'. True 'Eco-tourism', however, requires a proactive approach that seeks to mitigate the negative and enhance the positive impacts of nature tourism. The International Eco-tourism Society defines Eco-tourism as responsible travel to natural areas that conserves the environment and sustains the well-being of local people.

This definition not only implies that there should be a recognition of, and positive support for, the conservation of natural resources, both by suppliers and consumers, but also that there is a necessary social dimension to Eco-tourism. The term 'community-based Eco-tourism' takes this social dimension a stage further. This is a form of Eco-tourism where the local community has substantial control over, and involvement in, its development and management, and a major proportion of the benefits remain within the community.

How the community is defined will depend on the social and institutional structures in the area concerned, but the definition implies some kind of collective responsibility and approval by representative bodies. In many places, particularly those inhabited by indigenous peoples, there are collective rights over lands and resources. Community-based Eco-tourism should therefore foster sustainable use and collective responsibility. However, it must also embrace individual initiatives within the community.

Some further general characteristics of Eco-tourism have been identified by UNEP and the World Tourism Organisation as:

- involving appreciation not only of nature, but also of indigenous cultures prevailing in natural areas, as part of the visitor experience;
- containing education and interpretation as part of the tourist offer;
- generally, but not exclusively, organised for small groups by small, specialised and locally owned businesses (while recognising that foreign operators also market and operate Eco-tourism);
- minimising negative impacts on the natural and socio-cultural environment;
- supporting the protection of natural areas by generating economic benefits for the managers of natural areas;

- providing alternative income and employment for local communities; and
- increasing local and visitor awareness of conservation.

While definitions can be useful, what is more important is the appropriateness and quality of action, not what it is called.

The processes involved in Eco-tourism include all aspects of planning, developing, marketing and managing resources and facilities for this form of tourism. Visitor provision includes access to natural areas and cultural heritage, guiding and interpretative services, accommodation, catering, sales of produce and handicrafts, and transport.

Appropriate recreational and special interest activities, such as trail walking, photography and participatory conservation programmes, may also be part of Eco-tourism. In some locations, hunting and fishing may be included as appropriate activities, provided that they are carefully researched and controlled within a management plan that supports conservation. This kind of sustainable use relies on local knowledge, provides significant local income, and encourages communities to place a high value on wildlife, resulting in net conservation benefits.

Checking the Preconditions for Eco-tourism

It is important to avoid spending time pursuing Eco-tourism and raising expectations in circumstances which are highly likely to lead to failure. An initial feasibility assessment should be made before instigating a communitybased strategy.

Some preconditions relate to the situation at a national level, others to conditions in the local area. The main aspects to check are as follows.

Reasonable conditions for undertaking tourism business are:

- an economic and political framework which does not prevent effective trading and security of investment;
- national legislation which does not obstruct tourism income being earned by and retained within local communities;
- a sufficient level of ownership rights within the local;
- high levels of safety and security for visitors (both in terms of image of the country/region and in reality);

- relatively low health risks and access to basic medical services and a clean water supply; and
- practicable means of physical access and telecommunication to the area.

Basic preconditions for community-based Eco-tourism:

- landscapes or flora/fauna which have inherent attractiveness or degree of interest to appeal either to specialists or more general visitors;
- ecosystems that are at least able to absorb a managed level of visitation without damage;
- a local community that is aware of the potential opportunities, risks and changes involved, and is interested in receiving visitors;
- existing or potential structures for effective community decision-making;
- no obvious threats to indigenous culture and traditions; and
- an initial market assessment suggesting a potential demand and an effective means of accessing it, and that the area is not over supplied with Eco-tourism offers.

Some preconditions may be more relevant than others, depending on the local circumstances, and these may change over time. For example, in Namibia cross-border conflict in Caprivi has seriously affected market demand in that region but action is being taken to enable promising Eco-tourism initiatives there to resume when the situation stabilises.

If the preconditions are met, this does not necessarily mean that Eco-tourism will be successful, only that it is worth proceeding to the next stage of consultation and assessment.

Checking these preconditions will require informed judgement. The concept of preconditions and fast pre-feasibility checks is increasingly applied among donor agencies in the tourism field. A useful guide to this process, giving far more detail than can be attempted here, has been produced by GTZ (1999).

Adopting an Integrated Approach

The small scale of most community-based Eco-tourism initiatives means that their impact, both on nature conservation and on income and employment for the community as a whole, is limited. They can be more influential and successful if they are integrated within other sustainable development initiatives at a regional and local level.

Eco-tourism can be integrated with other sectors of the rural economy, creating mutually supportive linkages and reducing financial leakage away from the area. It can also be coordinated with agriculture, in terms of the use of time and resources and in providing markets for local produce.

In principle, multiple sector activity within local communities should be encouraged. Eco-tourism markets are small, seasonal and sensitive to external influences such as political changes or economic instability in the host or generating country. On the other hand, Eco-tourism can shield against threats to other sectors.

As well as horizontal integration within the community, the success of local Eco-tourism initiatives may depend on vertical integration with national level initiatives to support and promote responsible tourism. In addition to making linkages with what may already exist, efforts should be made to influence national policies in favour of Eco-tourism, including coordination between tourism and environmental ministries and policies. National level support is needed in terms of linking conservation and tourism activities and responsibilities, appropriate legislation and assistance towards small enterprises and community initiatives, and national and international promotion. In Brazil, for example.

At an early stage in work on Eco-tourism it is important to be aware of the work of other national and international agencies in this field and to seek mutually beneficial coordination.

Finding the Best Way to Involve the Community

Involving the community is a critically important and complex subject for successful community-based Eco-tourism. Opportunities and solutions will vary considerably in different areas and between communities. An important principle is to seek to work with existing social and community structures, though these can create challenges as well as opportunities. It can also help to identify potential leaders and people with drive. The main objective should be to achieve broad and equitable benefits throughout the community. Issues of gender may also be important and Eco-tourism can provide good opportunities for women. Community-based Eco-tourism requires an understanding, and where possible a strengthening, of the legal rights and responsibilities of the community over land, resources and development. This should apply in particular to the tenure of community-held lands and to rights over tourism, conservation and other uses on these lands, enabling the community to influence activity and earn income from tourism. It should also apply to participation in land use planning and development control over private property.

It is important to remember that Eco-tourism is a business. As well as community-led initiatives, private enterprise and investment should be encouraged where appropriate, within a structure which enables the community to benefit, and have decision-making power over the level and nature of tourism in its area.

There are various ways in which the community can relate to private enterprise. The degree of community involvement and benefit can develop over time. For example, there are some Eco-tourism initiatives in the Amazon where lodges, that have been built with private investment, offer a concession to the community, an agreement to hand the business over to them after a specified period, and provision for an employment and training programme for local people. Options for community involvement with enterprise include the following.

1 Private tourism businesses employing local people. Although a useful form of employment, it is very important to guard against poor wages and conditions and to ensure that training is offered to local people, including in management.

2 Local individuals selling produce and handicraft to visitors directly or through tourism businesses. This has often proved to be a good way of spreading benefits within a community.

3 Private tourism businesses (internally or externally owned) being granted a concession to operate by the community, in return for a fee and a share of revenue. There are many examples where this has worked well.

4 Individuals, with links to the broader community, running their own small tourism businesses. Success can vary and

lack of skill and tourism knowledge has often proved a weakness.

5 Communally owned and run enterprises. Sometimes these suffer from lack of organisation and incentive, but this can be overcome with time.

Action can be taken to strengthen relationships between the community and private partners. This includes:

- advice and training for communities on their rights and negotiating practies;
- ensuring transparent, simple and consistently applied deals give sufficient incentive to private enterprises, recognise commercial realities, and minimise administrative burdens and uncertainty; and
- establishing committees involving local people, private operators and possibly government agencies and NGOs, to ensure understanding and smooth operation of agreements, and to help local communication.

The method of distribution of income earned by communities to individual members needs careful attention. This can sometimes be covered in legislation relating to communal rights. There are examples where communally-earned income from Eco-tourism has been directly divided between households or placed in community development funds or separate trusts for use on community projects such as health or education programmes.

Working Together on an Agreed Strategy

All community-based Eco-tourism initiatives should be centred on a clear strategy agreed and understood by the local community and all other stakeholders with an interest in tourism and conservation.

The strategy should enable a comprehensive picture to be formed of needs and opportunities in an area, so that a range of complementary actions can be taken. One of the main benefits from working on a strategy is to provide the community with the tools and knowledge necessary for decision making.

The strategy should be community-led and community-focused. However, it is essential that people with experience and knowledge of tourism and conservation are involved in its preparation. People involved should include representatives of the local community, knowledgeable tourism operators, local entrepreneurs, relevant NGOs, conservation agencies including protected area managers, and local authorities. Links should be made as appropriate to the regional and national government level.

Inputs to the strategy should include:

- careful consultation within the community covering attitudes and awareness of tourism, possible opportunities and pitfalls, existing experience, concerns and level of interest;
- a comprehensive market assessment; and
- an assessment of the natural and cultural heritage, including opportunities presented for Eco-tourism and sensitivities and constraints.

It is also helpful to set out a clear statement of strengths, weaknesses, opportunities and threats.

The output of the strategy process should be an agreed vision for Eco-tourism over a specified period, together with an identification of aims, objectives and strategic priorities, an action plan, and a way of monitoring results. The action plan should identify practical initiatives, including a timescale and an indication of responsibility and resources required. It is very important, in order to avoid frustration, not to be too ambitious in terms of targets and timing.

The actions identified may include specific development or marketing projects. In some locations at least as much, or more, attention may need to be paid to action to manage tourism, including policies on development control and the handling of existing visitors. In many places, the relationship between the local community and a protected area may be an important element of the strategy, including agreed action on the level of any park admission fees and their subsequent use for conservation or within the community, which is an important issue for Eco-tourism.

Ensuring Environmental and Cultural Integrity

A fundamental characteristic of community-based Eco-tourism is that the quality of the natural resources and cultural heritage of an area should not be damaged and, if possible, should be enhanced by tourism. Adverse impact on the natural environment should be minimised and the culture of indigenous communities should not be compromised. Eco-tourism should encourage people to value their own cultural heritage. However, culture is not static and communities may wish to see change.

A practical approach is to identify the limits of acceptable change that could be brought by tourism and then to consider what level of tourism activity would generate this change. It is very important that communities decide on the level of tourism they wish to see. Consultation during the process of drawing up an Eco-tourism strategy should reveal the kinds of changes that might be viewed positively or negatively by local people. They can then be helped to consider what this might mean in terms of the numbers and types of visitor to look for, when they should come and their length of stay. For example, in one community in the Amazon it was felt that more than eight visitors per month would be disruptive. Two important principles are:

- products developed should be based on the community's traditional knowledge, values and skills; and
- the community should decide which aspects of their cultural traditions they wish to share with visitors.

A similar approach can be adopted with respect to determining limits of acceptable change and of acceptable use as far as the natural environment is concerned. Here scientific knowledge may be required to enable a judgement to be made, taking account of the conditions of different sites at various times of the year. Often it is found that the quantity of visitors at any one time is a more critical factor than the overall level of visitation. Useful tools in the management of visitors include the following.

1 Agreements with tour operators over the number and size of groups to bring.

2 Codes of conducts for visitors.

3 Application of systematic environmental, social and cultural impact assessment on all proposed development. This should also be concerned with details of what is offered to visitors, such as the choice of products sold to them (for example avoiding artefacts with a sacred significance) or the use of inappropriate sources of fuel.

4 Zoning both within and outside protected areas. This should cover both the siting of facilities and the degree of access allowed. In some locations, village communities have identified specific zones for Eco-tourism, both with respect to facility provision and wildlife conservation measures. A common approach is to locate tourist lodges some distance away from community villages.

The planning process should ensure that monitoring measures are in place so that it is possible to tell when limits of acceptable change have been reached. Furthermore, strategies for making the necessary adjustments to overcome any problems identified will need to be established.

There are many examples in the Mediterranean where environmental degradation has occurred but also places where sound planning control and community involvement have prevented over-exploitation.

Ensuring Market Realism and Effective Promotion

The main reason why many community-based Eco-tourism projects have failed is that they have not attracted a sufficient number of visitors. Often, assumptions made about the marketability of a particular location or experience have been unrealistic and not based on research. As a result, promotional activity has been misdirected. A problem has been the lack of tourism knowledge not only among local communities themselves but also among advisors and supporting agencies.

A thorough market assessment should be undertaken for the destination as a whole and for the individual Eco-tourism project. This should consider the following.

1 The patterns, profiles and interests of existing visitors to the area, based on visitor surveys. In principle, it is far easier to get more out of existing visitors than to attract new ones.

2 The location of the area with respect to established tourist circuits in the country. Proximity to these and opportunities for deflection make a considerable difference.

3 The level, nature and performance of existing Eco-tourism products which are competitors but also potential collaborators.

4 The activities of inbound tour operators and ground handling agents in the country and coverage by international tour operators.

5 Existing information and promotional mechanisms in the area.

The unique or particular qualities that an area might offer in comparison to other existing products should be identified. From knowledge of the market, an initial profile of target visitors should be drawn up. Attention needs to be paid to the different opportunities and requirements of experienced ecotourists, more general mid-market visitors who enjoy seeing nature and local culture, backpackers, and educational markets. In some areas, the domestic visitor market may offer more potential than international travellers.

The level and nature of marketing should also take into account the environmental and cultural integrity of the area and implications for visitor numbers. A marketing plan should be prepared for all projects, which relates market research to a promotional programme. A vital ingredient for many projects is to form a close working relationship with one or more specialist tour operators.

These should be selected carefully to ensure they are well established and are delivering reliable business. Contact, directly or through handling agents, should be made in the early stages, before the development of the offer has occurred, so that the operator can advise on what can be sold and adjustments, if necessary, can be made. Setting up a fully saleable programme can take time. An initial step may be to test market the programme with one or two groups. This also has the advantage of acquainting the community with the experience of handling guests.

It is not sufficient for community-based Eco-tourism projects to rely simply on tour operators to supply visitors. For example, although pre-arranged groups may be easier to handle, backpackers or independent travellers may often be better suited to the product in question, but tend not to purchase inclusive packages through operators in their home country. The marketing plan, therefore, will also need to address issues such as local information delivery, internet promotion, media and guidebook coverage, linkages with other projects, and promotion though national tourism campaigns.

Putting Forward Quality Products

A second common reason for failure concerns the quality of execution of the project, both in terms of what is offered and proper business planning. Quality is about delivering an experience that meets or exceeds visitor expectations. These, in turn, will vary according to the type of visitor coming, which reinforces the need for effective market research.

Although luxury and sophistication may not be sought, an important section of the Eco-tourism market, often handled by tour operators, is looking for a rich wildlife experience, comfortable and reliable accommodation and efficient business handling. It can sometimes be difficult for communities to deliver this. On the other hand, the special sense of discovery, welcome and privilege which a community visit can provide is something valued by many visitors. There are three key requirements.

1 Attention to detail, ensuring that what is offered, at whatever level, is well delivered.

2 Quality and accuracy of promotion and information, giving reassurance but also ensuring that expectations match reality. All visitors in this market are increasingly looking for a high level of information provision.

3 Authenticity and ambience. Ecotourists respond to genuine and traditional values and experiences and they do not want this to be manufactured for them.

Some issues relate to specific components of the offer.

1 The quality of the wildlife and landscapes, in terms of relative uniqueness, attractiveness and abundance. If this is high, a project has a greater chance of success. Without it, the quality of the associated facilities and derived experiences becomes more important.

2 The mix of natural and cultural experiences. Many visitors are looking for a combination.

3 Accommodation: cleanliness is of primary importance, but issues such as ablution and toilet arrangements, general functionality, privacy and overall design and ambience can be significant. Different requirements in terms of investment and sophistication exist between lodges and camping grounds.

4 Guiding and interpretation: a fine balance between local colour and story telling, and scientific knowledge and accuracy is often sought. This may require involvement of different people, including an opportunity for local people to be trained as guides and interpreters.

5 Local produce and handicrafts: although visitors may look for authenticity, it is very important to avoid the depletion of cultural artefacts and other resources. Quality products can be made and sold which reflect an area's traditions and creativity without devaluing them.

6 General experience of village life, including folklore: this can prove an experience highly valued by visitors. It can provide an incentive to keep local culture and pass on local knowledge.

7 Participation: some visitors value the opportunity to participate in activities.

Conservation participation programmes are a specific sub-sector of Eco-tourism and can be community-based.

Managing Impacts

Attention to detail in a number of aspects of both the development and operation of Eco-tourism projects can significantly improve their delivery.

The design of all new buildings should be carefully considered. Traditional styles and locally available materials should be used. In some communities, useful income has been earned through, for example, the supply of thatching. Often it can be better to use existing buildings rather than engaging in new development, and this should be considered first.

Action should be taken, both at the development stage and in operating facilities, to reduce consumption of water and energy, reduce waste and avoid pollution.

Low energy technologies appropriate to the location should be applied where possible. Recycling should be encouraged and all forms of waste disposal should be carefully managed, with a principle of taking as much waste away from the site as possible. Use of environmentally friendly transport should be positively favoured, both in the planning of programmes and in the information supplied.

In order to minimise economic leakage, every effort should be made to use local produce and services, and to favour the employment of local people. This may require action to identify local, sustainable sources. Producers can be assisted through the formation of local groups and networks, and help with contacts, marketing and pricing.

Local communities should be encouraged and helped to take account of these issues themselves without any effect on their living standards, through information, training and demonstration. Feedback to them from visitors will help. Influencing the actions taken by visitors and tour operators is very important. Some elements of good practice can be included as firm requirements in contracts with the private sector.

A number of national and international tourism certification schemes provide formal recognition of good practice in managing impacts on the environment and local communities. In selecting a scheme, the criteria it uses should be carefully considered. In particular, certification should be based on action taken rather than simply expressed intention.

Providing Technical Support

Communities will require ongoing access to advice and support in the development, management and marketing of responsible, good quality Eco-tourism products.

Many of the issues raised in these guidelines point to the importance of capacity building and training programmes with local communities. It is important to get the level of delivery and content right. This should be carefully discussed with the communities themselves. In general, it has been found that short, technical courses have had little impact. Longer courses, including learning by doing and on the job training, have proved necessary.

Important topics to consider include:

- product development issues;
- handling visitors, customer care and hospitality skills;
- marketing and communication;
- environmental management;
- working and negotiating with commercial operators;
- management skills, legal issues and financial control;

- guide training, including content and delivery; and
- basic language training.

A useful way of generating ideas, giving confidence and putting across knowledge is through contacting, visiting or meeting other projects which are already experienced in community-based Eco-tourism. There are various examples where this has been particularly successful.

Most projects require some form of financial support. However, the nature of the financial assistance must avoid inhibiting incentive and causing problems within and between communities. Soft loans and long-term credit, well targeted to local needs, may be most appropriate. The use of local committees to approve financial offers has proved successful in some areas. It is important to demonstrate to governments and donor agencies the success of small community-based projects, including appropriate credit schemes, in order to encourage more financial assistance programmes.

The importance of effective marketing has been covered under Guideline 7. As well as technical marketing advice, projects can be assisted through access to national research data, help with visitor surveys, and linkages to marketing outlets such as national tourist board promotions and websites. The establishment of registers of community-based Eco-tourism projects, if possible backed by efficient reservation systems, should be encouraged.

A very valuable way of providing technical support is through establishing networks between projects. Some countries have associations of communitybased tourism initiatives. These not only raise awareness and provide marketing support but can also promote common quality standards, deliver training and financial assistance and generally represent the sector in the commercial and political arena.

Obtaining the Support of Visitors and Tour Operators

Eco-tourism experiences should raise awareness of conservation and community issues among visitors and tour operators and include mechanisms for enlisting their support.

Significant additional benefits can be achieved through improving communication with visitors themselves and with the tour operators who bring them.

These benefits include greater awareness of environmental and social issues, modifying behaviour when visiting, and generating direct support for local communities and conservation causes. In almost all cases, the experience of a community-based tourism programme will have an impact on how people think in future about the area and habitats they have visited. However, this can be made more or less meaningful depending on the information they receive before, during and after the visit, and how it is delivered. Careful attention should be paid to the messages put out by tour operators to their clients and to the quality of guiding and interpretation on site. Mechanisms for follow-up contact should be explored. Visitors should be encouraged to 'multiply' their experience by writing and talking about it.

A number of codes of conduct for visitors have been produced. Some are generic, others are area or site specific. These tend to cover questions such as prior reading and understanding, selection of operators and destinations, respect for local cultures, minimising environmental impact, purchasing decisions, activities to avoid, and conservation issues to support. Similarly, codes for tour operators cover issues such as particular environmental and cultural issues in the destination concerned, selection of sites, relationship with indigenous communities, messages to put across to staff and clients, and more specific instructions and regulations. These codes can be adapted for all Eco-tourism destinations. Raising finance or other forms of support from visitors (such as participation in research) has become quite a common practice in Eco-tourism destinations. This is often through a levy applied by tour operators or through inviting donations. Although some operators resist this, the effect on tour prices can be relatively small. Visitors appear to applaud the opportunity to make a contribution, creating a marketing advantage for the operator. Money may be put into a local development fund. Visitors may be invited to discuss beneficiary schemes and to get to know them. These can be conservation initiatives or social programmes within the community.

Monitoring Performance and Ensuring Continuity

A recurring problem with many community-based Eco-tourism projects that have been established as part of externally funded and assisted initiatives, has been a tendency not to continue satisfactorily after the life of the aid programme. It is very important that:

- a reasonable time span is allotted to the project so that withdrawal of assistance does not occur too early;
- an 'exit strategy' is worked out at an early stage;
- all bodies providing assistance take care to impart know-how to local individuals and organisations throughout the course of the project;
- a strategy of long-term local ownership is maintained; and
- use is made of national or local authority and private sector support that may be ongoing.

Projects will be considerably strengthened by regular monitoring and feedback to assess success and identify weaknesses that may need to be adjusted. Simple indicators should be agreed and made known to the community. These should cover economic performance, local community reaction and wellbeing, visitor satisfaction and environmental changes. Monitoring should be kept simple and feedback should be obtained from visitors, tour operators and local people. Training of local participants in monitoring processes may be required. Certification and award schemes can play a role in maintaining as well as establishing good practice. To ensure maximising benefits from Eco-tourism and minimising negative impacts on natural environments and surrounding communities, all stakeholders must commit themselves to following some principles and guidelines in their operations, in a concerted effort. WTO has identified the following principles and guidelines for Eco-tourism development and management, which need to be adapted to suit the special conditions of each country, region and local destination:

1. Eco-tourism must contribute to the conservation and improvement of natural areas and to the sustainable development of adjacent areas and communities.
2. Eco-tourism requires specific policies, strategies and programmes for each particular destination; it cannot be sustainability developed by simply copying what has been done elsewhere, let alone be left to grow in a disorderly and anarchic manner.

3. Eco-tourism needs practical and effective systems of coordination between all the players involved, including governments, private enterprises and the local community.
4. The planning of Eco-tourism must include strict criteria for territorial zoning, including in surrounding seas, designating reserves, low-and medium-impact areas. These criteria should be strictly enforced and respected by all parties.
5. The physical planning and design of eco-tourist facilities –especially hotels and other means of accommodation, restaurants, information centres in national parks and the like-should be carried out in a manner to avoid or minimise any negative impact they may have upon the natural and cultural environment. Building materials, architectural styles, furniture and decor should ideally be local, while low pollution energy sources should be used.
6. Similarly, the means of transport and communications to access Eco-tourism areas should be low contaminating. Sports involving noisy or highly polluting means of transport should definitely be prohibited in these areas.
7. The practice of Eco-tourism in national parks and protected areas should strictly comply with the management rules governing such areas.
8. Reciprocally, these management plans should take into account the fact that they will be used by tourists, and make suitable provisions for a sustainable use and visitation.
9. The carrying capacity of island systems in relation to tourism is all-important, and integrated long-term strategies and plans must take into account these carrying capacities.

Bibliography

Clark, Mona: *Interpersonal Skills for Hospitality Managers,* London, Chapman Hill, 1995.

David L: *International Tourism Policy, New York,* Van Nostrand and Reinhold, 1990.

Donald M.: *Customer Service in the Hospitality and Tourism Industry,* Englewood Cliffs, Prentice Hall, 1994.

Eberts, Marjorie: *Careers in Travel, Tourism, and Hospitality,* Lincolnwood, VGM Career Horizons, 1997.

Elliott, James: *Tourism: Politics and Public Sector Management,* London, Retailed, 1997.

Hoffman, Edward: *Project Management Success Stories: Lessons of Project Leaders,* New York, John Wiley & Son, 2000.

Hubert, B.: *A Host of Opportunities: An Introduction to Hospitality Management,* Chicago, Irwin, 1996.

Ireland, Lewis: *Quality Management for Projects and Programs,* Upper Darby, PMI, 1991.

Larkham, P J: *Building a New Heritage: Tourism, Culture & Identity in the New Europe,* London, Routledge,1994.

Lewis, Robert C.: *Cases in Hospitality Marketing and Management,* New York, John Wiley, 1997.

Lucas, Rosemary E.: *Managing Employee Relations in the Hotel and Catering Industry,* London, Cassell, 1995.

Madhukar Manoj : *Hospitality Industries in Next Millennium,* Rajat, Delhi, 2001.

Martin, B.S. : *The Efficacy of Growth Machine Theory in Explaining Resident Perceptions of Community Tourism Development,* Clemson University, 1996.

Moscardo, G. : *Tourism Community Analysis,* London and New York: Routledge, 1999.

Murphy, P.E. : *Tourism: A Community Approach*, London: Methuen, 1985.

Nijkamp, Peter: *Sustainable Tourism Development*, Aldershot, Avebury, 1995.

Norman G.: *Hotel, Restaurant, and Travel Law: A Preventive Approach*, Albany, Delmar Publishers, 1993.

Peter J.: *College & University Foodservice Management Standards*, Westport, AVI Pub. Company, 1985.

Prentice, R: *Conceptualising The Experiences of Heritage Tourists*, 1997.

Ratti Manish : *Hospitality Management : Theories and Practices*, Rajat Pub, Delhi, 2007.

Richards, G. : *Culture, Crafts and Tourism: A Vital Relationship*, Tilburg: Atlas, 1999.

Robert C.: *Cases in Hospitality Marketing and Management*, New York, John Wiley, 1997.

Rosemary E.: *Managing Employee Relations in the Hotel and Catering Industry*, London, Cassell, 1995.

Rosenzweig, J. E.: *Organisation and Management*, New York, McGraw Hill International, 1963.

Sabharwal Rajiv : *Tourism and Hospitality Management in Liberalised Era*, Pacific, Delhi, 2011.

Sharma Sunil : *Planning and Development of Tourism and Hospitality*, Rajat Pub, Delhi, 2007.

Slinn, Judy A: *Tourism: Management of Facilities*, London, Pitman: M & E, 1993.

Stallworthy, E.: *Waste Management Towards a Sustainable Society*, Auburn House, New York, 1990.

Swarbrooke, J.: *Marketing Tourism, Hospitality and Leisure in Europe*, London, International Thomson Business Press, 1996.

Timothy R.: *Cases in Hospitality Management: A Critical Incident Approach*, New York, Wiley, 1995.

Tribe, John *Corporate Strategy for Tourism, London*, International Thomson Business Press, 1997.

Var, Turgut: *Tourism Planning*, London, Retailed, 2002.

Index

O

P

R

S

T

W

❑❑❑